D1088937

DIGITAL CONTINUOUS-SYSTEM SIMULATION

GRANINO A. KORN

Professor of Electrical Engineering
University of Arizona

JOHN V. WAIT

Professor of Electrical Engineering
University of Arizona

Prentice-Hall, Inc., Englewood Cliffs, New Jersey 07632

Library of Congress Cataloging in Publication Data

KORN, GRANINO ARTHUR, 1922–
    Digital continuous-system simulation.

    Bibliography: p.
    Includes index.
    1. Digital computer simulation. I. Wait, John V.,
joint author. II. Title.
QA76.9.C65K67   001.4'24   77-505
ISBN   0-13-212274-X

To *Terry*, *Anne*, **and** *John Korn*
    Sharon, *Katherine*, **and** *Kira Wait*

©1978 by Prentice-Hall, Inc.
Englewood Cliffs, New Jersey

10   9   8   7   6   5   4   3   2   1

Printed in the United States of America

PRENTICE-HALL INTERNATIONAL, INC., *London*
PRENTICE-HALL OF AUSTRALIA, PTY. LTD., *Sydney*
PRENTICE-HALL OF CANADA, LTD., *Toronto*
PRENTICE-HALL OF INDIA PRIVATE LIMITED, *New Delhi*
PRENTICE-HALL OF JAPAN, INC., *Tokyo*
PRENTICE-HALL OF SOUTHEAST ASIA PTE. LTD., *Singapore*
WHITEHALL BOOKS LIMITED, *Wellington, New Zealand*

Contents

iii

6. *High-Performance Simulation Techniques   126*

A. *APPENDIX: Integration Routines   169*

B. *APPENDIX: More on the FORTRAN Package* 185

C. *APPENDIX: Tricks and Treats: Some Numerical Techniques*   206

Preface

Simulation is experimentation with models. Simulation for research and design, education, training, and partial-system tests is dramatically cost-effective, whereas real experiments are expensive, dangerous, slow, and/or not yet physically possible. *Continuous-system simulation*, in particular, implements models of "dynamic" systems described by differential equations, practically always with the aid of an electronic computer.

Useful computer simulation models of aerospace vehicles, chemical or nuclear reactors, biological systems, or social systems can be quite complicated. There may be hundreds of differential equations and many nonlinear functions. Nevertheless, the simulation user would like to be as free as possible from the details of computer programming as such in order to concentrate on his model experiments.

In this book we introduce engineers, researchers, and students to digital-computer techniques designed specifically to free the user from programming details:

1. **Equation-oriented simulation languages** permit the user to enter first-order differential equations in essentially unchanged mathematical form. He does not even have to know FORTRAN. Sophisticated users are still free to include FORTRAN subprograms in their simulation programs.
2. **Simple output commands** produce solution time histories, cross plots, listings, and reports. Either large or small digital computers may be used.
3. **Interactive minicomputer systems** permit keyboard entry and editing of system equations and yield solution plots at the touch of a button. The

user can immediately change the parameters and the model to investigate the effects of successive changes on line.

In addition, it is possible to program *multirun simulation studies*, producing cross plots, statistics, or optimizations on the basis of multiple differential-equation-solving runs.

Continuous-system-simulation software is available from a number of computer manufacturers and software houses. We believe that readers will find the simple DARE (Differential Analyzer REplacement) systems developed at the University of Arizona especially easy to learn and use. Use of DARE P (for large computers) or DARE/ELEVEN (interactive minicomputer system) with this book will, in particular, greatly simplify meaningful simulations and homework assignments in courses on physics; control theory; aeronautical, chemical, and nuclear engineering; population dynamics; and ecology. *Simple problems are regularly programmed by college sophomores*, who need not learn about the more sophisticated language features available to advanced users, *with only a half-hour's introduction to the simulation language.*

We believe that digital simulation can and should replace analog/hybrid computation in most applications. Interactive digital simulation (whose convenience and computing power must be experienced to be believed) has significant advantages:

Better man-machine interaction

Better accuracy and reproducibility

Vastly more convenient programming and report generation

Radically lower equipment cost

Digital-simulation costs will be still further reduced because the minicomputers (and also new inexpensive 32-bit machines) used are *mass-produced* for a growing nonsimulation market, while analog computers are special-purpose machines.

In Chapter 1 we introduce *continuous-system models* and *computer simulation*. In Chapter 2 we describe the computer routines required for differential-equation solving and present a package of standard FORTRAN routines designed for this purpose. This program package will run on any machine which supports FORTRAN and is intended for users who, for hardware or for other reasons, lack access to a true simulation-language system. Other readers might wish to go directly to Chapter 3.

Chapter 3 is a basic description of *equation-oriented continuous-system simulation languages* (*CSSL languages*, roughly standardized by the CSSL Committee of the Computer Simulation Society). The discussion proceeds from simple applications to advanced language features, function generation, and multirun studies, and describes currently available CSSL systems (CSMP III, CSSL III). In Chapter 4 we then specifically teach the use of the *DARE P language*, a new easy-to-learn

CSSL system which will run on any medium-sized or large computer which supports FORTRAN.

In Chapter 5 we describe the design and application of *minicomputer interactive simulation systems*, in particular the ultra-convenient DARE/ELEVEN system implemented, with complete interactive graphics, on a $45,000 Digital Equipment Corporation PDP-11/40 or larger machines. Display editing and interactive operation procedures, including multirun simulation, are discussed.

In Chapter 6 we describe methods for *increasing the computing speed* of digital-simulation systems for *real-time simulation* and *fast multirun studies*. In this chapter we describe high-speed fixed-point and floating-point *block-diagram simulation languages*, combined equation/block-diagram languages, and a multi-microprocessor system for fast simulation. *Interconnections of real hardware with a minicomputer simulation system* is discussed. We close the chapter with a *performance comparison* of different computer simulation systems.

Three appendices include some reference material on *numerical integration*, *specific computer routines*, and *special simulation techniques*, such as perturbation methods, steepest-descent optimization, and difference equations. The reader is referred to the bibliography for more material on integration routines, a by no means settled field. We note that interactive computer experiments are an especially neat way for selecting integration methods for specific problems.

Our text includes many worked and programmed examples from control, nuclear, and aerospace engineering and population dynamics, and a simple blood-circulation simulation. This is, however, a book about special computer techniques (simulation-language systems), *not* a book on model design and model validation. We do not discuss partial differential equations or discrete-event simulation (business games, scheduling) and give only literature references to the history of simulation software.

We are grateful to the National Science Foundation for supporting the DARE I/II, DARE III, and DARE/ELEVEN projects under NSF Grants GK-1860, GK-15224, and GK-38840. Nine different interactive and batch-processed DARE simulation systems were written by

John Goltz	Claude Wiatrowski
Thomas Liebert	John Lucas
Hans Aus	Ralph Martinez
William Moore	Steven Conley
Alexander Trevor	

Many other students made contributions, in particular, J. Puls, M. Carnes, W. Huey, E. Clish, J. Fertig, and D. Clarke. Finally, we want to thank Dr. R. H. Mattson, Chairman of the Electrical Engineering Department at the University of Arizona, for his encouragement of our computer simulation projects.

AVAILABILITY OF SIMULATION SOFTWARE

The following programs may be obtained at nominal cost by writing to:

Engineering Experiment Station
College of Engineering
University of Arizona
Tucson, AZ 85721
U.S.A.
Attention: Professor J. V. Wait

1. FORTRAN IV subroutine package (Chapter 2), suitable for a machine with $12,000_{10}$ memory, card reader, and 132-column line printer. Source code is available on *cards* (about $\frac{1}{2}$ box) or preferably *magnetic tape* (9-track IBM-compatible EBCDIC format), 7-track CDC (UPDATE or coded-file format), or DECtape (DEC-10).
2. DARE P CSSL-type simulation language (Chapter 4), suitable for a machine with a card reader, 132-column line printer, fast-access mass storage (preferably disk), and $24,000_{10}$ memory (might be overlayed on 16K). Source code is not available on cards but only on magnetic tape (as specified above).
3. DARE/ELEVEN requires a PDP-11/35, 40, 45, 50, or 70 with $24,000_{10}$ memory and an RK11-05 disk and currently runs under the DOS-11 operating system. Furnished on RK11-05 disk. A faster RT-11 version is in preparation.

G. A. KORN
J. V. WAIT

1

Models,
Simulation,
and Computers

INTRODUCTION

1-1. Models, Time Histories, and State Equations. Engineers and scientists describe the vast complexity of natural phenomena in terms of simplified **models. Model relationships** between **model objects** abstract useful and/or interesting properties of corresponding real objects and relations. Model objects and states are generally specified by sets of numbers related to real measurements, so that states predicted from model relationships can be checked and the model amended as needed. This technique is the basis of the scientific method and of rational engineering design. Examples of model-predicted relations are those among voltage, current, and resistance in electric circuits; between pressure and volume of a gas; and also between supply and prices of commodities. Well-defined relations between model objects are necessarily mathematical relations. Model relations and predictions are always simplified and idealized; model objects, however familiar (say electrons), are intellectual constructs and cannot be identical to real-world objects.

Many model descriptions must specify **time histories of model variables**, X, Y, ... :

$$X = X(T), \quad Y = Y(T), \quad ...$$

where the **independent variable** T is the time measured by an agreed-upon clock mechanism. For example, $X(T)$ might predict the distance traveled, current speed, or fuel remaining for an automobile or aircraft; the chemical composition of a reactor charge; or the current price of wheat. Some time histories can be adequately

1

predicted by simple formulas; thus for all T of interest, one might have approximately

$$Tire\ pressure = A * Absolute\ temperature$$

$$Drag = B * Velocity^2$$

where A and B are known constants. Figure 1-1 represents such relationships in terms of a *block diagram*; we can predict a block *output* time history whenever we know the *input* time history or time histories.

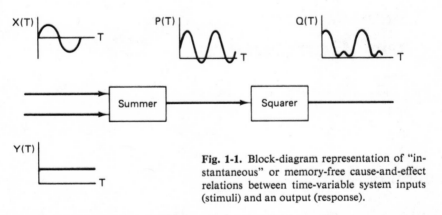

Fig. 1-1. Block-diagram representation of "instantaneous" or memory-free cause-and-effect relations between time-variable system inputs (stimuli) and an output (response).

But many inportant time histories cannot be specified through such "instantaneous" relationships because

> **1.** The effect of the input or inputs on the output is *delayed* (Fig. 1-2), and/or
> **2.** The output time history depends on its *initial value* in addition to a block input.

Such situations are very common indeed. Consider, for instance, time histories describing the "dynamics" of mechanical systems, of current transients in electrical circuits, of chemical reactions, and of biological population changes.

Many such phenomena are very successfully described and predicted through **state-transition models**. Assuming that we know the value $X(T)$ of a **state variable** X at some time T, a state-transition model specifies the value of X at some future time $T + \Delta T$ by a **state equation**,

$$X(T + \Delta T) = S[X(T), T, \Delta T] \qquad (1\text{-}1a)$$

i.e., **the future state $X(T + \Delta T)$ is a given function of the current state $X(T)$, of the current time T, and of the time increment ΔT.** Such a state-transition model can account for the effects of delays and initial conditions typical of many dynamic

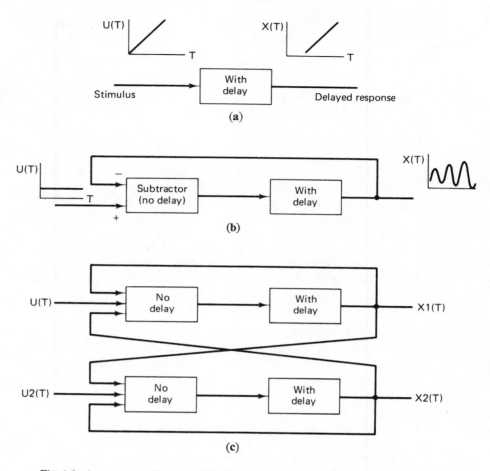

Fig. 1-2. A system or subsystem with delayed response (a), a system or subsystem with oscillatory response due to feedback of the delayed output (b), and a multiloop feedback system with delays (c). Feedback of delayed effects is typical of control systems and economic systems.

systems. If our model specifies the function S from empirical and/or theoretical considerations for even a small range of time increments $\Delta T\,(0 \leq \Delta T < h)$, then *Eq.* (1-1a) *permits recursive computation of the state variable* $X(T)$ *for all values of* T *once an initial value, say* $X(0)$, *is known.* It is only necessary to start with

$$X(\Delta T) = S[X(0), 0, \Delta T]$$

and to continue with

$$X(\Delta T + \Delta T') = S[X(\Delta T), \Delta T, \Delta T']$$

The state-transition model thus readily predicts future states.

The state-transition model is easily generalized. If the model state is specified by N state variables $X1, X2, \ldots, XN$, or by the column matrix (vector)

$$X = \{X1, X2, \ldots, XN\}$$

then Eq. (1-1a) can be interpreted as an N-element matrix (vector) equation which represents N state equations

$$XI(T + \Delta T) = SI[X1(T), X2(T), \ldots; T, \Delta T] \qquad (I = 1, 2, \ldots, N) \quad (1\text{-}1b)$$

which can be solved recursively with the aid of N initial conditions, say N given initial values $X1(0), X2(0), \ldots, XN(0)$. The state equations (1-1b) are *difference equations* to be satisfied by *solution values* $X(T)$ and $X(T + \Delta T)$.

The time increment ΔT is often a given *constant*. In that case, we specify and predict the state-variable values $X(T)$ at *uniformly spaced sampling times* $0, \Delta T,$ $2\Delta T, \ldots$. ΔT could be a millisecond, a month, a year, etc. This type of description works nicely for models involving *economic time series*. Another application is to *sampled-data instrumentation and control systems* which sample and control physical quantities every ΔT seconds with digital-logic circuitry.

1-2. Differential-Equation Models. Some of the most important state-transition models, especially in physics, assume *continuously variable T and X* (**continuous systems, continuous dynamic systems**) and express the state equations (1-1), for small ΔT, in the "incremental" form

$$
\begin{aligned}
X(T + \Delta T) &= X(T) + \Delta X(T) \\
&= X(T) + G[X(T), T]\,\Delta T
\end{aligned}
\qquad (1\text{-}2)
$$

In the limiting case $\Delta T \rightarrow 0$, $\Delta X \rightarrow 0$, the state equations then become (a system of N) **first-order ordinary differential equations**

$$\frac{dX}{dT} = G[X(T), T] \qquad (1\text{-}3a)$$

or

$$\frac{dXI}{dT} = GI[X1(T), X2(T), \ldots; T] \qquad (I = 1, 2, \ldots, N) \quad (1\text{-}3b)$$

These differential equations must be satisfied by the **solution** $X(T)$ or $X1(T),$ $X2(T), \ldots, XN(T)$ together with N initial-value conditions.

1-3. Applications, Choice of State Variables, and Examples. State-equation models for dynamic systems form much of the subject matter of physics and reaction-rate chemistry. More recently, such models have been used to describe plant growth, population dynamics in ecology, and economic and social systems.[2-7] In physics, state variables will, in general, describe energy storage. Thus, in electric-circuit problems, one can employ capacitor voltages and inductor currents as state variables.[2,4] In mechanical systems, position and velocity variables or the corresponding generalized coordinates in Lagrangian or Hamiltonian formulations are used.[4]

For systems already described in terms of second- or higher-order differential equations, such as

$$\frac{d^N z}{dT} = f\left(Z, \frac{dZ}{dT}, \frac{d^2 Z}{dT^2}, \dots, \frac{d^{N-1} Z}{dT^{N-1}}; T\right) \tag{1-4}$$

one simply introduces Z and its first $N-1$ derivatives as state variables $X1$, $X2, \dots, XN$ to obtain *first-order* equations:

$$\left.\begin{array}{l} \dfrac{dX1}{dT} = X2, \quad \dfrac{dX2}{dT} = X3, \quad \dots, \quad \dfrac{dX(N-1)}{dT} = XN \\[2ex] \dfrac{dXN}{dT} = f(X1, X2, \dots, XN; T) \end{array}\right\} \tag{1-5}$$

The state variables $X1$, $X2, \dots$ obtained in this manner are sometimes referred to as *phase variables*. Special approximation techniques are needed if it is impossible to solve explicitly for the highest-order derivative as in Eq. (1-4).

State-transition models permit the formulation of *very convenient and general natural laws* in state-equation form. Surely the best known example is that of Newton's or Lagrange's equations of motion in mechanics; these state equations specify a huge class of *different motions*, in terms of force functions, in a manner *entirely independent of the initial state of motion* (Fig. 1-3).

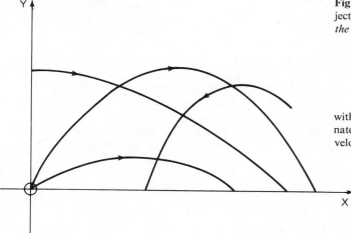

Fig. 1-3. All the different projectile trajectories shown here are derived from *the same* state-equation model

$$\frac{dX}{dT} = \dot{X}, \qquad \frac{dY}{dT} = \dot{Y},$$

$$\frac{d\dot{X}}{dT} = 0, \qquad \frac{d\dot{Y}}{dT} = -G,$$

with different initial-position coordinates $X(0)$, $Y(0)$ and different initial-velocity components $\dot{X}(0)$, $\dot{Y}(0)$.

In many problems, the *choice of state variables* seems obvious, because the model is already given in differential-equation form. In other problems, there are several different possibilities, all related by appropriate transformations. The simulation designer's physical knowledge of his problem often leads him to natural choices. We shall present examples to illustrate useful approaches, and many books on analog/hybrid computation provide information which is equally useful for designing digital simulations.

The following examples will be used in computer solutions described later in this book.

Example 1-1: Motion of a Falling Body. The motion of a body in free fall (no air resistance) with constant acceleration $G = 32.2$ ft/sec² is described by the second-order *equation of motion*

$$\frac{d^2H}{dT^2} = -G \tag{1-6}$$

We use the altitude H and its derivative $\dot{H}$ (velocity) as state variables and find

$$\frac{dH}{dT} = \dot{H}, \qquad \frac{d\dot{H}}{dT} = -G \tag{1-7}$$

with initial conditions giving $H(0)$ and $\dot{H}(0)$.

There is, of course, little need for computer solution of such a simple system. The problem becomes more interesting, however, if we consider that the acceleration of gravity G is actually a function of the altitude coordinate H, and also add a drag force D dependent on altitude (air density) and velocity:

$$\frac{dH}{dT} = \dot{H}, \qquad \frac{d\dot{H}}{dT} = -G(H) - \frac{D(H, \dot{H})}{M} \tag{1-8}$$

where M is the mass, and the functions $G(H)$ and $D(H, \dot{H})$ may be given in the form of tables or curves obtained from experimental data. Note that the problem no longer has an analytical solution.

Example 1-2: Population Dynamics. In this problem, the state variables represent numbers of three *populations which interreact by affecting each other's growth and decay*. Models of this type are used in studies of chemical reactions and of biological populations (predator/prey dynamics, habitat studies in ecology, bacterial growth); there may be hundreds of interreacting populations.

Our simple example describes the spread of an infectious disease (epidemic), where recovery results in immunity. We use three state variables:

SUSC	number of susceptible individuals
SICK	number of sick disease carriers
CURED	number of cured (and now immune) individuals

The total population POPUL will be a defined variable (Sec. 1-4). Although we clearly have integer-valued, *discrete* variables, we shall use the approximate differential-equation model

$$\frac{d}{dT}\text{SUSC} = -A*\text{SUSC}*\text{SICK}$$

$$\frac{d}{dT}\text{SICK} = A*\text{SUSC}*\text{SICK} - (B+C)*\text{SICK}$$

$$\frac{d}{dT}\text{CURED} = B*\text{SICK}$$

$$\text{POPUL} = \text{SUSC} + \text{SICK} + \text{CURED}$$

(1-9)

where the independent variable T is time measured in, say, days. A, B, and C are time rates of infection, recovery, and death associated with our epidemic; no other births and deaths are considered. Our model will describe the spread and eventual subsidence of the disease, starting with given initial values of the three state variables, SUSC, SICK, and CURED.

Computer solutions of this problem will be discussed in Secs. 2-10 and 3-6. In the meantime, can you solve this problem analytically? Can you guess the shape of each time-history curve?

Example 1-3: An Electric-Circuit Problem. The voltage V and the current I in the simple circuit of Fig. 1-4 satisfy the first-order differential equations

$$L\frac{dI}{dT} = E - V, \qquad C\frac{dV}{dT} = I - \frac{V}{R}$$

(1-10)

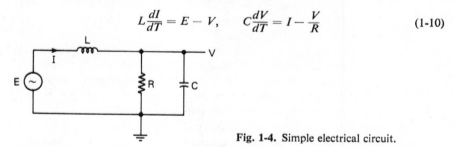

Fig. 1-4. Simple electrical circuit.

which express Kirchhoff's laws together with the definitions of inductance, capacitance, and resistance. One frequently eliminates I to obtain the second-order equation

$$\frac{d^2V}{dT^2} + \frac{1}{RC}\frac{dV}{dT} + \frac{1}{LC}V = \frac{E}{LC}$$

(1-11)

or, using phase variables V and $\dot{V}$,

$$\frac{dV}{dT} = \dot{V}, \qquad \frac{d\dot{V}}{dT} = -\frac{\dot{V}}{RC} - \frac{V}{LC} + \frac{E}{LC}$$

(1-12)

Note that the initial conditions for Eq. (1-12) are directly given by the "natural" initial inductance current $I(0)$ and capacitor voltage $V(0)$, while the initial value of the phase variable $\dot{V}$ must be computed from

$$\dot{V}(0) = \frac{I(0)}{C} - \frac{V(0)}{RC}$$

(1-13)

We shall present additional useful examples in later chapters.

1-4. Defined Variables, Output Variables, Input Variables, and System Parameters.
In many applications of state-transition models, it is useful to introduce, in addition
to the *state variables* $X(T)$, a set of **defined variables** with the aid of memory-free
(undelayed) relations

$$Y(T) = F[X(T),\ Y(T),\ T] \tag{1-14a}$$

or

$$YI(T) = FI[X1(T),\ X2(T),\ \ldots\ ;\ Y1(T),\ Y2(T),\ \ldots\ ;\ T]$$
$$(I = 1, 2, \ldots, M) \tag{1-14b}$$

The $YI(T)$ are **output variables** (whose time histories have physical significance and
are to be displayed or read out) and/or **intermediate results** introduced to simplify
the computation of the functions S or G in a state equation such as Eq. (1-1), (1-2),
or (1-3). Thus, in Example 1-2 of Sec. 1-3, the total population

$$\text{POPUL} = \text{SUSC} + \text{SICK} + \text{CURED}$$

is an example of an *output variable* computed as a function of the three *state variables* SUSC, SICK, and CURED. Although the right-hand side of Eq. (1-14) may
contain defined variables Y, one usually avoids "implicit" definitions which require
the solution of equations for defined variables (*algebraic loops*; Sec. 3-2).

All or some of the time dependence of the functions S, G, and F in the model
equations (1-1), (1-2), (1-3), and (1-4) is often conveniently expressed in terms of
input variables $U(T)$, which can be physically interpreted as *forcing functions* or
stimuli causing state changes. And the model-defining functions S, G, and F may
contain **system parameters** P (or $P1$, $P2$, ...) which remain constant for each simulation
but can be changed to modify the model. Figure 1-5 shows a general block-
diagram representation of a differential-equation model with state variables, defined
variables, input variables, and system parameters. Completely analogous representa-
tions apply to difference-equation models. Such block diagrams are often used
by control-system engineers[4] (see also Chapter 6).

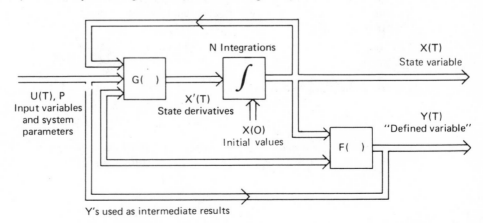

Fig. 1-5. General structure of a continuous dynamic system. Note that X, X', Y, U, and
P each will, in general, represent a set of variables, e.g., $X1$, $X2$, $X3$, $X4$.

COMPUTER SIMULATION SYSTEMS

1-5. Simulation: Experimentation with Models. **Simulation** is **experimentation with models** representing systems to be studied. A differential-equation-solving **simulation run** implements the model state equations and defined-variable equations as accurately as practical from $T = 0$ to $T = $ TMAX to produce desired solution time histories. A **simulation study** involves **multiple runs** designed to investigate the effects of different system parameters, initial conditions, and model changes. Although simulation could utilize paper and pencil, game boards, etc., **all practical dynamic-system simulation employs computers**, i.e., *hardware implementations of mathematical models.*

Computer simulation provides convenient, easy-to-change "live mathematical models" for experiments which might be slow, expensive, or impossible with the real-world system or situation being simulated. Computer simulation is needed for

Engineering design (e.g., control-system simulation)

Research (e.g., matching different dynamic models to real-world data)

Education (dynamic-system behavior)

Training (e.g., flight simulation, nuclear reactor operator training)

Partial-system tests (e.g., test of autopilot components with a simulated aircraft)

Play (toys)

Applications of simulation to each of these areas form the subject of much interesting literature, including the proceedings of important computer conferences. In this book, though, we shall concentrate on computer techniques for simulation as such; we shall use various applications as illustrative examples.

1-6. Computer Simulation. Multirun Simulation Studies. A **computer simulation system** implements a "live mathematical model" for convenient experimentation. **Programming convenience is very important, for simulation users are not computer engineers and would like to concentrate on their simulation experiments, not on a computer system. Criteria for the design of practical simulation systems are**

1. Computing speed. In particular, simulations incorporating human-operator tests or tests with real equipment require **real-time solution speed.**
2. Simple program entry and modification, either by direct entry of state equations and defined-variable equations (equation-oriented simulation language) or through specification of *block diagrams* (block-diagram language, analog-computer patching).
3. Convenient entry and modification of system parameters and initial conditions, without reprogramming.
4. Output of nicely labeled and scaled time-history plots, cross plots of

different variables, and numerical listings on convenient **displays** or as **hard copy**, without much programming effort (no FORTRAN FORMAT statements).

5. Output of commented programs for **report preparation** and **program storage** (tape, disk, stored patchboards) for later reruns.

6. The simulation system must permit sophisticated preprogramming of **simulation studies** involving **multiple simulation runs.**

The last point is important, for a computer simulation system is not simply a machine for solving differential equations or difference equations. Most simulation problems really involve multirun simulation studies, which may

1. Cross-plot or cross-list effects of parameter or initial-condition changes or solutions.

2. Make **iterative parameter or initial-condition changes** so as to **optimize a criterion function (iterative optimization).**

3. Measure statistics over multiple runs with random inputs, parameters, or initial conditions (**Monte Carlo simulation studies**).

Computer simulation can be **interactive**, i.e., the experimenter may modify parameters or model in response to his solution output and run the program again to test the effects of his modifications. Interactive operation of a simulation system is not restricted to interactive model changes between single runs but applies very much to *interactive multirun studies* (interactive optimization, statistical experiments—Chapters 5 and 6).

By contrast, **batch-processed** simulation delivers the results of preprogrammed runs with a range of preselected parameter values and model situations. Interactive simulation is especially fruitful, but it may be good to try a few interactive runs and then to produce batch-processed results overnight.

1-7. Digital Continuous-system Simulation. Integration Methods. Digital-computer state-transition models always implement difference equations. To approximate the solution of a differential-equation model

$$\frac{dX}{dT} = G(X, T) \tag{1-15}$$

(where G can also involve defined variables as needed), one can write an approximating difference equation

$$X(T + DT) = X(T) + G[X(T), T]\, DT \tag{1-16}$$

where DT is a small time increment (*integration-step size*). One starts with the known initial state $X(0)$ for $T = 0$ and computes successive values $X(T + DT)$ recursively by alternating two subroutines,

1. A derivative computation (derivative call) producing $G[X(T), T]$, and
2. An integration routine producing the new $X(T + DT)$ and T.

until $T = $ TMAX. We remember that Eqs. (1-15) and (1-16) are, in general, matrix (vector) equations yielding multiple state variables and that computation of the derivative G can involve defined-variable equations (*Secs.* 1-4 and 3-1).

Equation (1-16) defines the **open Euler integration routine** which, although it is intuitively clear, can approximate a differential-equation solution within acceptable errors only for very small integration steps DT. The resulting large number of integration steps increases computing effort and roundoff-error accumulation, so that practical digital simulation requires better integration routines than Eq. (1-16). The two most frequently employed integration schemes are

1. Multistep formulas, which extrapolate $X(T + DT)$ not by the simple *linear* extrapolation formula (1-16) based on $X(T)$ and one derivative value [Fig. 1-6(a)] but as a polynomial extrapolation based on past X and G values for $T - DT, T - 2DT, \ldots$ [Fig. 1-6(b)].
2. Runge-Kutta formulas, which precompute two or more approximate derivative values in the interval $(T, T + DT)$ by Euler steps and then use an average of these derivative values instead of G in Eq. (1-16) [Fig. 1-6(c)].

The choice of integration methods is further discussed in Appendix A.

1-8. Analog/Hybrid Computers. Electronic analog computers used for simulation represent problem variables by **continuously variable (analog) voltages (machine variables)**. **Multiple parallel computing elements** (summers, coefficient-setting potentiometers, integrators, multipliers, function generators), one for each mathematical operation, enforce the model equations, including fast, continuous integration of state-variable derivatives (Figs. 1-7 and 1-8).

Since the analog voltages are necessarily restricted to some finite range (± 1 **machine unit**, typically ± 10 V or ± 100 V), each problem must be **scaled**, i.e., problem variables must be represented by proportional machine variables (voltages) which cannot "overload" computing-element outputs and thus render computation invalid. Procedures for scaling will be treated in Sec. 6-5 in connection with fixed-point digital simulation.

Example 1-4: Analog-Computer Setup for the Epidemic Problem (Example 1-2). Referring to Eq. (1-9), for a benign disease with death rate $C = 0$, the population POPUL will remain constant, and it is sufficient to study the two-variable system

$$\frac{d}{dt}\text{SUSC} = -A * \text{SUSC} * \text{SICK}$$

$$\frac{d}{dT}\text{SICK} = A * \text{SUSC} * \text{SICK} - B * \text{SICK}$$

(1-17)

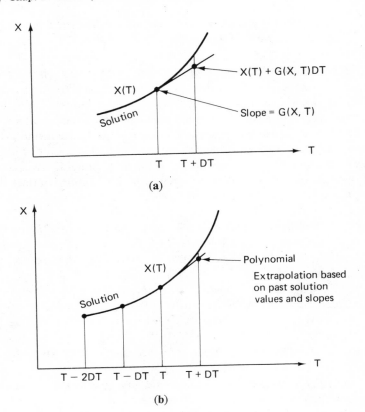

(a)

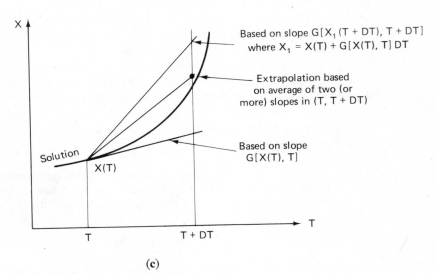

(c)

Fig. 1-6. Numerical integration.

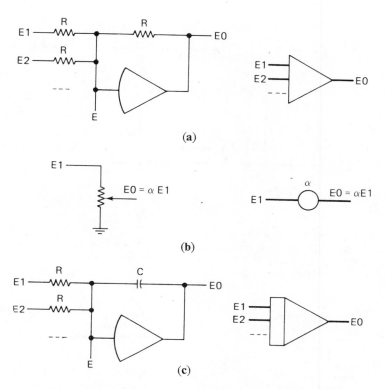

Fig. 1-7. Analog *summing amplifier* (a), *coefficient-setting potentiometer* (b), and *integrator* (c), with block-diagram symbols. In the operational-amplifier circuits (a) and (c), high-gain feedback reduces the summing-point voltage E to zero, so that Kirchhoff's current-summing law implies

$$E0 = -(E1 + E2 + \ldots) \qquad \text{(summing amplifier)},$$

$$E0(T) = -\frac{1}{RC} \int_0^T (E1 + E2 + \ldots)\, dT + E0(0) \qquad \text{(integrator)}.$$

The initial-condition voltage $E0(0)$ is supplied by electronic switching circuits designed to charge all integrator capacitors C to the desired initial voltages (RESET mode) and to release them at $T = 0$ (COMPUTE mode of the electronic analog computer). Additional analog computing elements include *multipliers* and *function generators*.

We are given

$$\text{Infection rate} = A = 0.001 \qquad \text{(individuals per day)}$$
$$\text{Recovery rate} = B = 0.07 \qquad \text{(individuals per day)}$$

and the initial conditions

$$\text{SUSC}\,(0) = 620, \qquad \text{SICK}\,(0) = 10$$

To scale the problem, we note that neither SUSC nor SICK can possibly exceed 1000 and introduce the scaled machine variables [SUSC/1000], [SICK/1000]. We simply substitute

$$\text{SUSC} = 1000 \left[\frac{\text{SUSC}}{1000} \right], \qquad \text{SICK} = 1000 \left[\frac{\text{SICK}}{1000} \right]$$

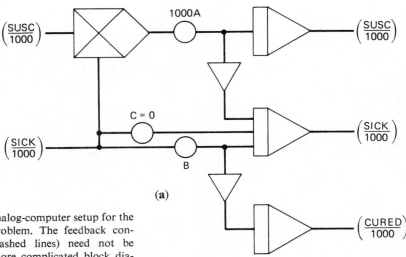

Fig. 1-8. Analog-computer setup for the epidemic problem. The feedback connections (dashed lines) need not be drawn in more complicated block diagrams.

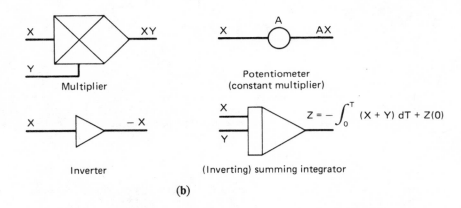

(b)

in the given problem equations (1-17) to find the *scaled machine equations*

$$\frac{d}{dT}\left[\frac{SUSC}{1000}\right] = -1000A\left[\frac{SUSC}{1000}\right]\left[\frac{SICK}{1000}\right]$$

$$\frac{d}{dT}\left[\frac{SICK}{1000}\right] = 1000A\left[\frac{SUSC}{1000}\right]\left[\frac{SICK}{1000}\right] - B\left[\frac{SICK}{1000}\right]$$

(1-18)

which are implemented by the analog-computer setup of Fig. 1-8 if 1 day corresponds to 1 second of machine time. For faster or slower simulation, we simply change all integrator gains proportionately (**time scaling**; see also Sec. 6-5).

Pure analog simulation is obsolete. Practical analog simulations tend to be fairly large (Sec. 1-9) and require a digital computer and an **interface** which implements analog-digital-analog **data conversion** and digital control of analog-computer operation (coefficient setting, integrator resetting, repeated runs). The resulting system is a **hybrid analog-digital computer**. The digital machine can

1. Store and set coefficients and initial conditions (possibly hundreds) and check for correct propagation of initial conditions (**setup** and **static** check).
2. *Take, store, process,* and *output data* from the analog computer.
3. Command repeated analog-computer runs, with new coefficients, initial conditions, and/or switch settings determined by a digital-computer program (**iterative analog computation**).
4. Take over part of the simulation computations, in particular generation of functions of two, three, or more variables (**combined simulation**).

At their best, hybrid computers combine analog-computer speed with the decision-making ability, storage, and input/output facilities of digital machines. But inherent problems of low analog-computer precision and sampled-data errors in the interface necessitate very clever programming, which can be quite difficult and time-consuming. Analog/hybrid computation is discussed in detail in References 11, 12, and 13.

1-9. Analog/Hybrid Versus Digital Simulation. New integrated circuits have improved analog as well as digital computers, although this has benefited instrumentation and control more than simulation, which requires high accuracy. We note that

1. Analog/hybrid computers have limited component accuracy (at best within 0.01 to 0.05% of half-scale).
2. Analog computation is fast (0.1% half-scale component accuracies at sine-wave frequencies up to 500 to 1000 Hz with commercially available general-purpose machines). **Parallel operation** of multiple analog computing elements (summers, integrators, etc.) makes computing speed more or less independent of the problem size.
3. Analog/hybrid computers are expensive, since they involve high-precision components produced for a limited market. It is necessary to stock enough analog computing elements for the largest problem (Table 1-1).
4. Problem preparation, scaling, and checkout tends to be complicated and expensive.
5. Analog computers interface easily with flight tables, instruments, etc., used for real-time partial-system tests, but this is also true for small digital computers.

Interactive operation of small analog-computer models has traditionally provided great insight into block-diagram dynamics (manual patching and modification of model interconnections, observing results of manual coefficient-potentiometer settings). This analog "feel" is lost in modern large hybrid computers, where the analog computer is simply another peripheral device in a digital-computer system operated in the batch or interactive mode.

For more efficient operation, new hybrid computer systems replace conventional plug-in interconnections (patching) of the computing elements with electronic switching matrices. Such **autopatch systems**, together with digital coefficient setting, permit quick problem changes, so that the *expensive hybrid computer can be time-shared* by different users. Such automatic systems, moreover, permit *more convenient programming with the aid of digital-computer software* (analog/hybrid "compiler" such as APSE or ACTRAN), which *translates simulation-language statements into appropriate interconnections and coefficient settings*. Scaling is usually done with the aid of a preliminary digital simulation.

TABLE 1-1. Estimated Cost of a Medium-Sized Hybrid Computer

120 Integrators	180 Gates
95 Summers	24 Flip-flops
215 Inverters	24 Registers
160 Digital coefficient units	16 Analog-to-digital channels
95 Multipliers	16 Multiplying digital-to-
60 Limiters	analog converters,
10 Sin/cos units	interface logic
60 Comparators	2 Consoles, display, power

1 Minicomputer, 32K memory

Cost: $750,000

Cost with *automatic patching:* $1,100,000

Note: A $40,000 minicomputer system can solve the same problem equations, but solutions can be 10 to 400 times slower.

In contrast to such precision-made special-purpose systems, digital simulation employs ever-cheaper off-the-shelf hardware mass-produced for a large general-purpose market. Accuracy can be improved at will at the expense of computing speed, and inexpensive mini/microcomputers can be paralleled to speed up larger simulations (Sec. 6-10). But **with off-the-shelf hardware, digital-simulation bandwidths, in the foreseeable future, will remain less than those attainable with analog/hybrid computers.**

As a case in point, a $75,000 minicomputer system can solve the same problem equations as the $750,000 to $1,100,000 hybrid computer of Table 1-1. The small digital computer can produce real-time outputs at a few Hz (floating-point) and up to 100 Hz (fixed-point; see Sec. 6-1). Digital solutions will be 10 to 400 times slower than the fastest hybrid-computer solutions.

It follows that the **relatively expensive analog/hybrid computers will be cost-effective only where their computing speed and parallel operation are really important.** This is especially true in large simulations requiring hundreds of amplifiers and thousands of differential-equation-solving "runs," as with larger aerospace-vehicle or process-plant models (Fig. 1-9). Time-shared simulation, if available, can also help to pay the cost of a large hybrid installation. Smaller simulation studies will be much more cost-effective on digital computers, which can also be time-shared.

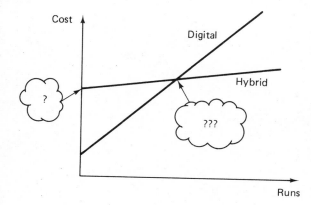

Fig. 1-9. When many differential-equation-solving runs are needed, hybrid computation may pay for its higher acquisition, programming/checkout, and maintenance costs by the lower cost *per run*. Unfortunately, no two persons seem to agree on *quantitative* slopes and intercepts for such cost curves (based on Reference 15).

REFERENCES AND BIBLIOGRAPHY

1. KORN, G. A., and T. M. KORN, *Mathematical Handbook for Scientists and Engineers*, 2nd ed., McGraw-Hill, New York, 1968.

2. MCLEOD, J., *Simulation, Dynamic Modelling of Systems and Ideas with Computers*, McGraw-Hill, New York, 1968.

3. GORDON, I., *System Simulation*, Prentice-Hall, Englewood Cliffs, N.J., 1971.

4. MELSA, J., and D. SCHULTZ, *State Functions and Linear Control Systems*, McGraw-Hill, New York, 1967.

5. FORRESTER, J. W., *Industrial Dynamics*, M.I.T. Press, Cambridge, Mass., 1961.

6. FORRESTER, J. W., *Urban Dynamics*, M.I.T. Press, Cambridge, Mass., 1969.

7. FORRESTER, J. W., *World Dynamics*, Wright-Allen, Cambridge, Mass., 1971.

8. CHU, Y., *Digital Simulation of Continuous Systems*, McGraw-Hill, New York, 1969.

9. JENTSCH, W., *Digitale Simulation Kontinuierlicher Systeme*, Oldenbourg, Munich, 1969.

10. ROSKO, W., *Digital Simulation*, Prentice-Hall, Englewood Cliffs, N.J., 1973.

11. BEKEY, G. A., and W. J. KARPLUS, *Hybrid Computation*, Wiley, New York, 1968.

12. HAUSNER, A., *Analog and Analog/Hybrid Computer Programming*, Prentice-Hall, Englewood Cliffs, N.J., 1971.

13. KORN, G. A., and T. M. KORN: *Electronic Analog and Hybrid Computers*, 2nd ed., McGraw-Hill, New York, 1972.

14. WAIT, J. V., "State-Space Methods for Designing Digital Simulations of Continuous Fixed Linear Systems," *IEEETEC*, June 1967.

15. KORN, G. A., "Recent Computer-System Developments and Continuous-System Simulation," *Ann. AICA*, April 1974.

16. ORD-SMITH, R. J., and J. STEPHENSON, *Computer Simulation of Continuous Systems*, Cambridge University Press, New York, 1975.

Periodical Literature

Useful references will be found in the journal *Simulation* and in the *Proceedings of the Summer Computer Simulation Conferences* (*Proc. SCSC*), both published by the Society for Computer Simulation, La Jolla, Calif.

2

Anatomy of Digital Simulation Programs, and a Portable FORTRAN Subroutine Package for Simulation

INTRODUCTION

In this chapter, we shall describe a **FORTRAN subroutine package** which provides the essential operations for continuous-system simulation. **In later chapters we shall describe more convenient user-oriented simulation languages, including a detailed treatment of the DARE family of CSSL-type languages. If the reader has access to a computer with such a language implemented, he may wish to skip to these later discussions.** We choose, however, to describe the use of this basic subroutine package at this point for two reasons:

> **1.** The core of most simulation languages is a similar package of run-time routines which perform the basic simulation run, and a study of our package will facilitate understanding the operations involved.
>
> **2.** Some readers may not have a computer of sufficient size, and with the required peripherals, to implement a full simulation language. Nevertheless, **anyone with access to a computer with a reasonably standard FORTRAN IV compiler should be able to use major portions of our subroutine package.**

The package, as described here, assumes that the user has an 80-column card reader or equivalent input device and a 132-column (or larger) output printer. Potential compatibility problems are discussed in Appendix B.

The package described here is dimensioned to accommodate systems of up to the 20th order (i.e., 20 state variables); there is space for 10 additional output variables. Standard subroutines for initialization and output display are provided; special jobs may require their alteration, since we cannot anticipate all requirements in a relatively compact package.

A FORTRAN SUBROUTINE PACKAGE

2-1. Structure of a Simulation Program. Regardless of programming details, a simulation job generally has the structure illustrated in Figs. 2-1 and 2-2. Here we are describing the function, not the program names. Three basic functions are

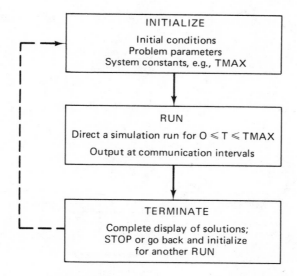

Fig. 2-1. Major operations in a simulation job.

1. INITIALIZE. This is a phase where the stage is set for the simulation run. Three classes of quantities are usually initialized:

(a) The **initial values** of the **state variables** in the problem equations are set.

(b) Values of adjustable **parameters** in the problem equations are set.

(c) **Simulation-system parameters** associated with the preprogrammed system routines are adjusted to fit the job. For example, a value for TMAX, the upper bound on the time variable, always must be selected.

2. RUN. This is the **main phase** of the program, where the problem equations are used to generate solutions. A RUN subroutine performs several interrelated functions:

(a) Call upon an **integration algorithm** (subroutine INTEG) to increase the problem time T to a new value $T + DT$ and to update all problem variables. The integration subroutine obtains the problem equations and thus the **state-variable derivatives**, from a user-furnished subroutine

DIFFEQ. The RUN subroutine checks to determine when the solution has reached a **communication time** when **output** should be delivered to a display device, or at least temporarily stored for later display.

(b) When $T = $ TMAX, RUN returns control to the calling program.

3. TERMINATE. This phase may depend considerably on the purpose of the simulation job. Typical functions that may be required are

(a) *The output of solutions is completed.* For example, plotting routines may be called to display arrays of solution values which have been developed during execution of RUN.

(b) Tests of solution results may be made to determine if another run is desired or whether the program should STOP.

More detail is provided in Fig. 2-2, where individual subroutines are identified.

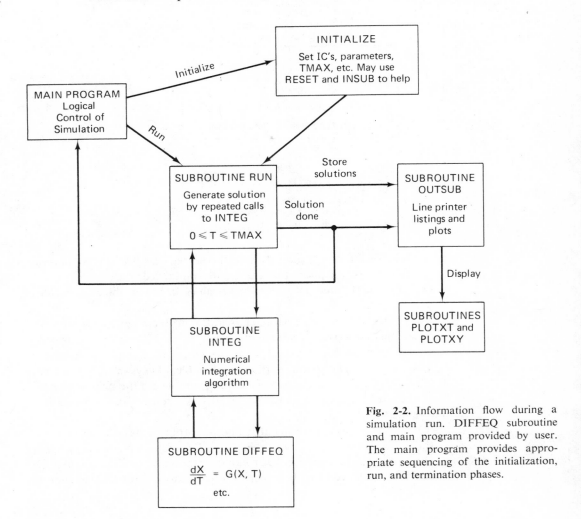

Fig. 2-2. Information flow during a simulation run. DIFFEQ subroutine and main program provided by user. The main program provides appropriate sequencing of the initialization, run, and termination phases.

We shall discuss the use of each of the routines in turn; in Appendix B we provide added detail about coding, options, etc.

2-2. Subroutine Linkage: Important Variables. Sets of problem variables and parameters usually needed for a simulation job are passed between subprograms through standard labeled COMMON **blocks,** specifically

STATEV	contains the **state variables** and **defined** (output **variables** (dimensioned 30); state variables are in first 20 locations and additional variables in last 10
STADER	contains the current values of the **state derivatives**
UNDVAR	contains **problem parameters,** to be specified as data or by other calculations
SYSVAR	contains important **simulation system parameters** in the following order:

T	independent variable
DT	current integration step size
TMAX	maximum value for T
TNEXT	value of T at which output is next required
DTMAX, DTMIN	maximum and minimum values of DT (used with variable-step integration rules)
EMAX, EMIN	maximum and minimum values of per-step error (used with variable-step rules only)
S1, S2, S3	spare real-valued system variables
NORDER	**order of system being simulated** (i.e., number of state variables, 20 maximum)
NPARAM	**number of problem parameters** (20 maximum)
NPOINT	number of points where output is required ($0 \leq T \leq TMAX$)
K1, K2, K3	spare integer-valued system variables
INIT	a logical variable used to initialize a problem run
OUTPUT	a logical variable used to signal that output is required
L1, L2, L3	spare logical-valued system variables
OUTVAR	contains a special set of variables to provide information to output subroutines, as follows:

	NLIST	**number of variables to be listed** (optional)

NPLOT	**number of variables to be plotted** (optional)
NOUT	an index indicating the current number of output points already generated
TITLE	an array of 16 titles for output (assumes A5 format requires only one word)
V	an array of **REAL output variables** to be displayed (dimensioned 10)
IV	an array of **integer-valued output variables** (dimensioned 10)
ISEL	an array (dimensioned 25) which stores indices for commands to special version of OUTSUB, discussed in Sec. 2-8 and Appendix B
W	a 101 × 4 array which may be used to store arrays for subsequent plotting

Note that all variables must be properly declared (REAL, LOGICAL, INTEGER, etc.) and treated as declared in all programs linked via the above blocks. We assume that one machine word is used per variable. On short-word-length machines, special care may have to be taken, especially with real variables and with character strings. In simple problems, the variables in the OUTVAR array need not be dealt with, although the index NOUT is often useful. On a first reading, the user should become familiar with the STATEV, STADER, UNDVAR, and SYSVAR blocks only; in the latter block, the most important variables are T, TMAX, NORDER, NPARAM and NPOINT.

2-3. Specifying the Differential Equations: Subroutine DIFFEQ. To use our subroutine package, **the user must prepare a special subroutine named DIFFEQ**, which specifies the problem equations for the particular problem to be studied. Special operations can, of course, be implemented with additional subprograms called upon by DIFFEQ. The following general form is required:

```
SUBROUTINE DIFFEQ
DIMENSION Y(30),G(20),P(20)
COMMON/STATEV/Y/STADER/G
COMMON/UNDVAR/P if used
```

COMMON/SYSVAR/T,SV(10), NORDER, NPARAM, INIT(4),
LOGIC(5)
LOGICAL LOGIC
DATA NORDER, NPARAM/*n, m*/

> Problem specification with
> Y(I) as state variables, $I = 1, 20$, or output variables,
> $I = 21, 30$.
> G(I) as derivative functions, and
> P(J) as parameters to be specified
> by data provided to UNDVAR block.
> In some time-varying systems, T is used.

RETURN
END

```
      PROGRAM DARE(INPUT,OUTPUT)
C        SIMPLIFIED USE OF SUBROUTINES
C     SECOND-ORDER DAMPED SYSTEM STEP RESPONSE
C     JAN. 1975
C     ESTABLISH LINKING COMMON BLOCKS
      COMMON/STATEV/Y(30)
      COMMON/UNDVAR/P(20)
      COMMON/SYSVAR/T,DT,TMAX,A(8),NORDER,NPARAM,NPOINT,K(3),
     1INIT,OUTPUT,L(3)
      LOGICAL L
C     SET INITIAL CONDITIONS AND PARAMETERS
      Y(1)=0.0
      Y(2)=0.0
      P(1)=0.1
      TMAX=50.
      DT=0.01
      NPOINT=21
      OUTPUT=.TRUE.
      CALL RUN
      STOP
      END
```

Fig. 2-3. (a)

Fig. 2-3. Primitive program to list solution values for a simple second-order system step response. (a) Main program; (b) DIFFEQ subroutine; (c) a simple version of INTEG (rectangular or Euler integration); (d) a simple version of OUTSUB which merely outputs a special title and lists T and Y(1); (e) program output.

```
      SUBROUTINE DIFFEQ
C
C     STEP RESPONSE OF SECOND-ORDER SYSTEM
      COMMON/STATEV/Y
      COMMON/STADER/G
      COMMON/UNDVAR/P
      COMMON/SYSVAR/T,X(10),NORDER,NPARAM,INT(4),LOGIC(5)
      DIMENSION G(20),Y(30),P(20)
      LOGICAL LOGIC
C     BE SURE TO ASSIGN PROPER VALUES FOR
C          NORDER AND NPARAM
C     COULD ALSO BE DONE IN MAIN PROGRAM
      DATA NORDER,NPARAM/2,1/
C     STATE EQUATIONS FOLLOW
      G(1)=Y(2)
      G(2) = -Y(1)-P(1)*Y(2) + 1.0
      RETURN
      END
```

Fig. 2-3. (b)

```
            SUBROUTINE INTEG
C           VERSION 2, DEC. 1970
C           EULER OR RECTANGULAR INTEGRATION
            COMMON/STADER/G
            COMMON/STATEV/Y
            COMMON/UNDVAR/P
            COMMON/SYSVAR/T,DT,TMAX,TNEXT,DTMAX,DTMIN,EMAX,EMIN,S1,S2,S3,
           $NORDER,NPARAM,NPOINT,K1,K2,K3,INIT,OUTPUT,L1,L2,L3
            DIMENSION G(20),Y(30),P(20)
            LOGICAL INIT,OUTPUT,L1,L2,L3
            IF(INIT) GO TO 300
1           CALL DIFFEQ
            DO 100 I=1,NORDER
100         Y(I)=Y(I)+ G(I)*DT
            TEM=K
            T=TEM*DT
            K=K+1
            RETURN
C           INITIALIZATION
300         K=1
            INIT =.FALSE.
            GO TO 1
            END
```

Fig. 2-3. (c)

```
            SUBROUTINE OUTSUB
            COMMON/STATEV/Y(30)
            COMMON/UNDVAR/P(20)
            COMMON/SYSVAR/T,X(10),I(6),L(5)
            LOGICAL L
C           THIS SIMPLE ROUTINE MERELY LISTS FIRST STATE VARIABLE
C           AND TIME
            IF(T.EQ.0) PRINT 100, P(1)
100         FORMAT(1H1,26H STEP RESPONSE, DAMPING = ,E10.3,//,
           15H TIME,10X,1HY,/)
            PRINT 200,T,Y(1)
200         FORMAT(E10.3,5X,E10.3)
            RETURN
            END
```

Fig. 2-3. (d)

```
        STEP RESPONSE, DAMPING =   1.000E-01

        TIME                Y

        0.                  0.
        2.500E+00           1.688E+00
        5.000E+00           8.149E-01
        7.500E+00           7.153E-01
        1.000E+01           1.555E+00
        1.250E+01           4.342E-01
        1.500E+01           1.366E+00
        1.750E+01           9.286E-01
        2.000E+01           8.099E-01
        2.250E+01           1.329E+00
        2.500E+01           6.817E-01
        2.750E+01           1.192E+00
        3.000E+01           9.789E-01
        3.250E+01           8.764E-01
        3.500E+01           1.193E+00
        3.750E+01           8.221E-01
        4.000E+01           1.100E+00
        4.250E+01           9.992E-01
        4.500E+01           9.213E-01
        4.750E+01           1.113E+00
        5.000E+01           9.011E-01
```

Fig. 2-3. (e)

The COMMON blocks link the variables in DIFFEQ to the rest of the package. Figure 2-3 shows a typical example program for the second-order linear differential equation

$$\frac{d^2 Y}{dT^2} + D\frac{dY}{dT} + Y = 1.0$$

with $D = P(1) = 0.1$. The equation is solved once with zero initial conditions and TMAX $= 50$.

Note that we normally establish the order of the system, NORDER, and the number of parameters, NPARAM, by a DATA statement in DIFFEQ. This is easy to remember. Otherwise, one could use an arithmetic replacement statement, e.g.,

NORDER $= 2$

but this wastes computer time, since the statement is redundantly executed every time DIFFEQ is called, which may be hundreds of times. Also, one could designate these system constants in the main program and link them to the DIFFEQ routine, etc., via the SYSVAR block. We find the technique shown (viz., the use of the DATA statement) easy to do once the habit is developed.*

Several examples in this chapter will indicate how the DIFFEQ subroutine looks for specific problems.

2-4. Subroutine RUN. Figure 2-4 shows one of the most important routines in the package, **subroutine RUN**. It implements a simulation run starting with T $= 0$ and terminates the run when T = TMAX. RUN also ensures that output is delivered to routine OUTSUB at the desired communication intervals.

Before calling RUN, **the calling program should make sure that the following has been done:**

1. OUTPUT = .TRUE. if output is to be made during a run.
2. System variable TMAX must be initialized to some positive value.
3. The number of output points, NPOINT, should be set to two or more (see below for more about choosing NPOINT).
4. The initial conditions (STATEV block) and the parameters (UNDVAR block) should be given proper initial values.

Subroutine RUN will set the integration step size DT initially to 0.005 TMAX, if a positive nonzero value of DT has not been set prior to the first call to RUN. Note that we assume that output is desired at equally spaced communication intervals and that to cover N time intervals $N + 1$ output points are required.

---

*Some older operating systems have loaders which do not permit variables in COMMON blocks to be specified by DATA statements; in this case, the user will have to use one of the suggested alternatives.

```
      SUBROUTINE RUN
C     VERSION 2, DEC. 1970
C     MODIFIED AUG. 24, 1972
C     CONTROLS RUN-TIME EXECUTION
C     RETURNS WITH DT AND ICS RESTORED
C     MAKE OUTPUT=.TRUE.  FOR OUTPUT TO SUBROUTINE OUTSUB
C     OUTPUTS AT PRECISE TIMES WITH VARIABLE STEP RULES
      COMMON/STADER/G
      COMMON/STATEV/Y
      COMMON/UNDVAR/P
      COMMON/OUTVAR/NLIST,NPLOT,NOUT,TITLE,V,IV,ISEL,W
      COMMON/SYSVAR/T,DT,TMAX,TNEXT,DTMAX,DTMIN,EMAX,EMIN,S1,S2,S3,
     1NORDER,NPARAM,NPOINT,K1,K2,K3,INIT,OUTPUT,L1,L2,L3
      DIMENSION TITLE(32),V(10),IV(10),ISEL(25),W(101,4)
      DIMENSION G(20),Y(30),P(20),Z(20)
      LOGICAL INIT,OUTPUT,L1,L2,L3
      DO 1 I=1,NORDER
    1 Z(I)=Y(I)
      DTSAV=DT
    2 INIT=.TRUE.
      IF(TMAX.LE.0.0)GO TO 13
      IF(DT.GT.0.0)GO TO 3
      DT=0.005*TMAX
      PRINT 14,DT
    3 IF(NPOINT.GE.2)GO TO 5
      NPOINT=101
      PRINT 4, NPOINT
    4 FORMAT(/,10H NPOINT = ,I3,/)
    5 NOUT=1
    6 SPACES=NPOINT-1
      COMINT=TMAX/SPACES
      TOL=-0.0001*COMINT
      TMAXP=TMAX+TOL
      TNEXT = COMINT
      T=0.
      IF(DT.GT.COMINT)GO TO 7
      GO TO 8
    7 DT = COMINT
      PRINT 14,DT
    8 CALL DIFFEQ
      IF(OUTPUT)CALL OUTSUB
    9 CALL INTEG
C     HAS OUTPUT POINT BEEN REACHED
      IF((T-TNEXT).LT.TOL)GO TO 9
      NOUT=NOUT+1
      IF(OUTPUT)CALL OUTSUB
      A=NOUT
      TNEXT=A*COMINT
   10 IF(T-TMAXP)9,11,11
   11 CONTINUE
      DO 12 I=1,NORDER
   12 Y(I)=Z(I)
      DT=DTSAV
      GO TO 16
   13 PRINT 15
      STOP
   14 FORMAT(/,20H DTSTART CHANGED TO ,E20.7)
   15 FORMAT(21H FAULTY RUN-TIME DATA,)
   16 RETURN
      END
```

Fig. 2-4. Subroutine RUN. This routine supervise one simulation run for $0 \leq T \leq TMAX$ and calls OUTSUB at NPOINT communication times over that range.

Thus typical values of NPOINT are 101 (for 100 intervals,), 51, etc. RUN calculates a communication interval

$$COMINT = TMAX/(NPOINT-1)$$

which establishes the time interval associated with each call by RUN to the output subroutine OUTSUB. Other system variables may need special values; e.g., DTMAX, DTMIN, EMAX, and EMIN normally have to be initialized for the use of most variable-step integration rules (see Sec. 2-9 and Appendix A).

If OUTPUT = .TRUE., then RUN will call subroutine OUTSUB (which will be discussed further below). In special situations, e.g., when one is doing iterative runs to find an optimum value for a parameter or initial condition, the user may want to suppress the calls to OUTSUB by temporarily setting OUTPUT = .FALSE. and then making it .TRUE. for a final run to get a solution for the optimum parameter value.

RUN finishes with the original values of DT, and the state variables are restored: it is important that the user remember this in iterative computations.

2-5. An Example

Example 2-1: Step Response of a Linear Second-Order System. Before discussing additional routines in our package which facilitate larger jobs, let us look at a very simple example, which develops a solution to

$$\frac{d^2Y}{dT^2} + D\frac{dY}{dT} + Y = 1.0 \qquad (2-1)$$

With a positive value of D, and $Y(0) = dY/dT = 0$, we shall get a stable step response. In Fig. 2-3, we have *not* used special routines, such as INSUB and RESET (discussed below), to initialize the problem. Also we use only a rudimentary version of OUTSUB, which merely lists a coarsely spaced set of values of Y and dY/dT for $0 \leq T \leq TMAX = 50.$ at 21 points.

Even in this simple example, we see the basic things that must be done, such as

1. Proper initialization of state variables and parameters (here done in the main program).
2. A CALL RUN is used to generate a solution time history.
3. Subroutine OUTSUB provides the desired output.
4. Subroutine INTEG is used by RUN to provide the numerical algorithm to generate the solution points.

We here show a simple open or explicit Euler integration rule (see Appendix A), which works reasonably well on this simple problem but is not suitable for accurate general-purpose simulation.

It is recommended that the reader study the listings for this first problem carefully to gain some "feel" of the manner in which the subroutines work together. In particular, the main program does the initialization; note which variables were involved. Note also how OUTSUB was used to provide an identifying message, titles for the columns, and the solution values.

2-6. More Complete Output: Use of Line-Printer Plotting. The printed output in our first example does not give the best possible insight into the nature of the solution. More complete output and **graphic output** are greatly preferable. Figure 2-5 shows an improved version of OUTSUB which not only lists the two state variable values but provides a **line-printer plot** of Y versus T, via the subroutine PLOTXT. We also have used the more effective four-point Runge-Kutta integration algorithm (Appendix A), which permits the step size to be ten times larger and still provides a more accurate solution. *Note that there are actually only $\frac{4}{10}$ as many calls to DIFFEQ in this example* as in the previous one.

The version of OUTSUB shown in Fig. 2-5 is a basic general-purpose routine, which might be used with other problems. It performs the following functions:

> **1.** Up to four state variables are **listed**. The routine automatically outputs Y(1), . . . , Y(NLIST), where NLIST = MINO(NORDER, 4).
>
> **2. Titles** for the state variables may be used as headings; these are via the OUTVAR block, which now appears in the main program.
>
> **3.** As the solution proceeds, OUTSUB generates an array W containing successive values of the first state variable, Y(1). After NPOINT values have been generated, a call to PLOTXT generates the **line-printer plot** indicated. Since PLOTXT is a self-scaling routine, it is necessary to build up the entire array of solution points prior to plotting any. This procedure must always be followed when using self-scaling routines.

Note that the main program initializes the "values" of the titles with Hollerith string definitions for TITLE(1) and TITLE(2).

Listings for two plotting routines, PLOTXT and PLOTXY, and their associated subprograms appear in Appendix B (Fig. B-3). They are easy to use once the required arrays of points to be plotted have been generated. Note that **these routines are self-scaling but that the user may override this feature.** The calling procedures are as follows:

To plot arrays versus a constant time increment,

```
CALL PLOTXT (TO,DT,X,NXDIM,NFUN,NPNT,XMINZ,XMAXZ)
```

where TO is the starting value of the independent variable,
 DT is the increment of the independent variable,
 X(NXDIM,NFUN) is an array of values of dependent variables,
 NXDIM is the first dimension of X (as declared in the dimension statement for X),
 NFUN is the number of functions of the dependent variables to be plotted,
 NPNT is the number of points from each function to be plotted (not necessarily NXDIM),
 XMINZ, XMAXZ are limits on the dependent variable; they should be set equal for autoscaling.

```
                PROGRAM DARE(INPUT,OUTPUT)
        C          SIMPLIFIED USE OF SUBROUTINES
        C       SECOND-ORDER DAMPED SYSTEM STEP RESPONSE
        C       ESTABLISH LINKING COMMON BLOCKS
                COMMON/STATEV/Y(30)
                COMMON/UNDVAR/P(20)
                COMMON/SYSVAR/T,DT,TMAX,A(8),NORDER,NPARAM,NPOINT,K(3),
               1INIT,OUTPUT,L(3)
                LOGICAL L
        C       SET INITIAL CONDITIONS AND PARAMETERS
                Y(1)=0.0
                Y(2)=0.0
                P(1)=0.1
                TMAX=50.
                NPOINT=101
                DT=0.1
                OUTPUT=.TRUE.
                CALL RUN
                STOP
                END
```

Fig. 2-5. (a)

Fig. 2-5. Step response of a second-order system with line-printer plotting. (a) Main program; (b) DIFFEQ subroutine; (c) improved version of OUTSUB, which calls PLOTXT; (d) fourth-order fixed-step Runge-Kutta integration rule (subroutine INTEG); (e) solution listing; (f) line-printer plot of Y versus T.

```
                SUBROUTINE DIFFEQ
        C
        C       STEP RESPONSE OF SECOND-ORDER SYSTEM
                COMMON/STATEV/Y
                COMMON/STADER/G
                COMMON/UNDVAR/P
                COMMON/SYSVAR/T,X(10),NORDER,NPARAM,INT(4),LOGIC(5)
                COMMON/OUTVAR/NLIST,NPLOT,NOUT,TITLE,V,IV,ISEL,W
                DIMENSION G(20),Y(30),P(20)
                DIMENSION TITLE(32),V(10),IV(10),ISEL(25),W(101,4)
                LOGICAL LOGIC
        C       BE SURE TO ASSIGN PROPER VALUES FOR
        C           NORDER AND NPARAM
        C       COULD ALSO BE DONE IN MAIN PROGRAM
                DATA NORDER,NPARAM/2,1/
        C       TITLES CAN BE PUT HERE OR IN MAIN PROGRAM
        C       NOTE EACH TITLE TAKES TWO WORDS
                DATA TITLE(1),TITLE(2),TITLE(3),TITLE(4)/5H   Y  ,5H        ,5H YDOT,
               1 5H       /
        C       STATE EQUATIONS FOLLOW
                G(1)=Y(2)
                G(2) = -Y(1)-P(1)*Y(2) + 1.0
                RETURN
                END
```

Fig. 2-5. (b)

```
                SUBROUTINE OUTSUB
        C       SIMPLE VERSION TO LIST UP TO FOUR
        C       STATE VARIABLES AND PLOT THE FIRST
                COMMON/STADER/G
                COMMON/STATEV/Y
                COMMON/UNDVAR/P
                COMMON/OUTVAR/NLIST,NPLOT,NOUT,TITLE,V,IV,ISEL,W
                COMMON/SYSVAR/T,DT,TMAX,TNEXT,DTMAX,DTMIN,EMAX,EMIN,S1,S2,S3,
               1NORDER,NPARAM,NPOINT,K1,K2,K3,INIT,OUTPUT,L1,L2,L3
                DIMENSION TITLE(32),V(10),IV(10),ISEL(25),W(101,4)
                DIMENSION G(20),Y(30),P(20),A(4)
                LOGICAL INIT,OUTPUT,L1,L2,L3
                DATA TOUT/5H TIME/
                NLIST=MINO(NORDER,4)
                NTIT=2*NLIST
                IF(INIT) PRINT 101, TOUT,(TITLE(I),I=1,NTIT )
        101     FORMAT(1H1,10X,A5,15X,2A5,15X,2A5,15X,2A5,//)
                PRINT 135,T,(Y(I),I=1,NLIST)
        135     FORMAT(1X,5G25.13)
        60      W(NOUT,1)=Y(1)
        70      IF(INIT) COMINT=TNEXT
        80      IF(NOUT.EQ.NPOINT) GO TO 100
                RETURN
        100     PRINT 200
        200     FORMAT(1H1)
                CALL PLOTXT(0.0,COMINT,W,101,1,101,0.0,0.0)
                RETURN
                END
```

Fig. 2-5. (c)

```
          SUBROUTINE INTEG
C         VERSION 2, DEC. 1970
C         FOURTH-ORDER RUNGE-KUTTA
          COMMON/STADER/G
          COMMON/STATEV/Y
          COMMON/UNDVAR/P
          COMMON/SYSVAR/T,DT,TMAX,TNEXT,DTMAX,DTMIN,EMAX,EMIN,S1,S2,S3,
         $NORDER,NPARAM,NPOINT,K1,K2,K3,INIT,OUTPUT,L1,L2,L3
          DIMENSION G(20),Y(30),P(20)
          LOGICAL INIT,OUTPUT,L1,L2,L3
          DIMENSION RK1(20),RK2(20),RK3(20),YS(20)
          IF(INIT) GO TO 200
100       CALL DIFFEQ
          DO 101 I=1,NORDER
          RK1(I)= G(I)*DTO2
          YS(I)=Y(I)
101       Y(I)=YS(I)+RK1(I)
          T=T+DTO2
          CALL DIFFEQ
          DO 102 I=1,NORDER
          RK2(I)= G(I)*DTO2
102       Y(I)=YS(I)+RK2(I)
          CALL DIFFEQ
          DO 103 I=1,NORDER
          RK3(I)= G(I)*DT
103       Y(I)=YS(I)+RK3(I)
          AI=J
          T=AI*DT
          J=J+1
          CALL DIFFEQ
          DO 104 I=1,NORDER
          Y(I)=YS(I)+.166666666666667*
         $(2.0*(RK1(I)+RK3(I))+4.0*RK2(I)+ G(I)*DT)
104       CONTINUE
          RETURN
200       DTO2=0.5*DT
          J=1
          INIT =.FALSE.
          GO TO 100
          END
```

Fig. 2-5. (d)

TIME	Y	YDOT
0.	0.	0.
.5000000000000	.1204106333540	.4676376990027
1.0000000000000	.4450075636119	.8007897932163
1.5000000000000	.8863140506695	.9264536233214
2.0000000000000	1.333247688475	.8247381274537
2.5000000000000	1.678799763444	.5310238409193
3.0000000000000	1.845391821090	.1248178877394
3.5000000000000	1.801967206297	-.2913855541292
4.0000000000000	1.569138957002	-.6177034470291
4.5000000000000	1.211747156088	-.78059007431'
5.0000000000000	.8212172007733	-.749116'
5.5000000000000	.4924295059895	-.54'
6.0000000000000	.3008921739337	-
6.5000000000000	.2856533536298	
7.0000000000000	.4417541411792	
7.5000000000000	.7235590818583	
8.0000000000000	1.057638396094	
8.5000000000000	1.361659623954	
9.0000000000000	1.5644840057	
9.5000000000000	1.62260953'	
10.0000000000000	1.529212''	
10.5000000000000	1.313°	
11.0000000000000	1.0'	
11.50000000000		
12.00000000000		

Fig. 2-5. (e)

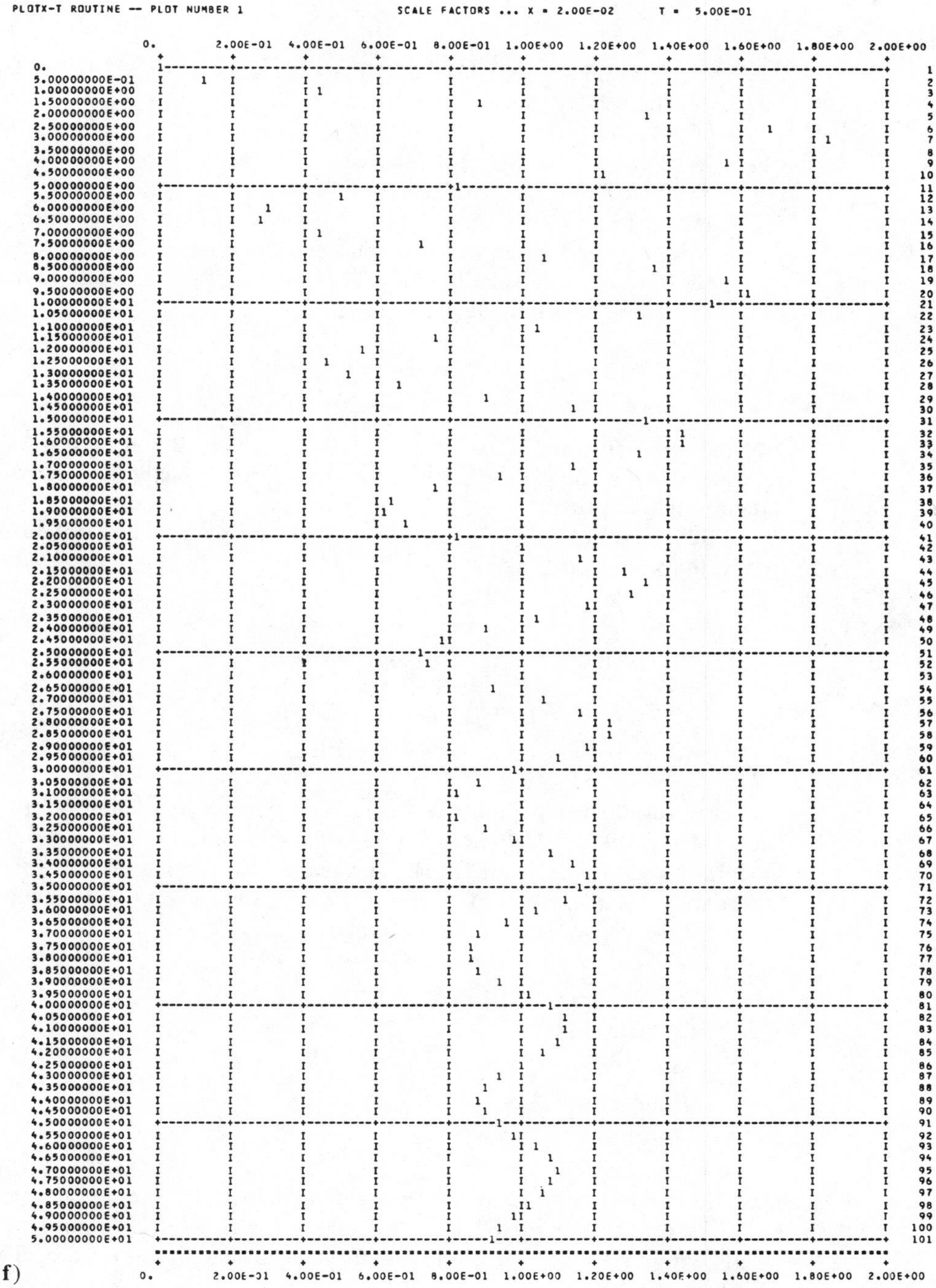
PLOTX-T ROUTINE -- PLOT NUMBER 1
SCALE FACTORS ... X = 2.00E-02 T = 5.00E-01
0. 2.00E-01 4.00E-01 6.00E-01 8.00E-01 1.00E+00 1.20E+00 1.40E+00 1.60E+00 1.80E+00 2.00E+00

Fig. 2-5. (f)

To plot arrays versus another array,

CALL PLOTXY (X,Y,NYDIM,NFUN,NPNT,MMN,XXMIN,XXMAX,
YYMIN,YYMAX)

where X(NYDIM) is the independent variable array,
Y(NYDIM, NFUN) is the array of dependent variables,
NYDIM is the dimension of Y as declared in its dimension statement,
MMN is the rate at which points are displayed; i.e., if MMN = 2, every
second point is displayed, etc.; if MMN = 0, PLOTXY determines the rate
for the best looking display.

Other variables are the same as defined above.

2-7. Initialization with RESET and INSUB. Appendix B contains listings of subroutines RESET and INSUB, which are provided to **facilitate input of run-time
data** and **initialization.**

RESET provides a general-purpose initialization, including default values of
important parameters, viz.,

EMAX = 0.001
EMIN = 0.00001
NPOINT = 101
OUTPUT = .TRUE.
INIT = .TRUE.

All other variables, including the Y and P arrays, are just initialized to zero. (See
Secs. 2-2 and 2-9 for a definition and use of system variables.)

Following a CALL RESET, one can then use subroutine INSUB to input run-
time data via card images. The data format is an alphanumeric-signal card, followed by associated data cards, as follows:

Signal (A5, left-justified)
Data card(s)
Signal
Data card(s)
etc.

Only the signals and data desired need be used. A set of data is terminated by a
signal card having a period in column 1, followed by four blanks. A program
STOP within INSUB can be initiated by an all-blank signal card. The signals
currently provided are

1. IC for initial conditions; the following cards should contain initial conditions Y(1) in format 4E20.13.

2. PARAM for undefined parameters in UNDVAR, again 4E20.13.

3. DT, step size (E20.13).

4. TMAX, run time (E20.13).

5. ERROR, error-control parameters; the next card should contain EMAX, EMIN, DTMAX, DTMIN (4E20.13). (Use with variable-step integration rules; see, e.g., Sec. 2-9.)

6. NPOIN (or NPOINT), number of points (I5).

7. IDENT, an 80-column problem-identification message should follow (16A5).

8. K; system variables K1, K2, K3 should follow in format 3I5.

9. L; logical system variables L1, L2, L3 should follow in format 3L1.

The following flags are intended for use with the special version of OUTSUB shown in Fig. B-2 in Appendix B:

10. LISTT; this flag signals that a set of variables from the Y array are to be listed (up to four); these can be any four indices from 1 through 30. If the indices point to output variables which are not state variables, then these variables must be properly defined in DIFFEQ. This flag is followed by a card which specifies the number of indices, and the indices, in format 5(I2,1X). For example, 04, 01, 02, 05, 21 directs listing of four variables, Y(1), Y(2), Y(5), and Y(21), every time OUTSUB is called.

11. STORE; this flag indicates that the following card will specify the number of items and the indices of variables from the Y array which are to be stored in a 101 × 4 array for later display. The format is 5(I2,1X).

12. Flags LISTW, PLOTT, and PLOTW may be used *following* a STORE flag; these flags signal that subsequent cards will specify indices of variables to be output from the array W, in particular

> LISTW lists from W against time.
>
> PLOTT plots from W against time.
>
> PLOTW initiates cross plotting of variables from W; the first index is for the abscissa, or independent variable, against which the others are plotted.

13. TITLE; this signals that two cards are to follow, with titles to be used for listing and plotting, as follows:

> (a) On the first card the user may furnish four 10-column titles to be used with normal OUTSUB listing via LISTT; a second group of four titles are used to title any variables listed from the W array via LISTW.
>
> (b) The second card provides two 40-character titles, the first to be used with PLOTT and the second with PLOTW.

INSUB will echo back current values of important variables. Remember that each signal card is followed by data, but a complete set of run-time data is terminated by a .bbbb card.

2-8. A General-Purpose Version of OUTSUB. The data implied by flags LISTT, STORE, LISTW, PLOTW, and PLOTT are intended for use with the special version of OUTSUB shown in Fig. B-2 in Appendix B. If output is desired (OUTPUT = .TRUE.) but no other output requests are made, the following *default* output is provided:

> **1.** *Listing against time* (LISTT) *of all the first four state variables* (up to a maximum of four).
> **2.** *Plotting against time* (PLOTT) *of the first two state variables* (if there are two; otherwise, plotting of just one against time).
> **3.** *Plotting of the first variable against the second* (this option is exercised only if there are two variables).

If explicit requests are made with LISTT, STORE, PLOTW, LISTW, and PLOTT, then a wide variety of outputs is possible. The examples in Sec. 2-10 illustrate how data cards can direct special output; further details are provided in Appendix B.

2-9. A General-Purpose Variable-Step Integration Rule. In Appendix A, we shall discuss some of the considerations bearing upon *the choice of a numerical integration rule*. In general, we prefer to use an algorithm which includes a means of local error estimation and associated step-size control. Figure B-4 in Appendix B shows a popular algorithm known as Runge-Kutta-Merson, which we have used as the primary integration routine in the FORTRAN package described in this chapter. In Appendix A, we shall discuss this type of rule in some detail. Our purpose here is to outline its use. Several *error-controlled parameters*, which are conveniently entered via INSUB, are involved:

EMAX	maximum estimated per step error allowed before DT is decreased
EMIN	minimum estimated value of per-step error allowed before DT is increased
DTMIN	minimum value of DT permitted, in order to avoid excessive computing time
DTMAX	maximum value of DT permitted: usually should be COMINT
K3	if 0, relative (fractional) error is used as a measure of accuracy; if a positive integer, then absolute error is used on $Y(K3)$ only
L3	if L3 = .TRUE., information on step size changes is printed

Our version of RESET establishes general-purpose default values of these parameters, which work well in most cases. These *default* values are

$$\text{EMAX} = 0.001, \quad \text{EMIN} = 0.00001$$
$$\text{K3} = 0, \quad \text{L3} = .\text{FALSE}.$$

In addition, DTMAX and DTMIN are set to 0.0, which causes the strategy shown in Fig. B-4(b) to set

$$\text{DTMAX} = \text{COMINT}, \quad \text{DTMIN} = 0.0625 \text{ DTMAX}$$

In most cases, these default values will yield accuracies of 0.1% or better with a 60-bit floating-point word, but tighter bounds on EMAX may be required.

2-10. More Examples. Use of the Complete FORTRAN Package. Our next example will utilize RESET and INSUB (Fig. B-1), the general-purpose output routine OUTSUB (Fig. B-2), and the variable-step Runge-Kutta-Merson integration routine (Fig. B-4) to treat the population-dynamics problem of Example 1-2. (See Appendix B for referenced listings.)

Example 2-2: Population Dynamics. Referring to Sec. 1-3, we rewrite the problem equations (1-9) as

$$\frac{dY1}{dT} = -P1 * Y1 * Y2$$

$$\frac{dY2}{dT} = P1 * Y1 * Y2 - P2 * Y2 \tag{2-2}$$

$$\frac{dY3}{dT} = P2 * Y2$$

since our FORTRAN package cannot use general symbol names. $Y1$ is the number of individuals *susceptible* to a disease, $Y2$ is the number of infectious *carriers*, and $Y3$ are the individuals recovered and *immune*. $P1$ and $P2$ are rate constants for susceptibility and recovery. We shall also compute the *epidemic curve* $-dY1/dT$.

Referring to Fig. 2-6, note that the main program is very simple and will permit reruns with new parameter values input via INSUB. Note in DIFFEQ that Y(21) is used to store the epidemic variable. All of the output, including the titles for the listing, was directed by data cards to INSUB. Figure 2-6(c) shows the complete data card set which generated the output of Fig. 2-6(d)–(f). Note how the titles were entered. Default values for DT, EMAX, etc., were used, and the initial conditions were set to

$$Y1 = 620. \quad Y2 = 10., \quad Y3 = 70.$$

The parameter values were

$$P1 = 0.001, \quad P2 = 0.072$$

and the solutions were generated with TMAX = 50. A final blank data card terminated the job; alternatively, new values of run-time parameters could be introduced. Only those values which are to be changed need be provided for another run.

Fig. 2-6. Solution of a population-dynamics problem (epidemic propagation) which uses the complete general-purpose package. (a) Main program; (b) DIFFEQ subroutine; (c) listing of data cards used; (d) output echo of initialization; (e) listing of solutions; (f) line-printer plot of solutions.

```
        PROGRAM EPIDEM(INPUT,OUTPUT)
    C
    C
3       CALL RESET
4   10  CALL INSUB
5       CALL RUN
6       GO TO 10
7       END
```

Fig. 2-6. (a)

```
        SUBROUTINE DIFFEQ
2       DIMENSION G(20),Y(30),P(20)
2       COMMON/STATEV/Y/STADER/G/UNDVAR/P
2       COMMON/SYSVAR/T,X(10),NORDER,NPARAM,INT(4),LOGIC(5)
2       LOGICAL LOGIC
2       DATA NORDER,NPARAM/3,2/
2       G(1)=-P(1)*Y(1)*Y(2)
14      G(2)=P(1)*Y(1)*Y(2)-P(2)*Y(2)
33      G(3)=P(2)*Y(2)
42      Y(21)=-G(1)
47      RETURN
47      END
```

Fig. 2-6. (b)

```
TMAX
50.0
IC
620.              10.                    70.
PARAM
0.001             0.072
IDENT
      EPIDEMIC  PROBLEM
TITLE
SUSCEPT   CARRIERS   IMMUNE     EPIDEM
          TIME PLOT
STORE
04 01 02 03 21
LISTT
04 01 02 03 21
PLOTT
04 01 02 03 21
.
```

Fig. 2-6. (c)

EPIDEMIC   PROBLEM

INITIAL CONDITIONS

   1   620.0000000000
   2   10.00000000000
   3   70.00000000000

PARAMETERS

   1   1.0000000000000E-03
   2   7.2000000000000E-02

DT =   0.   TMAX =   50.00000000000

NUMBER OF POINTS = 101

DTSTART CHANGED TO   2.5000000E-01

TERMINATED BY INSUB

Fig. 2-6. (d)

TIME	SUSCEPT	CARRIERS	IMMUNE	EPIDEM
0.	620.0000000000	10.00000000000	70.00000000000	6.200000000000
.5000000000000	616.4449892612	13.14098263844	70.4140281C034	8.100692901435
1.000000000000	611.8090685666	17.23338703517	70.95754439824	10.54358913479
1.500000000000	605.7901569059	22.54046272224	71.66938037184	13.65490093442
2.000000000000	598.C202503731	29.38091802344	72.59883160349	17.57059870625
2.500000000000	588.0636321548	38.12969397851	73.80767386663	22.42247341591
3.000000000000	575.4246180668	49.20336718823	75.37201474494	28.31343119645
3.500000000000	559.5709502041	63.04550232644	77.38354746940	35.27932375254
4.000000000000	539.9796439255	80.07080317598	79.94955289851	43.23781277228
4.500000000000	516.2102981552	100.5989019756	83.19079986918	51.93166378935
5.000000000000	488.0046406932	124.7589169718	87.23644233493	60.88450551268
5.500000000000	455.3992783167	152.3854401854	92.21528149782	69.39762745360
6.000000000000	418.8233946692	182.9330918666	98.24351346418	—
6.500000000000	379.1419777591	215.4477175857	105.4103046552	
7.000000000000	337.8092068754	248.6269218640	113.76387¹¹	
7.500000000000	295.7226016496	280.9759039642	1?? ⋅	
8.000000000000	255.0086578304	311.0249300528	— ⋅⋅⋅⁹	2.105135354113E-02
8.500000000000	216.8025336295	337.544755586⁶	⌐32494332	1.9573782507422E-02
9.000000000000	182.0866388909	2⁻⁻	629.7872382998	1.822351322226E-02
9.500000000000	151.4243417915		632.2608875616	1.6987614236618E-02
10.00000000000	124.9851087465	⌐/71755	634.6473697390	1.5854648153799E-02
10.50000000000	102.029274⁶⁻	.0003446B910	636.9497469940	1.4814480064655E-02
11.00000000000	84.0138⁶⁻		639.1709748535	1.3858112794665E-02
11.50000000000	68.6⁰⁻	58.46411963384	641.3139058202	1.2977544910548E-02
12.00000000000	5⁶	56.40301565517	643.3812928743	1.2165648097310E-02
12.50000000000		54.41440861791	645.3757928664	1.1416061051748E-02
13.00000000000	⌐9744933	52.49576422169	647.2999698037	1.0723097489303E-02
13.50000000000	..490668315238	50.64463513575	649.1562980326	1.0081666235146E-02
14.00000000000	.1941764824359	48.85865819638	650.9471653190	9.487201682700 3E-03
14.50000⁰⁰	.1895724872541	47.13555168356	652.6748758290	8.935603164035⁹E-03
⋅⋅⋅00000	.1852343512810	45.47311263634	654.3416530122	8.4231819955904E-03
45.00000000000	.18114333C9432	43.86921427E18	655.9496423907	7.9466151466074E-03
45.50000000000	.1772822613389	42.32180348270	657.5009142558	7.5029046325409E-03
46.00000000000	.173⁶354028187	40.82889832197	658.9974662750	7.0893418662750E-03
46.50000000000	.1701883042902	39.38858568320	660.4412260123	6.7034763103787E-03
47.00000000000	.166927⁶812414	37.99901⁶95522	661.8340533634	6.3430878670775E-03
47.50000000000	.1638413067356	36.65841578402	663.1777429091	6.0061625219083E-03
48.00000000000	.160917⁹138604	35.365C5589644	664.4740261895	5.6908708244159E-03
48.50000000000	.1561471083020	34.11727899081	665.7245739007	5.3955488466353E-03
49.00000000000	.1555192898874	32.91348269348	666.9309981164	5.1186813090526E-03
49.50000000000	.1530255820772	31.75212057967	668.0948538381	4.8588860557566E-03
50.00000000000	.150C6577685217	30.63170025747	669.2176419738	4.6149034948536E-03

Fig. 2-6. (e)

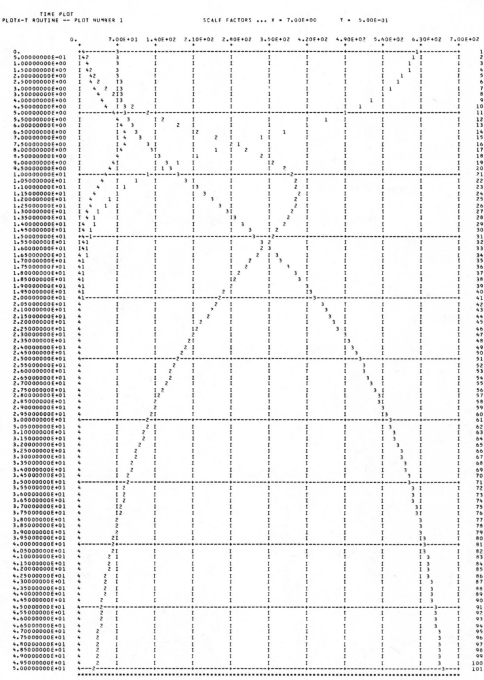

Fig. 2-6. (f)

Example 2-3: Van der Pol's Equation (stiff system, Fig. 2-7). The previous problem could have been run effectively with a simple two-point Runge-Kutta rule and a fixed step size, since the system is not "stiff" (see Appendix A for a discussion of stiffness criteria). Next we present the well-known *Van der Pol's equation*

$$\frac{d^2Y}{dT^2} + P\frac{dY}{dT}(Y^2 - 1) + Y = 0 \qquad (P \geq 0), \tag{2-3}$$

which describes a nonlinear oscillator whose amplitude-dependent damping eventually produces constant-amplitude (limit-cycle) oscillations for any nonzero initial values of Y and dY/dT. If the parameter P equals zero, we have a simple harmonic oscillator. As P increases, the nonlinearity becomes more and more pronounced. Indeed, for $P > 2$, this problem is difficult to solve directly on an analog computer, since the dynamic range of the second term in Eq. (2-3) becomes large.

If a simple fixed-step integration rule is used with a large value of P, one finds that a very small value of DT may be required; actually, a small step size is really needed only when Y is rapidly changing. *A variable-step algorithm is far superior for this type of problem.* Figure 2-7 shows a solution of Van der Pol's equation, using the variable-step Runge-Kutta-Merson rule. Note the limit-cycle behavior and the sharp peaks in $YDOT = dY/dT$. This solution uses a value of $P = 5$, which is too large for conventional analog computation.

Fig. 2-7. Solution of Van der Pol's equation (a stiff system). (a) Main program; (b) DIFFEQ subroutine; (c) listing of data cards; (d) output echo of initialization; (e) solution listing; (f) time plot; (g) phase-plane plot. Note that the plots were obtained as a default option without any special signal cards.

```
      PROGRAM VANO(INPUT,OUTPUT)
   C
   C
      CALL RESET
10    CALL INSUB
      CALL RUN
      GO TO 10
      END
```

Fig. 2-7. (a)

```
      SUBROUTINE DIFFEQ
   C  VAN DER POL EQUATION
      COMMON/STATEV/Y
      COMMON/STADER/G
      COMMON/UNDVAR/P
      COMMON/SYSVAR/T,X(10),NORDER,NPARAM,INT(4),INIT,OUTPUT,L(3)
      DIMENSION G(20),Y(30),P(20)
      LOGICAL LOGIC
   C  BE SURE TO ASSIGN PROPER VALUES FOR NORDER AND NPARAM
      DATA NORDER,NPARAM/2,1/
      G(1)=Y(2)
      G(2)=-Y(1)-(Y(1)*Y(1)-1.)*Y(2)*P(1)
      RETURN
      END
```

Fig. 2-7. (b)

```
IDENT
        VAN DER POL EQUATION
TITLE
Y           YDOT
      TIME PLOT                                        X-Y PLOT
TMAX
25.0
IC
1.0                    1.0
PARAM
5.0
.
```

Fig. 2-7. (c)

```
        VAN DER POL EQUATION

INITIAL CONDITIONS

    1               1.000000000000
    2               1.000000000000


PARAMETERS

    1               5.000000000000

DT =        0.                  TMAX =        25.00000000000

NUMBER CF POINTS =    101

DTSTART CHANGED TO        1.2500000E-01




TERMINATED BY INSUB
```

Fig. 2-7. (d)

```
        TIME                    Y                    YDOT

0.                          1.000000000000          1.000000000000
 .250000000000              1.196545228894           .5170335944498
 .500000000000              1.261344585261          4.1898765748634E-
 .750000000000              1.237419284798          -.2045989696729
1.000000000000              1.167312667711          -.34955428194
1.250000000000              1.062085194062          -.50090170?
1.500000000000               .9075904137271         -.7701894
1.750000000000               .6430087501336         -1.4871
2.000000000000             -3.4785860893845E-03     -4.3
2.250000000000             -1.609391776679          -5
2.500000000000             -2.016611364410          -
2.750000000000             -1.995394880762
3.000000000000             -1.961977073590
3.250000000000             -1.927326188687
3.500000000000             -1.891588088338
3.750000000000             -1.854655142°
4.000000000000             -1.816?°
4.250000000000
```

Fig. 2-7. (e)

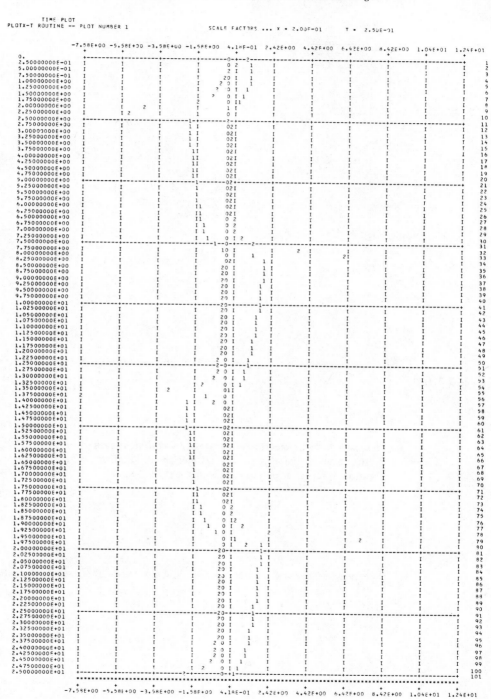

Fig. 2-7. (f)

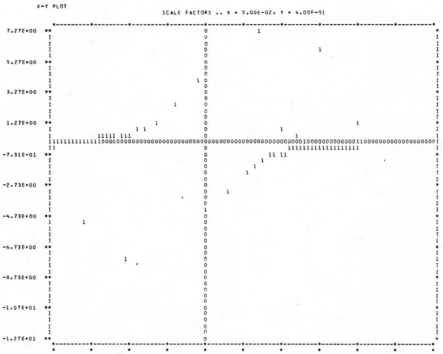

Fig. 2-7. (g)

Example 2-4: Calculation of a Satellite Orbit. If the only force acting on a satellite is the gravitational attraction of a spherical and uniform earth, then the equations of motion in terms of polar coordinates R (Fig. 2-8) are

$$\frac{d^2R}{dT^2} = -\frac{K}{R^2} + R\frac{d\theta^2}{dT}$$

$$\frac{d^2\theta}{dT^2} = -\frac{2}{R}\frac{dR}{dT}\frac{d\theta}{dT}$$

(2-4)

where K is the earth's inverse-square-law gravitational constant. We introduce

$$\frac{dY1}{dT} = Y3, \qquad \frac{dY2}{dT} = Y4$$

$$\frac{dY3}{dT} = -\frac{K}{Y1*Y1} + Y1*Y4*Y4$$

$$\frac{dY4}{dT} = -\frac{2*Y3*Y4}{Y1}$$

(2-5)

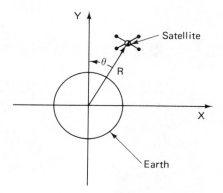

Fig. 2-8. Orbiting satellite; polar coordinates are used for state equations, and rectangular coordinates for orbit display.

which is a set of four first-order state equations in the form of Eq. (1-3). If we wish to output the orbit in terms of rectangular coordinates $X = Y21$, $Y = Y22$, we must add the defined-variable equations

$$Y21 = Y1 \cos Y2, \qquad Y22 = Y1 \sin Y2 \qquad (2\text{-}6)$$

(i.e., $X = R \cos \theta$, $Y = R \sin \theta$; Fig. 2-8).

It is convenient to establish the initial launch conditions in terms of the launch velocity VL. Assuming that, for simplicity, we launch tangential to the earth's surface, then the initial conditions are

$$Y1(0) = \text{Earth's radius} = 21.E + 06 \text{ ft}$$

$$Y2(0) = Y3(0) = 0.$$

$$Y4(0) = VL/Y1(0) \text{ ft/sec}$$

Figure 2-9 shows the coding required to generate an X-Y plot of the orbit, which follows the elliptical shape predicted by Kepler's laws. It is important to note that a variable-step integration rule is again of considerable importance here. We have used Runge-Kutta-Merson integration with absolute error control on the radius variable, setting EMAX = 1000 feet. Note that $K3$ was set to 1 for this purpose. As one orbit is traversed, the step size initially starts out at 400 seconds but increases to 800 as one leaves the strong influence of the gravitational field. We have used a launch velocity of feet per second, thereby achieving a translunar orbit. This problem was run on a CDC 6400, which has a 48-bit mantissa for floating-point variables. *On a computer with a word length shorter than 54 bits, one should use a double-precision version of the integration rule, since many steps accumulate to form the total solution.*

```
            PROGRAM  EARTH(INPUT,OUTPUT)
            COMMON/STATEV/Y(30)
            COMMON/UNDVAR/P(20)
            COMMON/OUTVAR/NLIST,NPLOT,NOUT,TITLE,V,IV,ISEL,W
            DIMENSION TITLE(16),V(10),IV(10),ISEL(25),W(101,4)
            CALL RESET
            CALL INSUB
            Y(4)=P(2)/Y(1)
            PRINT 100, Y(4)
    100     FORMAT(* THETADOT = *,E15.6)
            CALL RUN
            STOP
            END
```

Fig. 2-9. (a)

```
            SUBROUTINE DIFFEQ
    C       EARTH-ORBIT
            COMMON/STATEV/Y(30)
            COMMON/STADER/G(20)
            COMMON/UNDVAR/P(20)
            COMMON/SYSVAR/T,X(10),NORDER,NPARAM,INT(4),LOGIC(5)
            LOGICAL LOGIC
    C       P(1) IS G
    C       P(2) IS LAUNCH VEL.
    C       Y(1) IS R
    C       Y(2) IS THETA
    C       Y(3) IS RDOT
    C       Y(4) IS THETA DOT
            DATA NORDER,NPARAM/4,2/
            G(1)=Y(3)
            G(2)=Y(4)
            G(3)=-P(1)/(Y(1)*Y(1))+Y(1)*Y(4)*Y(4)
            G(4)=-2.0*Y(3)*Y(4)/Y(1)
            Y(22)=Y(1)*SIN(Y(2))
            Y(21)=Y(1)*COS(Y(2))
            RETURN
            END
```

Fig. 2-9. (b)

```
            IDENT
                    EARTH-ORBIT PROBLEM
            TMAX
            80000.
            TITLE

                                                            ORBIT

            IC
            21000000.
            PARAM
            1.42            E+16    33600.
            L
            FFT
            K
                            1
            ERROR
            1000.               1.0             3000.           100.
            STORE
            02 21 22
            PLOTW
            01 01 02
```

Fig. 2-9. (c)   .

```
              EARTH-ORBIT PROBLEM


    L1 = F  L2 = F  L3 = T


    K1 =     -0  K2 =     -0  K3 =        1


    EMAX =           1000.000      EMIN =        1.000000
    DTMAX =          3000.000      DTMIN =       100.0000

    INITIAL CONDITIONS

         1              21000000.00000
         2              -0.
         3              -0.
         4              -0.



    PARAMETERS

         1          1.4200000000000E+16
         2          33600.00000000

    DT =      0.                   TMAX =         80000.00000000


    NUMBER OF POINTS =     101

    THETADOT =     1.600000E-03

    DTSTART CHANGED TO          4.0000000E+02
    DT HALVED,NEW DT =          2.0000000E+02
    DT HALVED,NEW DT =          1.0000000E+02
    DT DOUBLED, NEW DT =         2.0000000E+02
    DT DOUBLED, NEW DT =         4.0000000E+02
    DT DOUBLED, NEW DT =         8.0000000E+02
    DT HALVED,NEW DT =          4.0000000E+02
    DT HALVED,NEW DT =          2.0000000E+02
    DT HALVED,NEW DT =          1.0000000E+02
    DT DOUBLED, NEW DT =         2.0000000E+02
    DT DOUBLED, NEW DT =         4.0000000E+02
    DT DOUBLED, NEW DT =         8.0000000E+02
    DT HALVED,NEW DT =          4.0000000E+02
    DT HALVED,NEW DT =          2.0000000E+02
    DT HALVED,NEW DT =          1.0000000E+02
    DT DOUBLED, NEW DT =         2.0000000E+02
    DT DOUBLED, NEW DT =         4.0000000E+02
    DT DOUBLED, NEW DT =         8.0000000E+02
    DT HALVED,NEW DT =          4.0000000E+02
    DT HALVED,NEW DT =          2.0000000E+02
    DT HALVED,NEW DT =          1.0000000E+02
    DT DOUBLED, NEW DT =         2.0000000E+02
```

Fig. 2-9. (d)

Fig. 2-9. Computer generation of satellite orbit. (a) Main program; (b) DIFFEQ subroutine; (c) listing of data cards; (d) output echo of initialization and history of step size as several orbits are traversed; (e) plot of orbit.

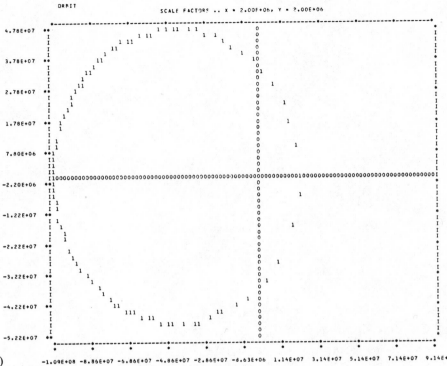

Fig. 2-9. (e)

REFERENCE

1. WAIT, J. V., and J. M. BRABSON, "FORTRAN Subroutines for Continuous-System Simulation (Version 3)," *CSRL Report 223*, Department of Electrical Engineering, College of Engineering, The University of Arizona, Tucson, Aug. 1973.

3

Programming
with an Equation-Oriented
Simulation Language.
Language Features
and Simulation Studies

INTRODUCTION AND SURVEY

The most important approach to digital continuous-system simulation employs **equation-oriented languages**, which permit **convenient problem entry directly in state-equation form** (Sec. 3-1). Problem equations are automatically translated into a FORTRAN program, which is compiled, loaded, and executed to produce time histories of the problem variables; these can be displayed, plotted, and printed through simple output commands (Secs. 3-2 and 3-3). The use of FORTRAN as a host language not only permits one to employ existing compilers but also offers knowledgeable users full use of FORTRAN functions and procedures in simulation problems (Secs. 3-7 to 3-10). **Multirun simulation studies** are easily controlled by powerful FORTRAN **control programs** which call repeated simulation runs for cross plotting, statistics, or optimization (Sec. 3-12). Nevertheless, these more advanced language features are transparent to elementary users, who can quickly learn to solve systems of differential equations without any knowledge of FORTRAN.

Many features of equation-oriented simulation languages have been reasonably standardized by the Society for Computer Simulation's CSSL Committee.[1] Our examples employ the conventions of the University of Arizona's DARE project,[2-7] which has produced a powerful interactive minicomputer system (DARE/ELEVEN; Chapter 5)[7] and the only portable simulation software for larger digital computers (DARE P; Chapter 4).[6] Special features of other language systems such as CSMP III and CSSL III are also reviewed in Sec. 3-16.

SIMPLE SIMULATION-LANGUAGE PROGRAMS

3-1. Programming State Equations and Defined Variables. Consider, as a simple example, the *Newtonian equations of motion of a point mass* (*spherical cannonball*) *with air resistance* in a constant-gravity field. Referring to Fig. 3-1, we have

$$\frac{dX}{dT} = \dot{X}, \qquad \frac{dY}{dT} = \dot{Y}$$

$$\frac{d\dot{X}}{dT} = -\frac{\text{DRAG}}{\text{MASS}} \cos\theta = -\frac{\text{DRAG}}{\text{MASS}} \frac{\dot{X}}{V}$$

$$\frac{d\dot{Y}}{dT} = -G - \frac{\text{DRAG}}{\text{MASS}} \sin\theta = -G - \frac{\text{DRAG}}{\text{MASS}} \frac{\dot{Y}}{V} \qquad (3\text{-}1)$$

$$V = \sqrt{\dot{X}^2 + \dot{Y}^2}$$

where the drag force DRAG will be a given function of the velocity V. We shall want time histories of X, Y, $\dot{X}$, $\dot{Y}$, and V and a trajectory plot $Y(T)$ vs. $X(T)$.

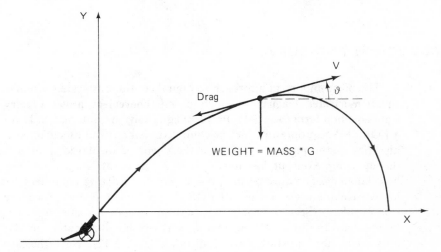

Fig. 3-1. Ballistic weapon system, anno 1776.

An **equation-oriented continuous-system simulation language** (**CSSL**) lets us program such a simulation problem directly in the state-equation form (3-1). We write **state derivatives** such as dX/dT as X' (or as X. for computer systems whose character set may lack the apostrophe, Chapter 4). Moreover, variables and parameters are not restricted to fixed symbols such as X1, X2, ... , P1, P2, ... but can have useful **symbolic** names such as XDOT, DRAG, and AMASS. Using DARE language conventions (References 2 to 6; see also Chapter 4), we can enter the problem equations as a program segment called a **derivative file** (**derivative block, dynamic region**):

$$X' = XDOT$$
$$Y' = YDOT$$
$$XDOT' = -(DRAG*XDOT/V)/AMASS \qquad (3\text{-}2a)$$
$$YDOT' = -G - (DRAG*YDOT/V)/AMASS$$
$$V = SQRT(XDOT*XDOT+YDOT*YDOT) \qquad (3\text{-}2b)$$

We have four **state equations** and a **defined variable** V. We shall need an additional equation defining DRAG as a function of the projectile velocity V. In the simplest practical case (low-speed square-law air resistance),

$$DRAG = A*V*V \qquad (3\text{-}2c)$$

we would simply substitute Eq. (3-2c) into Eq. (3-2a) and cancel V (Example 3-1). But it will pay to keep Eq. (3-2c) as a defined-variable equation if we want to substitute more complicated drag functions later.

Note that we have two possible reasons for introducing defined variables:

1. We may want time histories of these variables (output variables).
2. We may want to avoid recomputation of an intermediate result in two or more problem equations (e.g., V in our example).

Since our DARE equations will be translated into a FORTRAN program (Sec. 3-4), we agree to a FORTRAN convention. **The names of state variables, defined variables, functions** (Sec. 3-9), **and nonintegral parameters must contain only alphanumeric characters and must begin with a letter other than** I, J, K, L, M, or N.

It is possible to have *integer parameters*. DARE/ELEVEN will accept "mixed-mode" expressions such as

$$Y = 7*X - I + 0.5$$

You must check this in your system manual for other language systems.

3-2. Avoiding Algebraic Loops. Defined-variable expressions may contain other defined variables. But there is an important restriction on these expressions. **It must be possible to express all defined variables in terms of state variables by explicit substitutions, not "implicitly" by solving equations.** Otherwise, the software will not be able to sort the defined-variable equations into **procedural order**, so that the computer can make the required substitutions in turn [e.g., V in Eqs. (3-2) must be computed before DRAG].

We see that

$$Q = P*E-X$$
$$E = X-Y+R$$
$$P = X+Y$$
$$R = X*Y$$

is legal, but that

$$Q + X = 2.0*Q$$

or

$$Q = P-X$$
$$P = Y+Q$$

creates illegal **algebraic loops**, which would require equation solving (see also Sec. 3-3).

Computation of implicitly given variables (**implicitly defined functions**) can be unavoidable or advantageous in some simulation problems. Several special programming techniques for this purpose exist and will be discussed in Secs. 3-18a and C-2 (Appendix C).

3-3. Initial Values and Parameters. Initial values for each state variable X, Y, XDOT, and YDOT and values for the **parameters** AMASS and G will be entered into a **problem data file** together with needed **simulation parameters**, such as the *integration step size* DT, the *integration time* TMAX, and a code for the *integration method* to be used. With *interactive* DARE simulation systems, the user need not even remember which data items must be entered: the system display will request all needed items automatically (Sec. 5-2).

3-4. What the Simulation Software Does. To run a problem such as our example, the user must enter only the state equations and defined variables, plus data (Sec. 3-3) and output commands (Sec. 3-5) as needed. To generate useful reports when the program is listed, one can enter **comment lines** (with a suitable delimiter) anywhere in the program, as shown in our examples.

Our program equations (3-2) are written using FORTRAN symbol conventions for multiplication, real numbers, etc., but they are not FORTRAN statements, nor is knowledge of the FORTRAN language needed to solve such simple simulation problems. When the program is to be compiled, a **simulation-language translator** scans the program equations (3-2) and **translates** them into a FORTRAN program similar to that discussed in Chapter 2:

> **1.** Defined-variable equations are **sorted** into "procedural order" (e.g., V must be computed before DRAG) and copied into a subroutine DIFFEQ. The state equations (which need not be sorted) follow.
> **2.** The state equations become FORTRAN replacement statements, generating new values of the state derivatives, which form the output of DIFFEQ for each "derivative call."
> **3.** COMMON statements for all variables and parameters are generated.
> **4.** Special statements (TERMINATE, run-time display, etc.; see below) are translated into appropriate FORTRAN statements or subroutine calls.

5. The DIFFEQ routine is combined with an integration routine INTGRX (precompiled library routine) and suitable initialization and RUN/output routines for repeating integration steps (Chapter 2).

The resulting FORTRAN program is now **compiled, loaded** with the necessary library routines, and **run** using the ordinary compiler, loader, and operating system for the computer used. *After any differential-equation-solving computer run, one may change parameters or initial conditions in the problem data file without retranslation or recompilation* (changing the integration routine requires relinking the load module).

The translator and compiler will print out, or display, indications of **programming errors** (illegal symbols, algebraic loops, expression syntax, etc.).

3-5. Simulation Output

a. The communication interval. A CSSL system solves the given problem equations between $T = 0$ and $T = \text{TMAX}$, unless the solution is terminated earlier (Sec. 3-7). Every state variable and defined variable will be computed at every integration step. Since integration steps may be very small and need not be constant, time-history output to displays and/or disk files is not produced with every DT step, but at the end of constant **communication intervals**

$$\text{COMINT} = \frac{\text{TMAX}}{\text{NPT} - 1} \tag{3-3}$$

where NPT is the number of points per time history. NPT normally defaults to 512 or 256 for interactive minicomputer systems with cathode-ray-tube displays.

COMINT can usually be *changed* as a data item. To obtain high-resolution time histories, one reduces TMAX (and possibly DT) and makes repeated runs without resetting initial conditions (Sec. 3-12). It is also possible to include FORTRAN output statements in procedural blocks (Sec. 3-10).

b. Time-history files and output commands. Some simulation systems normally produce **time-history files (time files)** *for all state variables and defined variables* and store them on the system disk for later output. DARE/ELEVEN (Sec. 5-1) saves computing time by storing only variables specified by a STORE statement in the derivative file, say

STORE   X,YDOT,V

After a computer run, an output program (**output file, output block**) loads the required time-history disk files into the computer memory and produces output in response to simple **output commands,**

DISPLAY	X,Y,T	(time histories)
PLOT	XDOT,X	XDOT vs. X
PRINT	X,Y,V,T	(table with headers)
LIST	X,Y,V,T	(same on CRT terminal)

if the appropriate peripheral devices are available.

A succession of output commands can be *preprogrammed* in the output file, but commands may also be used *interactively* at the user's convenience.

One may specify displays and plots with *optimal scaling* (as large as possible) for each variable, or *equal scales* can be forced to make comparisons easier.[2] *Print intervals can be varied*, if desired. Special commands can operate special plotters and strip-chart recorders [Fig. 6-3(d)] and may also display, plot, or print the *difference* between two time histories for error studies. Examples of simulation output are shown throughout this book.

Ordinarily, the time-history files of a simulation will be *overwritten* during the next run. The DARE output command

$$\text{SAVE X1,X2, . . .}$$

will, however, **save** up to 100 named time-history files as more permanent consecutively numbered SAVE **files** for later **run-to-run comparisons.** We can retrieve numbered SAVE files after any run with ordinary output commands such as

DISPLAY 15,X,T   (time-history display of SAVE file 15 and X from last run)

c. Run-time displays. In interactive DARE systems, one simple display command such as DISPLAY X, V, T or DISPLAY Y, X can be entered anywhere in a *derivative file*. The translator processes this command to generate a **run-time display** (usually on a cathode-ray oscilloscope) *while the solution proceeds*. The run-time display does not replace the regular output program but informs the operator quickly about results and possible errors in his simulation; he can, for instance, save time by aborting faulty runs quickly.

3-6. Examples

Example 3-1: Epidemic Propagation. Figure 3-2 shows a complete DARE program and solution display for the epidemic-propagation problem of Example 1-2.

Example 3-2: Nuclear-Reactor Dynamics. Figure 3-3 similarly illustrates the solution of a simple nuclear-reactor-dynamics problem.[17] The state variables used are the neutron density DN and the densities $D1$, $D2$, $D3$, and $D4$ of four fission products. The problem is interesting in that the neutron density can range over many decades in the course of the chain reaction.

Note that the comment lines for each example contain descriptive text and definitions of parameters, so that the computer can prepare complete reports.

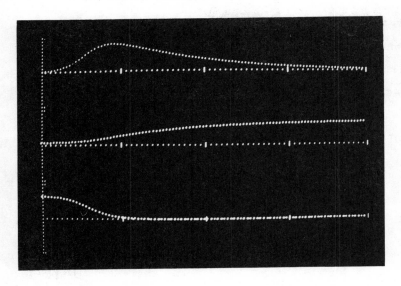

* DERIVATIVE BLOCK:

* EPIDEMIC MODEL — PRODUCES TIME HISTO-
* RIES OF SUSCEPTIBLE, SICK, AND CURED/
* NOW IMMUNE POPULATIONS:
*

      SUSC'   = −A*SUSC*SICK
      SICK'   = A*SUSC*SICK−(B+C)*SICK
      CURED' = B*SICK
      POPUL = SUSC+SICK+CURED

* A,B,C ARE INFECTION, CURE, AND DEATH
* RATES.
      DISPLAY POPUL,SICK,T

* DATA:

DT = 0.5E+00
TMAX = 5.0E+01
SUSC = 620
SICK   = 10
CURED = 70
A = 0.001
B = 0.07
C = 0.01

Fig. 3-2. DARE program and solution for the epidemic-propagation problem of Example 1-2. The star serves as a comment delimiter.

```
* DERIVATIVE BLOCK:

*SIMULATION OF NUCLEAR-REACTOR KINETICS
*     DN IS NEUTRON DENSITY
*     DI IS DENSITY OF ITH FISSION PRODUCT
*     REACT IS EXCESS REACTIVITY
*     RI IS ITH NEUTRON FRACTION
*     OI IS ITH DECAY CONSTANT
*     TL IS PROMPT-NEUTRON LIFETIME
*

        DN'=REACT*S-D1DOT-D2DOT-D3DOT-D4DOT

        D1'=D1DOT
        D2'=D2DOT
        D3'=D3DOT
        D4'=D4DOT
*
        D1DOT=P1*S-O1*D1
        D2DOT=B2*S-O2*D2
        D3DOT=B3*S-O3*D3
        D4DOT=B4*S-O4*D4
        S=DN/TL
        DISPLAY DN,D1,T

* DATA:

DT   =1.0E-02
T 1AX = 3.9E+00
DN   = 0.1
D1   = 0.1
D2   = 0.1
D3   = 0.1
D4   = 0.1
REACT = 0.0063
TL   = 2.0F-04
B1   = 0.0002
B2   = 0.0016
B3   = 0.0021
B4   = 0.0024
Q1   = 0.013
Q2   = 0.032
Q3   = 0.154
Q4   = 0.456
```

Fig. 3-3. Program and solution for a simple nuclear reactor-dynamics problem.

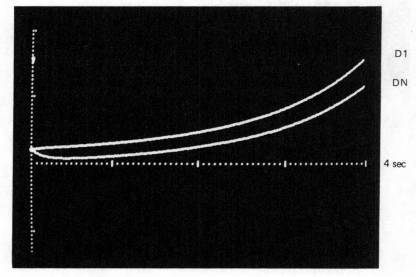

REACT = 0.005

Example 3-3: Damped Pendulum. Finally, Fig. 3-4 shows a phase-plane plot ($\dot{X}$ vs. X) for the angular displacement of a damped pendulum. Such *phase-plane plots* are useful in studies of nonlinear oscillations (see also Sec. 6-5).

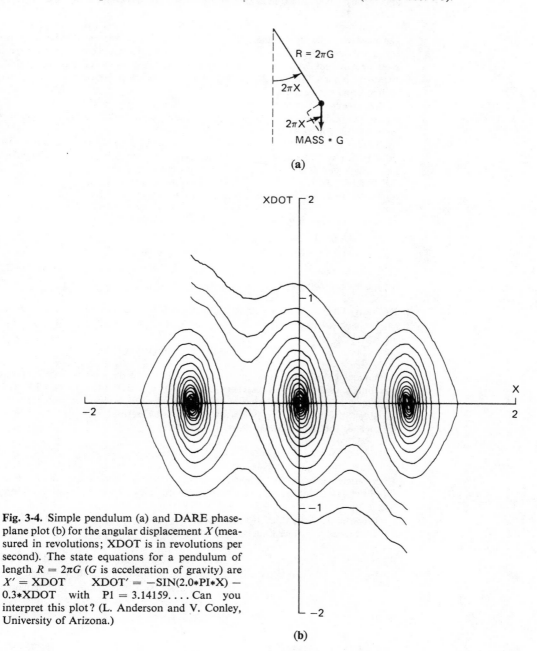

Fig. 3-4. Simple pendulum (a) and DARE phase-plane plot (b) for the angular displacement X (measured in revolutions; XDOT is in revolutions per second). The state equations for a pendulum of length $R = 2\pi G$ (G is acceleration of gravity) are $X' = \text{XDOT}$ $\text{XDOT}' = -\text{SIN}(2.0*\text{PI}*X) - 0.3*\text{XDOT}$ with $\text{PI} = 3.14159\ldots$. Can you interpret this plot? (L. Anderson and V. Conley, University of Arizona.)

TABLE 3-1. DARE Equation-Language Summary*

---

1. **Variables, Parameters, Expressions, and Functions**
   (a) **State variables** and **defined variables** are named REAL FORTRAN variables (names must not start with I, J, K, L, M, **or** N), respectively defined by state equations and defined equations (see below). T represents the **independent variable,** typically problem time.

   All other named quantities (FORTRAN REAL and/or INTEGER quantities) are **undefined variables** or **parameters,** which must be defined as data (DARE data file or data cards) and may be changed without recompilation. Some parameters are **simulation-system parameters (system variables, system parameters,** e.g., DT, TMAX, COMINT; see also Table 4-2). The other parameters are parameters describing the system being simulated.

   Variables and parameter names must begin with a letter and must contain only alphanumerical characters. *No subscripted variables are permitted,* although there may be variables such as X1, X2, ...

   (b) **Expressions** in DARE state equations and defined equations (see below) are valid FORTRAN expressions and named *functions* containing the above variables and parameters, plus REAL and INTEGER constants.

   DARE/ELEVEN accepts mixed-mode expressions (Sec. 3-1).

   (c) **DARE functions** (Secs. 3-8, 3-9, and 3-10.a) include

   > **FORTRAN library functions** (e.g., SIN(X); Table 3-2)
   >
   > **DARE library functions** (e.g., DELAY; Table 3-3)
   >
   > **FORTRAN functions** defined in DARE FORTRAN files
   >
   > **DARE table functions** defined by one- and two-dimensional tables in DARE table files (Sec. 3-8)

2. **Derivative File (derivative block)** defines a dynamic system (or subsystem) in terms of
   (a) **State equations** (first-order ordinary differential equations; Sec. 3-1):

   $$SVAR' = FORTRAN\ expression$$

   A minimal DARE program consists of one derivative file with at least one state equation, plus data cards (DARE P; Chapter 4), or a data file (DARE/ELEVEN; Chapter 5). Each state equation must be supplied with an initial value for its state variable (SVAR) as data, or assigned a default value (zero).
   (b) **Defined-variable equations** (Secs. 3-1 and 3-2):

   $$DVAR = FORTRAN\ expression$$

   Each defined variable (DVAR) must be *explicitly* defined in terms of state variables, other defined variables, system variables, and/or parameters (no algebraic loops; Sec. 3-2).
   (c) **Procedural blocks** (Sec. 3-10.b), which can produce defined variables by FORTRAN procedures other than simple expressions:

   PROCED P, Q, . . . = X, Y, . . .   (FORTRAN program producing defined variables P, Q, . . . explicitly in terms of state variables, other defined variables, system variables, and/or parameters X, Y, . . .)

   ENDPRO

*See Chapters 3 to 5 for examples.

Procedural blocks may contain any valid FORTRAN program *without declarative statements* (type declarations, COMMON, DIMENSION, etc.; hence no subscripted variables). But declarative statements and subscripted variables can be put into *subroutines* called by procedural blocks (subroutines will be in DARE FORTRAN files; see below).

Different procedural blocks must not duplicate FORTRAN statement numbers.

(d) DARE special statements:

STORE	(Sec. 3-5.b)
DISPLAY	(Sec. 3-5.c)
TERMINATE	(Sec. 3-7)

Some DARE/ELEVEN systems implement *simulation-language macros* (Sec. 3-17) and simple *matrix operations* (Sec. 3-18).

3. Data File

The problem data file contains statements of the form

$$PARAM = value$$

which assign numerical values to all simulation-system parameters, undefined variables in derivative files, and in logic-control-file input lists.

4. DARE Logic-Control File (logic block; Secs. 3-3 and 5-2)

The logic-control file is a FORTRAN program which calls at least one simulation run and controls parameters and initial values before, after, and between runs. *This program may contain any valid FORTRAN statements except type declarations and* IMPLICIT *statements.* COMMON and DIMENSION statements (and hence subscripted variables) are allowed. The DARE translator automatically inserts COMMON statements linking all state variables, defined variables, and parameters to the logic-control program, so the user need not bother with this. *Exception:* No declaratives are allowed in logic-control files containing INLIST statements for block-diagram derivative blocks (Chapter 6).

The logic-control file can contain FORTRAN calls to DARE library and system routines, including RUN, RESET, DIFFEQ, STORE, SAVE, STROF, and STRON (refer carefully to Secs. 3-12 and 3-13).

The special statements

INPUT	*list of names separated by commas*
OUTPUT	*list of names separated by commas*

must, respectively, precede the use of variables input from the data file and output to a CROSS file (Sec. 3-13).

COMMON statements for all state variables, defined variables, and parameters are automatically supplied. No END statement is needed.

5. FORTRAN and Assembly-Language Subroutine Files

These contain user-written routines for functions and subroutines called in derivative and logic blocks (and possibly in other subroutine blocks). FORTRAN files are compiled together with the main program and thus have access to DARE-variable COMMON. Assembly-language subroutines must satisfy FORTRAN-linkage conventions for the machine used and have proper external references. Each subroutine must have an END statement. *Note:* DARE library and system subroutines such as RUN can be replaced with user-written subroutines entered, each under the corresponding name, in a DARE FORTRAN or assembly-language subroutine file.

6. Table Files

See Sec. 3-8 and the system manual for the DARE system used.

WE ADD LANGUAGE FEATURES

3-7. TERMINATE Statements. At times, it will be economical to *terminate* a simulation run as soon as some state variable or defined variable takes a predetermined value (e.g., when the projectile in our example strikes the ground, i.e., $Y = 0$). In most systems (e.g., DARE P), the statement

$$\text{TERMINATE Y}$$

in a derivative file will cause termination when $Y = 0$. Y could also be an expression, so that TERMINATE(Q−0.5) would cause termination when $Q = 0.5$. DARE/ELEVEN has TERMINATE statements similar to FORTRAN IF conditions:

$$\text{TERMINATE(X1.GT.5.0.AND.X2.LT.5.5)}$$

which will terminate a run if $X1 > 5$ *and* $X2 < 5.5$. Figure 3-6 shows an example.

3-8. Tabulated Functions. Very often a continuous function (e.g., DRAG as a function of V in our example) is given in terms of a *table* listing corresponding argument and function values (*breakpoint coordinates*). For $F = F(X)$, say, one is given

$$F_1 = F(X_1)$$
$$F_2 = F(X_2)$$
$$\vdots$$

Digital simulation languages will include routines which accept such a table (in a specified format) and use the linear-interpolation formula

$$F \approx F_i = \frac{F_{i+1} - F_i}{X_{i+1} - X_i}(X - X_i) \qquad (X_i \leq X < X_{i+1}) \tag{3-4}$$

to produce a *piecewise-linear (polygonal) approximation* for each value* of the argument X. The breakpoint abscissas $X_1, X_2, \ldots$ need not be uniformly spaced;

---

*It is customary to use

$$F = F(X_1) \qquad (X \leq X_1), \qquad F = F(X_n) \qquad (X \geq X_n) \tag{3-5}$$

where X_1 and X_n are the smallest and largest breakpoint abscissas.

if $Y(X)$ is originally given as a continuous function (formula or empirical curve), one must choose the breakpoints judiciously for good approximation with a given number of breakpoints.[8-10]

The DARE translator will automatically insert an interpolation formula (3-4) for any reference to a **named function**, e.g.,

$$DRAG = BOBO(V) + 20.1$$

The appropriate breakpoint coordinates must be entered in a **table file**, one for each function used. DARE/ELEVEN uses the format

BOBO,N
0.0, 1.2
0.8, 3.7
2.1, 9.2
. . . .

Each line contains a breakpoint abscissa and ordinate. Lines are ordered, starting with the lowest breakpoint abscissa, and **N** is the number of breakpoints (or lines) provided.

Good simulation systems also provide similar facilities for **functions of two variables**. For $F_{ik} = F(X_i, Y_k)$, one uses the interpolation formula

$$F \approx F_{ik} + \frac{F_{i+1,k} - F_{ik}}{X_{i+1} - X_i}(X - X_i) + \frac{F_{i,k+1} - F_{ik}}{Y_{k+1} - Y_k}(Y - Y_k)$$

$$+ \frac{F_{i+1,k+1} + F_{ik} - F_{i+1,k} - F_{i,k+1}}{(X_{i+1} - X_i)(Y_{k+1} - Y_k)}(X - X_i)(Y - Y_k) \qquad (3\text{-}6)$$

Refer to your simulation-language manual for the specific table-entry format used.

3-9. Special Functions

a. FORTRAN Library functions. FORTRAN-based simulation languages can freely employ the usual **FORTRAN library functions**, such as SQRT in Eq. (3-2b). Table 3-2 lists common library functions available with most FORTRAN systems.

Note: The FORTRAN library function AINT(X) returns the largest integer $\leq$ X and can be used to simulate *quantization*, as in analog-to-digital converters. AMOD(X,Y) returns the *remainder* of X/Y and can be used as a sawtooth-signal generator.

TABLE 3-2. FORTRAN Library Functions Available with Typical
Simulation-Language Systems[2]

Function Name	Definition	No. of Arg.	Type of Arg.	Type of Function
ABS	Absolute value	1	REAL	REAL
IABS	Absolute value	1	INTEGER	INTEGER
AINT	Truncation	1	REAL	REAL
INT	Truncation	1	REAL	INTEGER
AMOD	Remainder	2	REAL	REAL
AMAX0	Choosing largest value	2 or more	INTEGER	REAL
AMAX1	Choosing largest value	2 or more	REAL	REAL
MAX0	Choosing largest value	2 or more	INTEGER	INTEGER
MAX1	Choosing largest value	2 or more	REAL	INTEGER
AMIN0	Choosing smallest value	2 or more	INTEGER	REAL
AMIN1	Choosing smallest value	2 or more	REAL	REAL
MIN0	Choosing smallest value	2 or more	INTEGER	INTEGER
MIN1	Choosing smallest value	2 or more	REAL	INTEGER
FLOAT	Convert to REAL	1	INTEGER	REAL
IFIX	Convert to INTEGER	1	REAL	INTEGER
EXP	e^a	1	REAL	REAL
ALOG	$\log_e (a)$	1	REAL	REAL
ALOGT	$\log_{10} (a)$	1	REAL	REAL
SIN	$\sin (a)$	1	REAL	REAL
COS	$\cos (a)$	1	REAL	REAL
TANH	$\tanh (a)$	1	REAL	REAL
SQRT	$\sqrt{a}$	1	REAL	REAL
ATAN	$\arctan (a)$	1	REAL	REAL
ATAN2	$\arctan (a_1/a_2)$	2	REAL	REAL

Simulation-language systems provide additional useful library functions, including
the dead-space, dual-limiter (saturated amplifier), and comparator transfer char-
acteristics needed for control-system applications (Table 3-3). Special driving functions of the independent variable T (e.g., pulse generators) are often provided.

In addition, simulation laboratories or individual users can use FORTRAN
functions and procedures (Sec. 3-10) to generate special functions (and libraries of
functions) for individual applications.

b. Noise generators and time delays. Simulation-language **noise generators** are
usually called as FORTRAN library functions, say RANF(Q), where Q is a dummy
parameter, which can be given any value. Each time RANF(Q) is called, it returns
independent floating-point samples uniformly distributed between -1.0 and $+1.0$.
A simulation system may also include a noise generator for *Gaussian (normally
distributed) samples* and a *random-integer generator*. Noise samples are most often
generated by a pseudo-random-number routine[18]; minicomputers can also employ
hardware noise generators.[2]

TABLE 3-3. Some DARE Library Functions[2]

Y = DXONE(X, A, B)	Y = 0, if A ≤ X ≤ B
	Y = 1. if X > B
	Y = −1. if X < A
Y = COMPR(X)	Y = 0. if X = 0.
	Y = 1. if X > 0.
	Y = −1. if X < 0.
Y = DEADX(X, A, B)	Y = 0. if A ≤ X ≤ B
	Y = X − B if X > B
	Y = X − A if X < A
Y = SATAM(X, A, B)	Y = A if X < A
	Y = B if X > B
	Y = X if A ≤ X ≤ B
Y = SAMPL(X, S)	Y = X/DT if S ≤ T < S + DT
	(approximates an impulse of area X)
	Y = 0. otherwise
Y = HOLD(X, N, S)	Y = X if T ≤ S
	Y = constant = value of X when S = T if T > S
	N = INTEGER constant between 1 and 20 which must be different each time this function is used in the same problem
Y = SENSE(A)	Y = 0. if sense switch A is off or A is out of range
	Y = 1. if sense switch A is on; A may vary from 1. to 5.

Independent noise samples generated once per derivative call approximate wide-band flat-spectrum noise (*white noise*) as long as the integration step DT is constant. The noise spectrum can be shaped with simulated filters (Sec. 6-5). Such *random-process simulation* is discussed in References 19 and 20.

A **time-delay operator**, as in

$$Y = DELAY(TAU, STEP, I, XINIT, X) \tag{3-7}$$

is called as a simulation-system library function and approximates

$$Y(T) = \begin{cases} XINIT & (T < TAU) \\ X(T\text{-}TAU) & (T \geq TAU) \end{cases} \tag{3-8}$$

where TAU is the **fixed or variable delay time**; an error will be returned if TAU is erroneously made negative in the course of a simulation. Different integers I = 1, 2, . . . are assigned to different input variables (X in our case) to be delayed (Fig. 3-5).

The delay algorithm actually stores samples of the input X at T = 0, STEP, 2∗STEP, . . . and interpolates linearly between delayed values. STEP is prevented from becoming smaller than the integration step DT. The maximum delay TAU is usually limited to, say, 100∗STEP or 1000∗STEP to conserve memory.

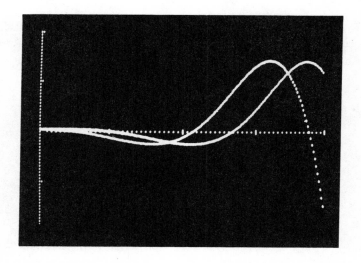

Fig. 3-5. DARE display of a delayed variable DX1(T) = X1(T-TAU) with zero initial value. The delayed output was obtained by linear interpolation with about 100 samples. (G. Lykos, University of Arizona.)

3-10. Special FORTRAN Procedures

a. FORTRAN functions. As we saw, **there is no need to know FORTRAN for simple simulations, but more sophisticated users can employ the full power of FORTRAN procedures in their simulation-language programs**. A DARE user can introduce his own **special FORTRAN functions,** as in

$$\text{FLOW} = \text{VALVE (PRES1, PRES2, RES)} \qquad (3\text{-}9)$$

by simply defining them as FORTRAN procedures in a FORTRAN file. The DARE translator simply appends subprograms written into such files to its DIFFEQ subroutine (Sec. 3-4).

Example 3-4: Representation of Flow Through a Check Valve (based on Reference 13). Equation (3-9) (the function call) is to describe the flow through a check valve with input pressure PRES1, output pressure PRES2, and flow resistance RES. The function definition is entered in a DARE FORTRAN file:

```
FUNCTION           VALVE (P,Q,R)
IF  (Q.GT.P) GO TO 2
VALVE = (P − Q)/R
GO TO 3
2  VALVE = 0.0
3  RETURN
END
```

P, Q, and R are *dummy variables;* the function VALVE would be called, as often as desired, with different arguments.

b. Procedural blocks. Another way to utilize special FORTRAN procedures in a simulation program is to include **procedural blocks** in a derivative file. A procedural block is a FORTRAN program section which produces a set of defined variables P, Q, . . . from a set of state variables, defined variables, and/or parameters X, Y, ... We enter

PROCED   P, Q, . . . = X,Y, . . .   (FORTRAN program producing

P, Q, . . .)

ENDPRO

in a derivative file, just as we would enter a set of defined-variable equations for P, Q, ... Note that a procedural block may produce two or more defined variables, which it must define explicitly to avoid algebraic loops (Sec. 3-2). The translator sorting process (Sec. 3-4) keeps each procedural block together as one entity and then simply enters the FORTRAN statements among the defined-variable statements.

Since procedural blocks will appear in the middle of a translator-output FORTRAN file, *they must not contain declarative statements* (e.g., type declarations, COMMON, DIMENSION and, therefore, no subscripted variables). *But procedural blocks may call FORTRAN functions and/or subroutines which can contain declaratives and subscripted variables.* Each function or subroutine definition is usually entered in a separate DARE FORTRAN file to avoid cluttering the procedural block. This also makes the function or subroutine easily available for use with other DARE programs.

A procedural block can do away with the need to define a rarely used function. This could speed execution with some FORTRAN compilers. Thus, Eq. (3-9) could be replaced by

```
PROCED           FLOW = PRES1, PRES2, RES
IF (PRES2.GT.PRES1)  GO TO 2
FLOW = (PRES1 − PRES2)/RES
GO TO 3
2  FLOW = 0.0
3  CONTINUE
ENDPRO
```

In Sec. 4-11 we shall show another example. Note also that *procedural blocks can neatly control external equipment* (special displays, partial-system tests) through FORTRAN input/output statements or by calling *assembly-language subroutines.* Such FORTRAN subprograms can, for instance, compute values of *implicit functions* (Sec. 3-2) by iterative or algebraic equation-solving and may even implement READ *and* WRITE *operations.* In Chapter 5, we shall describe even more powerful simulation systems which can employ assembly-language subprograms as well as FORTRAN procedures and are especially suitable for real-time simulations involving human operators and/or real equipment (partial-system tests).

NOTE: Multiple procedural blocks must not duplicate FORTRAN statement numbers.

SIMULATION STUDIES AND MULTIPLE RUNS

3-11. Simulation Studies. A simulation-language system must not only solve differential equations but must permit *convenient programming of insight-producing experiments with the simulation model.* Such experiments are called **simulation studies.**[1] They will almost always involve **multiple differential-equation-solving runs.** One requires programs for

1. **"Initial" computation of model parameters and/or initial conditions** before a run (Example 3-5).
2. **"Terminal" processing of results** from a run, e.g., functions of time-history samples.
3. **Calling multiple simulation runs** with parameters and/or initial conditions either **preprogrammed** or **determined by results from earlier runs** (**iterative** simulation experiments, optimization, model matching[21,22]).
4. **Saving time histories from multiple runs.**
5. **Cross-plotting** results and parameters in multirun studies.
6. **Computation of statistics from multiple runs** with random inputs (**Monte Carlo simulation**[20]).

CSSL systems implement these operations through a FORTRAN main program, which calls simulation runs as needed.

3-12. The DARE Simulation Control Program. The DARE **logic-control file** or **logic block** is explicitly programmed as a distinct file separate from any derivative block specifying differential equations. The logic block, written in FORTRAN, serves as the "main program", which calls differential-equation-solving simulation runs, as needed, with the FORTRAN subroutine calls CALL RUN, and CALL RESET. Before, between, and after these calls, FORTRAN statements can, then,

set and modify parameters and initial conditions. The FORTRAN program can read and use values of state variables and defined variables at the end of each run. Values at a specified time T1 *before* termination are read with the aid of the HOLD (X,N,T1) function (Table 3-3 and Example 3-6), which simulates a *sample-hold circuit*.

More specifically,

CALL RUN	saves state-variable values at the time of the call (for later RESET) and *makes one simulation run*. Solutions run to T = TMAX unless terminated earlier (Sec. 3-7). All variables are left at their termination values.
CALL RESET	resets T = 0 and restores state variables, *but not defined variables*, to their initial conditions at the start of the last run preceded by RESET.

In DARE P, the *first* RESET of a simulation study resets the state variables to the initial values given in the problem data file.

NOTE: In the batch-processed DARE P simulation system (Chapter 4), CALL RESET *must* precede the first CALL RUN. But in the interactive DARE/ELEVEN system (Chapter 5), the initial-reset operation is done automatically by the keyboard command to run, and *no* CALL RESET *must precede the first* CALL RUN *in the logic file* (this would reset all state variables to zero).

Successive CALL RUNs without a CALL RESET "continue" a run which was terminated to take data or to make parameter changes, using the last-attained value of each variable as its new initial value. Portions of such "continued" runs can be displayed with high resolution in time.

NOTE: FORTRAN statements intended to change a state-variable initial value before a run must *follow* CALL RESET, which would nullify such changes. Defined variables normally assume their correct initial values only at the start of RUN. To set all defined values to their initial values *before* a run (e.g., for use in static checks, prerun computations), you must *first* CALL RESET, *then* modify state-variable initial values if desired, and *then* CALL DIFFEQ.

3-13. Special Logic-Block Statements and Routines. The DARE logic block is a FORTRAN program linked to the rest of the simulation program through COMMON statements automatically added by the translator and by the simple special statements

INPUT	*list of names separated by commas*
OUTPUT	*list of names separated by commas*

INPUT *lists logic-block parameters to be supplied in the data file* (Example 3-6).

OUTPUT *lists the names of variables and/or parameters whose values are to be stored on the disk whenever the FORTRAN statement*

CALL STORE

is encountered in the logic block. If, for instance, CALL STORE is programmed after each successive simulation run, then each item in the OUTPUT list will produce an entry in a named file (*CROSS file*). *When all runs are finished, the DARE output program (Sec. 3-5) can then list, display or plot* OUTPUT *quantities as functions of the run number or cross-plot them* (Example 4-5).

The logic-block statement

CALL SAVE(VAR,N)

used *after* a CALL RUN in DARE/ELEVEN*, will *store the time history of the variable* VAR *in SAVE file* N (Sec. 3-5.b), so that it can be output later. CALL SAVE may be used repeatedly for different variables (see also Sec. 4-7).

In most iterative and interactive multirun simulation studies, it would be a waste of computer time to store time histories from intermediate runs on the disk. The logic-block statement

CALL STROF

will kill all time-history disk storage until the *logic-block statement*

CALL STRON

reenables the storage operation (Example 3-6; see also Sec. 5-5).

The DARE logic block is *optional* and must have at least one CALL RUN. An equation-language logic file may contain any valid FORTRAN statement except type declarations and IMPLICIT statements, and DIMENSION statements (and hence subscripted variables) are allowed.** The logic block can freely refer to DARE table and FORTRAN files for functions and subroutines. The DARE translator automatically inserts COMMON statements for all state variables, defined variables, and parameters, so the user need not bother with this. No END statement is needed.

3-14. Examples

Example 3-5: "Initial" Computation for a Ballistic Trajectory. In the cannonball-trajectory example of Sec. 3-1, one is usually given the initial values of the velocity V

---

*But SAVE is used before CALL RUN in DARE P; Sec. 4-8.
**Refer to Table 3-1 for the case of logic files used with block-diagram-language programs.

and the flight-path angle θ rather than the initial values of the state variables $\dot{X}$ and $\dot{Y}$. The DARE program of Fig. 3-6(a) shows how initial values of

$$\dot{X} = V\cos = V\cos\left(\frac{\pi}{180}\text{THETA}\right)$$

$$\dot{Y} = V\sin = V\sin\left(\frac{\pi}{180}\text{THETA}\right)$$

(3-10)

```
*  DERIVATIVE BLOCK:

*BALLISTIC TRAJECTORY WITH AIR RESISTAN-
*CE. R IS AIR RESISTANCE COEFFICIENT
*OVER PROJECTILE MASS: G IS ACCELERATION
*OF GRAVITY.
*
        X'=XDOT
        Y'=YDOT
        XDOT'=-R*V*XDOT
        YDOT'=-R*V*YDOT-G
        V=SQRT(XDOT*XDOT+YDOT*YDOT)
        TERMINATE Y
        DISPLAY Y,X

*  LOGIC BLOCK:

*PRECOMPUTATION OF INITIAL VELOCITY
*  COMPONENTS, AND CONVERSION OF INI-
*  TIAL ANGLE TO DEGREES.
        INPUT THETA, V0
        XDOT=V0*COS(THETA*3.14159/180.)
        YDOT=V0*SIN(THETA*3.14159/180.)
        CALL RESET
        CALL RUN

*  DATA:

DT   = 0.5E-01
TMAX = 5.0E+01
X    = 0.0
Y    = 0.0
XDOT = 0.0
YDOT = 0.0
R    = 7.5E-05
G    = 32.2
THETA = 10.
V0   = 900.
```

(a)

```
*  DERIVATIVE BLOCK:

*ALTERNATIVE FORMULATION OF TRAJECTORY
*  PROBLEM, USING WIND AXES.
*
        V'=-G*SIN(THE)-R*V*V
        THE'=-G*COS(THE)/V
        X'=V*COS(THE)
        Y'=V*SIN(THE)
        TERMINATE Y
        DISPLAY Y,X

*  LOGIC BLOCK:

*RESCALING INITIAL TRAJECTORY
*  IN DEGREES.
*
        INPUT THETA
        THE=THETA*3.14159/180.
        CALL RESET
        CALL RUN

*  DATA:

DT   = 1.0E-01
TMAX = 9.9E-00
V    = 900.
THE  = 0.0
X    = 0.0
Y    = 0.0
G    = 32.2
THETA = 10.
R    = 7.5E-05
```

(b)

Fig. 3-6. a, b. DARE programs for the cannonball-trajectory problem (Example 3-5) using earth axes (a) and wind axes (b). The logic-block precomputation of initial values replaces data-file entries for XDOT, YDOT, and THE. In the interactive DARE/ELEVEN system, the first CALL RESET is omitted (replaced by the keyboard run command: Sec. 3-12).

Y, 8200'

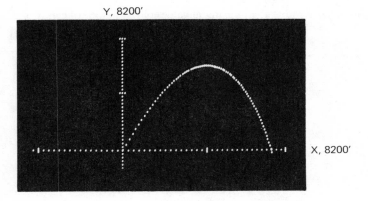

X, 8200'

Fig. 3-6. (c)

TIME	X	Y
0.00000	0.00000	0.00000
2.00000	630.617	1506.01
4.00000	1194.71	2730.90
6.00000	1709.07	3724.43
8.00000	2186.51	4520.46
10.0000	2632.68	5142.55
12.0000	3057.10	5607.29
14.0000	3463.70	5926.29
16.0000	3856.13	6107.50
18.0000	4236.79	6156.35
20.0000	4606.79	6076.83
22.0000	4966.00	5872.77

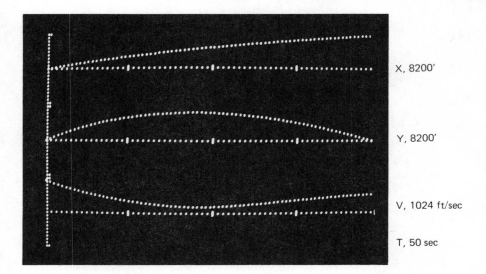

X, 8200'

Y, 8200'

V, 1024 ft/sec

T, 50 sec

DARE   OUTPUT LISTING   PAGE 1

TIME	X	Y	THETA
0.0000000	0.0000000	0.0000000	.26179939
.30000000	258.19660	67.744126	.25129783
.60000000	511.33213	131.29064	.24052768
.90000000	759.61406	190.74840	.22948813
⌐000000	1003.2371	246.21954	.21817862
⌐⌐	1242.3843	297.80008	.20659885
	1477.2276	345.58032	.19474886
	⌐⌐7.9291	389.64533	.18262898
		430.07536	.17023994
		466.94615	.15758280
		⌐⌐931	.14465904
		⌐	.13147057
			.10430939
			⌐342801E-02
			⌐6E-02
			⌐⌐

Fig. 3-6. c, d. Graphic output (c) and part of an output listing (d) for the DARE program of part (a).

(d)

(THETA in degrees) are precomputed in a DARE logic block, which then calls a differential-equation-solving run. We have used the low-speed drag formula (3-2c), so that

$$\frac{DRAG}{MASS} = RV^2 \tag{3-11}$$

An alternative approach is to introduce V and θ as state variables instead of $\dot{X}$ and $\dot{Y}$. We resolve forces and accelerations along, and at right angles to, the instantaneous velocity vector (*wind axes*) and find the four state equations

$$\frac{dX}{dT} = V\cos\theta \qquad \frac{dY}{dT} = V\sin\theta$$

$$\frac{dV}{dT} = -G\sin\theta - \frac{DRAG}{MASS} = -G\sin\theta - RV^2 \tag{3-12}$$

$$\frac{d\theta}{dT} = -\frac{G\cos\theta}{V}$$

Figure 3-6(b) shows a complete program, including logic-block precomputation of the initial angle in radians.

Example 3-6: A Simple Parameter-Optimization Problem.[21,22] In a simple servomechanism, the motor torque is proportional to the *error* $E = X - U$, where U and X are the servo input and output. The approximate (linearized) performance equation is

$$\frac{d^2X}{dT^2} = -GE - R\frac{dX}{dT} \qquad \text{with } E = X - U \tag{3-13}$$

We consider a step input $U = $ constant ($T > 0$). For fixed servo gain G, the output X will follow the input step slowly for large values of the damping coefficient R and quickly, but with more overshoot, for large R [Fig. 3-7(a)]. We want to optimize the servo step response by selecting R so as to minimize the mean-square error between $T = 0$ and $T = TF$, or

$$PF = P(TF) = \int_{0}^{T=TF} E^2\, dT \tag{3-14}$$

We compute PF as a sample $P(TF)$ of the state variable $P(T)$ defined by

$$\frac{dP}{dT} = E^2 \qquad \text{with } P(0) = 0 \tag{3-15}$$

We thus have a derivative block with three state variables X, $\dot{X}$, and P. To minimize PF as a function of the damping coefficient R, we start with $R = 0$, make another run with $R = dR$, and note the resulting change DF in PF. We now vary R in the direction of decreasing mean-square error PF until PF changes by less than a small present amount CRIT.

More sophisticated optimization problems, which may involve several unknown parameters and many different optimization strategies, are discussed in References 21 and 22. It is possible to link simulation-language programs to existing FORTRAN optimization-routine packages.[23,24]

3-15. Problem Segmentation: Multiple Derivative Blocks*

Modern simulation languages permit *problem segmentation into two or more derivative blocks* (*derivative files*; Sec. 3-1) whose state equations and defined-variable

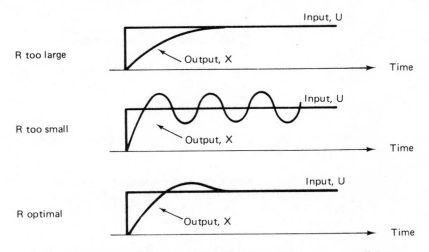

Fig. 3-7a. Servo step response for different values of the damping coefficient R.

*See also Sec. 6-9.

```
*  DERIVATIVE BLOCK:

*  FINDING OPTIMAL DAMPING PARAMETER R
*  FOR A SIMPLE SERVO WITH FIXED GAIN
*
*  SYSTEM STATE EQUATIONS
         X'=XDOT
         XDOT'=-G*E-R*XDOT
*  DEFINITION OF INTEGRAL SQUARE ERROR
         E=X-U
         P'=E*E
         PF=HOLD(P,1,TF)
*
*LOGIC BLOCK:
*
*  LIST OF PARAMETERS FROM DATA FILE
*                          USED IN LOGIC BLOCK
         INPUT CRIT, OPG, DR
*TURN OFF DISK STORAGE, MAKE INITIAL RUN
*                       WITH R=0, AND MEASURE PF
         CALL STROF
         NRUN = 0
         CALL RESET
         CALL RUN
*  PERTURB R, RUN, AND MEASURE CHANGE IN PF
         R = R + DR
15       PFOLD = PF
         CALL RESET
         CALL RUN
         DF = PF - PFOLD
*  FINISHED IF DF IS SMALL ENOUGH
         IF (ABS(DF).LT.CRIT) GO TO 17
*  IF NOT, CONTINUE IN GRADIENT DIRECTION
         NRUN = NRUN + !
         R = R - OPG*DF - DR
         CALL SHOW (NRUN, R, PF)
         GO TO 15
*  STORE TIME HISTORY OF OPTIMIZED RUN
17       CALL STRON
         CALL RESET
         CALL RUN
*
*  DATA
*
DT   = 0.01              U = 0.9
TMAX = 0.8               CRIT = 0.00005
X    = 0.                OPG = 12000.
XDOT = 0.                DR = 0.03
P    = 0.
```

Fig. 3-7b. DARE program for the parameter-optimization problem. Omit the first CALL RESET if DARE/ELEVEN is used.

equations represent a *subsystem* or a *temporary portion or version* of the total system to be simulated. With two derivative blocks, say, the logic-block statements CALL RUN1 and CALL RUN2 will, respectively, run derivative blocks 1 and 2 until terminated. CALL RUN will run *both* blocks together (although one could terminate before the other). We also have separate RESET1 and RESET2 statements as needed.

There are two principal uses for problem segmentation:

1. *Use of two (or more) different integration routines* for different subsystems (e.g., fast and slow subsystems; see also Sec. 6-9).
2. *"Switching" between different system configurations in the course of time* (Example 3-7).

The different derivative blocks and the logic block communicate through state-variable, defined-variable, and parameter COMMONs supplied automatically by the translator.

NOTE: Sorting (Sec. 3-4) is usually done *within* each derivative block only, and the user must guard against algebraic loops (Sec. 3-2) formed by defined variables in simultaneously run derivative blocks.

Example 3-7: Boost and Midcourse Simulation for a Space Vehicle. Derivative block 1 represents the boost configuration of a space vehicle and terminates at a specified time or altitude. Derivative block 2 represents the midcourse configuration and takes its initial values of altitude, range, pitch angle, etc., directly from their final values in derivative block 1. The logic block is simple:

```
CALL RESET       (both blocks)
CALL RUN1
CALL RUN2
```

If the simulation language starts T at $T = 0$ in each derivative block, we can define a new time variable TIME, e.g., by

```
TIME = T         in derivative block 1
TIME' = 1.0      in derivative block 2
```

OTHER SIMULATION LANGUAGES AND LANGUAGE FEATURES

3-16. Representative Equation Languages. CSMP III and CSSL III. References 11 and 16 sketch a history of early continuous-system simulation languages. Since modern FORTRAN compilers can generate efficient object code even for some minicomputers, all equation-oriented simulation languages in wide use translate into FORTRAN. We shall list the major languages of this type; block-diagram languages for fast simulation with small computers will be discussed in Chapter 5 and 6.

DARE P is "portable," i.e., transfers readily to different computers because the translator is written in FORTRAN (Chapter 4).[6] A simplified time-shared interactive version exists. **DARE/ELEVEN**, an interactive minicomputer system for the

Digital Equipment Corporation PDP-11 (Chapter 5), is unique in that it also incorporates a block-diagram language with very fast execution.[7]

CSMP III (formerly CSMP/360)[12] is supplied by the IBM Corporation for System/360 and 370 machines. An interactive-graphics version for IBM time-sharing systems with IBM 2250 graphic displays exists.

CSSL III, developed by Programming Sciences Corporation (no longer in existence), is supplied by Control Data Corporation for their 6000/7000 series computers.[13] A Sperry Univac version exists. **SL-I**, a related language for Xerox Data Systems' Sigma 5, 7, and 9, can be made interactive. **RSSL** (Raytheon Missile Division), **CSSL IV** (Levine and Nilsen), and **ACSL** (Mitchell and Gauthier Associates) are more recently improved versions of CSSL III, which are now commercially available for a variety of computers.

All these languages conform roughly to the CSSL-committee specifications of Reference 1 and are thus quite similar to the DARE language used in this book. Most systems will accommodate at least 200 state variables, 200 defined variables, and 200 parameters, depending on the computer memory available. Individual languages differ in

1. Delimiter conventions for separating the program entries into derivative blocks, logic block, FORTRAN files, etc.
2. Facilities for preparing labeled output listings, tables, and plots.
3. Features such as special library functions, function memory, macros, and matrix manipulation (Secs. 3-9, 3-17, and 3-18).

Note also that language features are sometimes changed and updated.

3-17. Simulation-Language Macros. Sometimes, groups of derivative-block statements (state equations, defined-variable equations, and/or procedural blocks) reoccur twice or more, or they occur often in different problems. It is then useful to define such a group as a named **simulation-language macro;** a one-line statement calling the macro with appropriate arguments (variables and parameters) will now cause the language translator to insert the previously specified group of statements with the correct arguments. We write a **macro definition** with general **dummy variables,** as in

$$\text{MACRO FILTER (P,Q,QDOT,R,G)}$$
$$\text{Q}' = \text{QDOT}$$
$$\text{QDOT}' = \text{P}-\text{R}*\text{QDOT}-\text{G}*\text{Q}$$
$$\text{MACRO END}$$

This macro defines a filter with input P and output Q such that

$$\frac{d^2Q}{dT^2} + R\frac{dQ}{dT} + GQ = P \tag{3-16}$$

with parameters R, and G and initial values $Q(0)$ and $\dot{Q}(0)$. Once the macro definition is included in a simulation-language program or in a *macro library* loaded together with the program, a **macro call**

$$\text{FILTER(STIM,RESP,DRESP,DAMP,GAIN)}$$

will automatically generate the two state equations

$$\text{RESP}' = \text{DRESP}$$
$$\text{DRESP}' = \text{STIM} - \text{DAMP} * \text{DRESP} - \text{GAIN} * \text{RESP}$$

and thus establish a relation (3-16) between STIM and RESP.

Simulation-language macros can be more than a convenient shorthand notation. They can be intuitively meaningful language elements which neatly represent subsystems and special operations. Groups of simulation-language statements suitable for macro representation include

> **1.** Performance equations for similar subsystems of a model (elements of electrical or hydraulic networks, mass-spring "lumps" of mechanical systems, component chemical reactions).
> **2.** Performance equations for one degree of freedom (generalized coordinate) of a dynamical system.
> **3.** Frequently used coordinate transformations and procedural blocks.

Macros may contain FORTRAN functions, procedural blocks (and hence subroutines), and other macros ("nesting" of macros). Frequently useful macro definitions can be stored in a library file and serve in different programs.

3-18. Additional Language Features

a. Implicit functions. As we noted in Sec. 3-2, simulation-language translators will reject derivative blocks containing algebraic loops, including implicit relations

$$Y = f(Y) \tag{3-17}$$

where $f(Y)$ is a given function of other defined variables, state variables, and/or T.

In reasonably posed simulation problems, a solution $Y = Y(T)$ of Eq. (3-17) will exist for each T, and if Eq. (3-17) cannot be solved explicitly for Y, one can include a numerical solution algorithm in a procedural block or FORTRAN function (Sec. 3-10). CSMP III and CSSL III provide a preprogrammed iterative solution algorithm which allows one to reprogram Eq. (3-17) in the form

$$\text{Y} = \text{IMPL (YO, ERROR, FOFY)} \tag{3-18}$$
$$\text{FOFY} = \text{F(Y)}$$

which "breaks" the algebraic loop and will be accepted by the translator. Y0 is an initial trial value for Y and could be a variable, and ERROR is a specified absolute fractional error used to stop the iteration. An error message is returned if convergence takes more than, say, 100 steps.

One usually employs the secant algorithm[18]

$$Y_{n+1} = \begin{cases} \dfrac{F(Y_n) - C_n Y_n}{1 - C_n} & (C_n \neq 1) \\ F(Y_n) & (C_n = 1) \end{cases}$$

$$C_n = \frac{F(Y_n) - F(Y_{n-1})}{Y_n - Y_{n-1}}$$

(3-18a)

for $n = 2, 3, \ldots$ with

$$Y_0 = Y0, \qquad Y_1 = 1.0001\, Y_0$$

(3-18b)

Even if the iteration takes only a few steps, the entire procedure repeats at each derivative call, which may be two to five times per *DT* step, depending on the integration routine used. We see that it will be best to avoid implicit functions whenever possible. If $F(Y)$ can be differentiated explicitly, the *steepest-descent technique* of Sec. C-2 is a good way out.

b. Function Memory. Function memory permits the user to store a time history obtained during a simulation run and to introduce this time history, as a function of T, into a following run. This is useful for iterative solution of integral equations[21] and for iterative optimization, e.g., of control systems.[22] Time-history samples may be stored once per integration step if enough memory is available, or interpolation between less frequent samples can be used as in the DELAY routine (which is also a form of function memory). One simple (but relatively slow) way to implement function memory is to recall SAVE files (Sec. 3-12) from the disk and to interpolate linearly.

c. Array and matrix operations. Simulation models may incorporate state equations or defined-variable equations such as

$$X_i' = \sum_{k=1}^{n} A_{ik} X_i + B_i \qquad (i = 1, 2, \ldots, n)$$

(3-19a)

$$Y_i = \sum_{k=1}^{m} C_{ik} X_i + D_i \qquad (i = 1, 2, \ldots, m)$$

(3-19b)

where n and m can be quite large (Example 4-4). It would be handy to enter such equations in matrix form,

$$X' = AX + B, \qquad Y = CX + D$$

(3-19c)

Unfortunately, existing CSSL languages do not have convenient facilities for entering and manipulating matrices. CSMP III handles subscripted state variables $X(I)$

with the aid of a special *integrator-array declaration*,[12] but otherwise *CSSL languages do not admit subscripted variables in state equations and defined-variable equations*. Matrix elements designated as X1, X2, ..., A11, A12, ..., etc., can be used and may be related to FORTRAN subscripted variables X(I), A(I,K) in procedural blocks or FORTRAN files containing FORTRAN matrix routines.[12,13] An experimental DARE language (DARE I-X[26]) admits matrix equations in the form of Eq. (3-19c) in one derivative block.

A simple way to abbreviate programs for matrix equations (3-19) is to introduce a **repetition operator** so that the statements

$$\text{REPT (I,N)}$$
$$\text{XI' = AI1 * X1 + AI7 * X7}$$

cause the simulation-language translator to generate N equations

$$\text{X1' = A11*X1 + A17*X7}$$
$$\text{X2' = A21*X1 + A27*X7}$$
$$\cdots \cdots \cdots \cdots \cdots \cdots \cdots$$

d. Transfer-function operators. CSMP III and CSSL III and some of the older DARE systems[2] provide special macros (or FORTRAN functions) which generate solutions of differential equations corresponding to transfer-functions such as

$$\frac{1}{As + 1}, \qquad \frac{Bs+1}{As+1}, \qquad \frac{1}{s^2 + Rs + G}, \qquad \text{etc.}$$

which are frequently useful in control-system simulation (*s* is a Laplace transform variable replacing the operator *d/dt*; see also Sec. 3-17). It will be necessary to supply values for the parameters *A, B, R, G,* ... and also for the initial conditions.

3-19. Miscellaneous Programming Aids. A simulation-language system must supply the user with **diagnostic error printouts or displays** that advise him of various programming errors. This is usually done at several levels. The simulation-language translator must catch errors such as illegal symbols or expressions and algebraic loops. If translation is successful, the FORTRAN compiler next reacts to the usual FORTRAN programming errors. Most simulation systems can also be loaded with a **debugging program** which permits preprogrammed HALTs, stepwise program execution, and memory readout and editing. Finally, the simulation system will have special commands to produce **translator and/or compiler output listings** and **memory maps.**

3-20. Addition of Special Features. Every CSSL-type language can be given a very wide variety of special features in terms of FORTRAN functions, subroutines, and procedures (Sec. 3-10). Integration methods can be added and changed. In addition, **DARE systems permit knowledgeable users to replace permanent system routines (RESET, RUN, function generation, output routines, etc.) with new user-**

written routines by simply entering similarly named **FORTRAN** routines (or **FORTRAN-called assembly-language routines**) in a **FORTRAN** file. It is, then, possible to rewrite substantial portions of a simulation system without having to start from scratch.

The system library is not permanently modified by this procedure. The special FORTRAN files can be stored and reused, or if they turn out to be generally useful, they can be made part of the permanent system library.

3-21. Programming Simplicity and Default Strategy. The simulation-language designer must compromise between the conflicting requirements for special language features and for programming simplicity; remember that **simulation languages are really intended for application-minded nonprogrammers.** DARE systems, which are used by college sophomores as well as by university and industrial researchers, attempt to resolve this compromise by making **all unused language features default to the simplest case.** The simplest simulation-language programs will contain only differential equations, initial-value and parameter data, and a simple output command, without any FORTRAN programming. *More advanced concepts, such as procedural blocks, FORTRAN subprograms, multiple derivative blocks, and even the control-logic, file, need not be learned until a user actually requires them.*

REFERENCES AND BIBLIOGRAPHY

1. SCi Software Committee, "The SCi Continuous-System Simulation Language," *Simulation*, Dec. 1967.

2. GOLTZ, J. R., "The DARE I On-Line Continuous-System Simulation Language," *Ph. D. thesis*, The University of Arizona, Tucson, 1970; see also *Proc. SWIEEECO*, Dallas, 1970.

3. KORN, G. A., "Project DARE: Differential Analyzer REplacement by On-Line Digital Simulation," *Proc. FJCC*, 1969.

4. AUS, H., and G. A. KORN, "The Future of On-Line Continuous-System Simulation," *Proc. FJCC*, 1971.

5. TREVOR, A. B., and J. V. WAIT, "DARE III B, A Digital Simulation System," *Simulation*, June 1972.

6. LUCAS, J., and J. V. WAIT, "DARE P, A Portable Continuous-System Simulation System," *Simulation*, Jan. 1975.

7. MARTINEZ, R., DARE/ELEVEN, "A Semi-portable Simulation System Using Both Fixed and Floating Point Derivative Blocks," Ph.D. thesis, The University of Arizona, Tucson, 1975; see also *Proc. DECUS Fall Symposium*, San Diego, 1974.

8. VAN STEENKISTE, G., "Optimal Generation of Continuous Functions," *Ann. AICA*, July 1967.

9. GOLDHIRSH, I. L., "Computation of Continuous Functions," *Simulation*, July 1968.

10. GRACON, T. J., and J. C. STRAUSS, "Application of Dynamic Programming to Function Generation," *Simulation*, Nov. 1968.

11. BRENNAN, R. D., and R. N. LINEBARGER, "A Survey of Digital Simulation," *Simulation*, Dec. 1964.

12. "Continuous System Modeling Program III and Graphic Feature," *Program No. 5734-X59 Manual*, IBM World Trade Corp., New York, 1972.

13. *Continuous System Simulation Language, Version 3, User's Guide*, Control Data Corp., Sunnyvale, Calif., 1971.

14. CHU, Y., *Digital Simulation of Continuous Systems*, McGraw-Hill, New York, 1969.

15. JENTSCH, W., *Digitale Simulation Kontinuierlicher Systeme*, Oldenbourg, Munich, 1969.

16. RECHENBERG, P., "*Simulationssysteme für Digitalrechner*," Ph.D. thesis, Technical University, Berlin, 1969.

17. HUSKEY, H. D., and G. A. KORN, *Computer Handbook*, McGraw-Hill, New York, 1962.

18. KLERER, M., and G. A. KORN, *Digital Computer User's Handbook*, McGraw-Hill, New York, 1967.

19. KORN, G. A., *Random-Process Simulation and Measurements*, McGraw-Hill, New York, 1966.

20. SHREIDER, Y. A., *Method of Statistical Testing*, Elsevier, Amsterdam, 1964.

21. BEKEY, G. A., and W. J. KARPLUS, *Hybrid Computations*, Wiley, New York, 1968.

22. KORN, G. A., and T. M. KORN, *Electric Analog and Hybrid Computers*, McGraw-Hill, New York, 1972.

23. HUELSMAN, L. P., *GOSPEL, a General Optimization Package*, Department of Electrical Engineering, The University of Arizona, Tucson, 1968.

24. STEMPLE, E., "The GOSPEL Optimization Package Linked to DARE IIIB," *CSRL Report No. 254*, Electrical Engineering Department, The University of Arizona, Tucson, 1974.

25. MITCHELL, E. E. L., and J. S. GAUTHIER, "A Table-Driven Continuous-System Simulation Language," *Proc. Summer Computer Simulation Conf. Montreal*, Simulation Councils, Inc., La Jolla, Calif., 1973.

26. MOORE, W. R., "An Expanded Simulation Language for Partitioned Systems," M.S. thesis, Electrical Engineering Department, The University of Arizona, Tucson, 1972.

4

A Machine-Independent CSSL System

INTRODUCTION

In this chapter we shall describe a specific example of an equation-oriented continuous-system simulation language.[1-3] DARE P system programs are coded entirely in ANSI FORTRAN IV. Unlike its predecessor DARE IIIB, which was written in CDC 6000 series assembly language, **DARE P is, therefore, essentially machine-independent or "portable"** (the acronym DARE P stands for Differential Amplifier REplacement, Portable).

DARE P is designed for **batch-mode processing** but can be run from an interactive time-sharing terminal without excessive modification. A true interactive version of DARE P is under development.

In this chapter we shall summarize DARE P language features with reference to the general discussion of Chapter 3 and illustrate applications to representative simulation programs. Additional documentation is available in the form of a user's manual[4] and an implementation guide.[5]

DARE P includes three main program modules: the *translator*, the *run-time system*, and the *output system*. The **translator** translates the user's original simulation program into FORTRAN-coded subprograms suitable for compilation and loading (see also Sec. 3-4). A communication table, which links problem and system variables between overlays, is also created. In the batch-processed DARE P system, the translator also puts user-entered **data** (initial conditions and parameters) into tables required by the run-time module, and output commands are processed for later use by the output module (see also Secs. 3-3 and 3-5).

Next, the conventional system **FORTRAN compiler** compiles the translated subprograms into relocatable code, which is subsequently loaded along with routines associated with the DARE run-time module. The **run-time module** then runs the problem and outputs solution-data files onto mass storage (usually a disk). The **output module** is then loaded and interprets user-furnished commands which direct the retrieval and display of solutions on a printer or plotter.

For the inexperienced user, all that is required is some understanding of how to phrase a simulation problem in state-variable equation form, using a FORTRAN-like notation (Chapter 3); no real knowledge of FORTRAN is needed. DARE P provides the more advanced user with the capability of doing one- and two-dimensional table lookup function generation and specifying special FORTRAN subroutines. He may implement complete multirun simulation studies with his own FORTRAN simulation control program.

BASIC FEATURES OF THE DARE P SYSTEM

4-1. Hardware Requirements for DARE P. We have attempted to keep the hardware requirements for DARE P to a practical minimum. Typically, one needs **a CPU with perhaps 24K words of memory** and the following peripheral devices:

1. **Output device:** An output device capable of printing 132 characters per line on wide computer output paper. With modifications, smaller-sized paper could be used.
2. **Input device:** A card reader for a batch environment or a TTY or CRT for an "interactive" environment.
3. **Mass-storage device:** High-speed disk/drum storage capability is almost essential to the implementation of DARE P. The amount of disk space required, like memory, will depend on the size of the system being simulated and on the amount of runs needed. Magnetic tape units can be substituted for a disk, but they will increase turnaround time and run time.
4. **Digital plotter:** DARE P is designed to provide CalComp-compatible plotter output for those installations with either CalComp off-line plotters or a CalComp-compatible on/off-line plotting device.

4-2. Using DARE P: Problem-Deck Format. A typical **problem deck** (see, e.g., Fig. 4-1) consists of three sections, each terminated by an END card:

1. **A problem descriptor deck or file,** including some or all of the blocks listed in Table 4-1. Here the differential equations are specified, and any other code required to describe the problem is entered. Special user-furnished routines may be introduced.

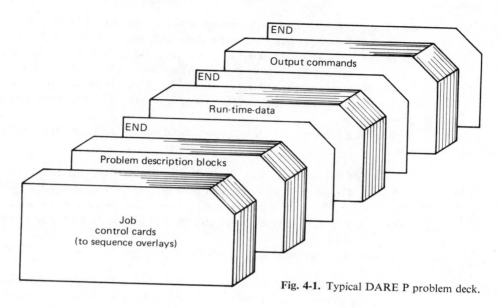

Fig. 4-1. Typical DARE P problem deck.

TABLE 4-1. DARE P Block Names*

Name	Block Name	Contents
Derivative block 1	$D1	Model equations describing system being simulated in derivative block 1
Derivative block 1	$D2	Model equations describing system being simulated in derivative block 2
Logic block	$L	FORTRAN code to control simulation runs
Table blocks	$T	Functions defined in tabular form
Function blocks	$F	FORTRAN functions or subroutines
Methods block	$Mn	Number selecting integration rule to be used
Own code block	$O	User-supplied integration rules

*Block name starts with the $ in column 2.

2. Free-form run-time data cards, specifying initial conditions, undefined parameters, solution time, and any special nondefault values of system parameters.

3. Output commands, which direct retrieval and display of solution histories.

The problem descriptor deck is subdivided into blocks, each block starting with an identifying block mark card (Table 4-1). *Derivative block 1 is the only block necessary for simple problems which require only one simulation run from T = 0 to T = TMAX.*

4-3. The Derivative Block. A **derivative block** consists of first-order differential equations (**state equations**) and **defined-variable equations,** which together specify the model to be simulated (see also Sec. 3-1). Both state equations and defined-variable equations can reference special functions (Secs. 3-8, 3-9, 4-9, and 4-10).

Equations may be entered in any order. The DARE translator will automatically sort the equations into the correct procedural order and will reject any algebraic loops (Sec. 3-2).

State and defined-variable equations must be written according to the following format:

1. Card columns 7 to 72, inclusive, are reserved for equations.

2. Equations may be broken over one or more card images by the placement of a $ character in card columns 3–6 of all continuation cards.

3. The derivative of a variable may appear only on the left-hand side of an equal sign.

4. The character Z may not be used as the last character of any variable name.

5. Variables and parameters must have REAL undimensioned FORTRAN-type names; i.e., *names must start with an alphanumeric character other than I, J, K, L, M, and N.*

6. State-variable names may be up to five characters long; other variable names can have up to six characters.

7. Variables appearing only on the right-hand sides of equations ("undefined variables") are considered as *parameters* to be input at run time.

8. *Simulation-system variables* (e.g., DT, TMAX; see Table 4-2) may be referred to in any equation, but the user must be cautious about redefining them in a derivative block.

9. A derivative block is terminated with an END card image, which contains the characters END in columns 1–3. For more advanced applications, DARE P admits **procedural blocks** (Sec. 3-10.b) in the form

$$\text{PROCED} \quad \underset{\text{output}}{A,B, \ldots} = \underset{\text{input}}{X,Y, \ldots}$$

$$\text{ENDPRO}$$

and **TERMINATE statements** such as

$$\text{TERMINATE } \textit{expression}$$

which will terminate a run *when the expression becomes less than or equal to zero.*

10. Normally all output variables are stored at each communication interval; however, a statement

$$\text{STORE list}$$

will cause *only* those variables in the list to be stored.

TABLE 4-2. DARE P System Variables

Name	Default Value	Function
T	0.0	Independent variable, time
TMAX	—	Maximum value of T
DT	COMINT	Initial integration-step size, not changed by fixed-step size rules
DTMAX	COMINT	Maximum allowable value for DT
DTMIN	DTMAX/16	Minimum allowable value for DT
EMAX	0.001	Maximum error bound for variable-step-size integration rules
EMIN	0.00001	Minimum error bound for variable-step-size integration rules
IRUNNO	1	Run number during multirun simulations
METHOD	1	Integration rule to be used
NPOINT	101	Number of points to be output during one run
COMINT	TMAX/(NPOINT-1)	Communication interval (time between output points)
SY(1-9)	0.0	Nine system variables—SY(1) and SY(6) used by Runge-Kutta-Merson integration rule
TALT DTA DTMXA DTMNA EMAXA EMINA		Alternative system variables for use in the second derivative block

4-4. Initial Conditions and Parameters. *Initial-condition entries* follow the derivative block END card image, together with entries for *system parameters* and parameters. In a free-format environment, all are entered in columns 1 through 72 of successive cards [Fig. 4-2(a)]. A value for such a variable is specified by the variable name followed by an "=", followed by the value to be assigned to that variable. More than one variable may be initialized per card image by separating assignments with a comma. An initialization of any entry may not be broken over two card images.

If some initial value of parameter is not entered, it will have value zero; system variables default to values shown in Table 4-2. The only variable which *must* be entered for each run is TMAX; otherwise a fatal error results.

A two-card example of initial-condition and parameter definition follows:

$$TMAX = 100.0, \quad X = 50.0$$
$$P = 2.5$$

Initialization is terminated by another END card with the characters END in columns 1–3.

Note that *arithmetic expressions may be entered in this section, e.g.*,

$$P = 215.1, \quad X = P/3.14159$$

but no sorting is done.

4-5. Output Commands. Simulation results are first output to the disk; Table 4-3 summarizes the types of files which may be created. The **output section (output block)** (Sec. 3-5) of the DARE P program specifies the extraction of results from the various output files by **output commands.** Output can take several forms, viz. , line-printer lists, line-printer plots (time-history plots or *XY* plots), and digital plotter output.

TABLE 4-3. Data Storage Files

File Name	Use
TIME	Time history of all output variables from a single simulation run. CALL RUN generates it, while CALL RESET destroys the contents of TIME from the previous run.
CROSS	Current values of all output variables at the points in time that a CALL STORE was issued in the logic block. Useful for comparing final values of various runs.
ZAVEF	Time history of simulation run for a user-selected subset of the output variables. Each run preceded by a CALL SAVE (list) creates a new ZAVEF record.
STASH	Magnetic tape or card file used to store results at output time for display and comparison with data from later simulation studies.

An **identification card** may be included as the *first* output request. It should begin with an asterisk; the information on the card will appear as problem output. Two forms are allowed:

1. *Func, list*
2. *Func (fnam,* P1, P2, P3) *list*

Func is one of the output functions
LIST, PLOT, PLOTXY, GRAPH, GRAPHY, GRAPHS, PLOTXS, STASH
fnam is one of the file names TIME or CROSS or a number indicating a ZAVEF file; default is TIME.
P1 is the lower bound of T; default is 0.
P2 is the upper bound of T; default is TMAX.
P3 is the increment of T; default is COMINT; note that P3 should be an integer multiple of COMINT.

The *list* above, is the list of output variables desired.

1. LIST produces a tabular listing of up to seven variables.
2a. PLOT plots up to eight variables on the line printer, versus time, or index on calls to STORE.
2b. GRAPH plots up to seven variables on the CalComp plotter versus the *first* variable in *list*.

3a. PLOTXY plots up to seven variables on the line printer versus the the first variable in the list.

3b. GRAPHY is like PLOTXY, except it uses the CalComp plotter.

4a. Overplotting of one variable from up to five **SAVE** files may be done by a command of the form

$$\text{PLOTXS (P1, P2, P3, P4, P5, P6, P7, P8) } Var$$

where P1–P5 are SAVE file numbers, listed in any order; at least one must be present,

P6 is the starting point for the plot;

P7 is the stopping point for the plot;

P8 is output increment;

Var is the variable name.

4b. GRAPHS may similarly be used with the CalComp plotter. Terminate the output request with a card containing END in columns 1–3.

5. STASH list may be used to store the variables listed on the disk or tape for subsequent processing after the DARE P job is over (see References 1 and 2).

4-6. Selection of Integration Rules ($Mn and $0 blocks) The signal $Mn allows the user to select one of a set of internally installed integration rules in the DARE P

TABLE 4-4. DARE P Integration Rules*

Number	*Method*
1	Runge-Kutta-Merson
	SY(1) = 0 relative error control
	SY(1) = n absolute error control on the nth-state variable (as output by the translator)
	SY(6) ≠ 0 print history of step sizes
2	Two-point Runge-Kutta (improved Euler or Heun's method), fixed-step
3	Not currently used
4	Fourth-order Runge-Kutta, fixed-step (classic)
5	Adam's two-point predictor (starts with two-point Runge-Kutta), fixed-step
6	Euler first-order predictor, fixed-step
7	Exponential rule (Pope's); variable step for stiff systems; SY(1)/ SY(6) used as in method 1, above
8	Gear's DIFSUB; SY(8) = 0.0 for implicit method; SY(8) = 1.0 for Adam's predictor-corrector; SY(7) = max. order, defaults to 5.0, may be up to 7.0 for implicit or 12.0 for Adam's
9	Calahan's third-order implicit Runge-Kutta rule, fixed-step
10	Runge-Kutta-Fehlberg 4(5)
11	Hindmarsh's EPISODE

*See also Appendix A.

system, where *n* is the number of the rule chosen. Table 4-4 lists the set currently provided. The user can introduce his own integration rule in the $0 ("oh," not zero) block. Reference 3 provides information on the structure of DARE P integration rules.

4-7. A Simple Example

Example 4-1: Step Response of a Linear Second-Order System (see also Sec. 2-3). Figure 4-2 illustrates the use of DARE P to find the step response of a simple second-order system specified by

$$\frac{d^2 Y}{dT^2} + D\frac{dY}{dT} + Y = 1 \qquad (T \geq 0) \tag{4-1}$$

Note that there are two first-order state equations. Unlike the more primitive program of Sec. 2-3, DARE P can employ user-furnished, intuitively suggestive names for variables and parameters, here *Y*, YDOT, and *D*. Figure 4-2(a) shows the complete problem deck. Note that initial conditions are set to default values of zero; other values could be entered. The only run-time data required are values for TMAX and the damping factor *D*. The output requests provide the line-printer display shown in Fig. 4-2(b) and (c).

```
DARE PORTABLE (VERSION 1.2)

UNIVERSITY OF ARIZONA


          $D1
          *
          *      STEP RESPONSE OF DAMPED SECOND-ORDER SYSTEM
          *
                 Y.=YDOT
                 YDOT.= -D*YDOT-Y+1.0
END
                 TMAX=50.,D=0.1
END
          LIST,Y,YDOT
          PLOT,Y
END                                    .
```

Fig. 4-2. (a)

Fig. 4-2. Step response of a simple second-order system. (a) Problem description; (b) solution listing; (c) solution plot.

```
                    LIST,Y,YDOT

                    RUN NUMBER    1

                   TIME              Y              YDOT
          0.                0.             0.
          5.00000E-01       1.20409E-01    4.67636E-01
          1.00000E+00       4.44964E-01    8.00774E-01
          1.50000E+00       8.86225E-01    9.26468E-01
          2.C0000E+00       1.33314E+00    8.24818E-01
          2.50000E+00       1.67873E+00    5.31178E-01
          3.00000E+00       1.84540E+00    1.25021E-01
          3.50000E+00       1.80209E+00   -2.91188E-01
          4.00000E+00       1.56937E+00   -6.17578E-01
          4.50000E+00       1.21205E+00   -7.80595E-01
          5.00000E+00       8.21512E-01   -7.49279E-01
          5.50000E+00       4.92633E-01   -5.405°
          6.00000E+00       3.00933E-01   -2.
          6.50000E+00       2.85497E-01
          7.00000E+00       4.41418E-01
          7.50000E+00       7.23113E-
          8.00000E+00       1.057]´
          8.50000E+00       1.36´
          9.00000E+00       ]
          9.50000E+00
```

Fig. 4-2. (b)

```
PLOT,Y
      PLOTX-T ROUTINE -- PLOT NUMBER 1                    SCALE FACTORS ... X = 2.00E-02     T = 5.00E-01

              0.      2.00E-01  4.00E-01  6.00E-01  8.00E-01  1.00E+00  1.20E+00  1.40E+00  1.60E+00  1.80E+00  2.00E+00
              +    +       +       +       +       +       +       +       +       +       +
      0.      1000000000000000000000000000000000000000000000000000000000000000000000000000000000000000000000001   1
5.00000000E-01   0    1       I       I 1     I       I       I       I       I       I       I   2
1.00000000E+00   0    I       I 1   1 I       I       I       I       I       I       I       I   3
1.50000000E+00   0    I       I       I   1 1 I       I       I       I       I       I       I   4
2.00000000E+00   0    I       I       I       I       I       I   1   I       I       I       I   5
2.50000000E+00   0    I       I       I       I       I       I       I   1   I       I       I   6
3.00000000E+00   0    I       I       I       I       I       I       I       I   1 1 I       I   7
3.50000000E+00   0    I       I       I       I       I       I       I       I       I 1   I   8
4.00000000E+00   0    I       I       I       I       I       I       I   1 1   I       I       I   9
4.50000000E+00   0    I       I       I       I       I       I   1   I       I       I       I   10
5.00000000E+00   0--------------------------------+-------1-------+-------+-------+-------+-------I   11
5.50000000E+00   0    I       I   1   1 I       I       I       I       I       I       I       I   12
6.00000000E+00   0    I   1   I       I       I       I       I       I       I       I       I   13
6.50000000E+00   0    I   1   I       I       I       I       I       I       I       I       I   14
7.00000000E+00   0    I     1 I 1   I       I       I       I       I       I       I       I   15
7.50000000E+00   0    I     1 I 1   I       I       I       I       I       I       I       I   16
8.00000000E+00   0    I       I       I   1   I       I       I       I       I       I       I   17
8.50000000E+00   0    I       I       I       I 1     I       I       I       I       I       I   18
9.00000000E+00   0    I       I       I       I       I       I   1 1   I       I       I       I   19
9.50000000E+00   0    I       I       I       I       I       I       I       I   I1   I       I   20
1.00000000E+01   0--------------------------------+-------+-------+-------+----1--+-------+-------I   21
1.05000000E+01   0    I       I       I       I       I       I       I   1   I       I       I   22
1.10000000E+01   0    I       I       I       I       I1      I       I       I       I       I   23
1.15000000E+01   0    I       I       I   1 1 I       I       I       I       I       I       I   24
1.20000000E+01   0    I       I   1   I   1 I       I       I       I       I       I       I       -   25
1.25000000E+01   0    I       I   1   I       I       I       I       I       I       I       I   26
1.30000000E+01   0    I       I   1 I       I       I       I       I       I       I       I   27
1.35000000E+01   0    I       I 1   I       I       I       I       I       I       I       I   28
1.40000000E+01   0    I       I       I   1   I       I       I       I       I       I       I   29
1.45000000E+01   0    I       I       I       I       I       I   1 I       I       I       I       I   30
1.50000000E+01   0--------------------------------+-------+-------+-------1-------+-------+-------I   31
1.55000000E+01   0    I       I       I       I       I       I       I   1 1   I       I       I   32
1.60000000E+01   0    I       I       I       I       I       I       I   1   I       I       I   33
1.65000000E+01   0    I       I       I       I       I       I   1   I       I       I       I   34
1.70000000E+01   0    I       I       I       I       I   1   I       I       I       I       I   35
1.75000000E+01   0    I       I       I       I   1   I       I       I       I       I       I   36
1.80000000E+01   0    I       I       I   1 I       I       I       I       I       I       I   37
1.85000000E+01   0    I       I       I1    I       I       I       I       I       I       I   38
1.90000000E+01   0    I       I       I 1     I       I       I       I       I       I       I   39
1.95000000E+01   0    I       I       I 1   I       I       I       I       I       I       I   40
2.00000000E+01   0--------------------------------+-------1-------+-------+-------+-------+-------I   41
2.05000000E+01   0    I       I       I       I       I   1   I       I       I       I       I   42
2.10000000E+01   0    I       I       I       I       I       I   1 1   I       I       I       I   43
2.15000000E+01   0    I       I       I       I       I       I   1   I       I       I       I   44
2.20000000E+01   0    I       I       I       I       I       I       I   1   I       I       I   45
2.25000000E+01   0    I       I       I       I       I       I   1   I       I       I       I   46
2.30000000E+01   0    I       I       I       I       I       I   1I    I       I       I       I   47
2.35000000E+01   0    I       I       I       I       I   1 1   I       I       I       I       I   48
2.40000000E+01   0    I       I       I   1   I       I       I       I       I       I       I   49
2.45000000E+01   0    I       I       I   1 1 I       I       I       I       I       I       I   50
2.50000000E+01   0--------------------------------+-------1-------+-------+-------+-------+-------I   51
2.55000000E+01   0    I       I       I   1   1 I       I       I       I       I       I       I   52
2.60000000E+01   0    I       I       I       I       I       I       I       I       I       I   53
2.65000000E+01   0    I       I       I       I   1   I       I       I       I       I       I   54
2.70000000E+01   0    I       I       I       I       I   1 1   I       I       I       I       I   55
2.75000000E+01   0    I       I       I   1   I       I       I   1 1   I       I       I       I   56
2.80000000E+01   0    I       I       I       I       I       I   I1    I       I       I       I   57
2.85000000E+01   0    I       I       I       I       I       I   I1    I       I       I       I   58
2.90000000E+01   0    I       I       I       I       I       I   1I    I       I       I       I   59
2.95000000E+01   0    I       I       I       I       I   1   I       I       I       I       I   60
3.00000000E+01   0--------------------------------+-------+---1---+-------+-------+-------+-------I   61
3.05000000E+01   0    I       I       I       I   1   I       I       I       I       I       I   62
3.10000000E+01   0    I       I       I       I 1   I       I       I       I       I       I   63
3.15000000E+01   0    I       I       I       I1    I       I       I       I       I       I   64
3.20000000E+01   0    I       I       I       I1    I       I       I       I       I       I   65
3.25000000E+01   0    I       I       I       I   1 I       I       I       I       I       I   66
3.30000000E+01   0    I       I       I       I       I1    I       I       I       I       I   67
3.35000000E+01   0    I       I       I       I       I   1 1 I       I       I       I       I   68
3.40000000E+01   0    I       I       I       I       I   1 1   I       I       I       I       I   69
3.45000000E+01   0    I       I       I       I       I   1 1   I       I       I       I       I   70
3.50000000E+01   0--------------------------------+-------+-------1-+-------+-------+-------+-------I   71
3.55000000E+01   0    I       I       I       I       I   1   I       I       I       I       I   72
3.60000000E+01   0    I       I       I       I       I1    I       I       I       I       I   73
3.65000000E+01   0    I       I       I       I   1   I       I       I       I       I       I   74
3.70000000E+01   0    I       I       I       I 1   I       I       I       I       I       I   75
3.75000000E+01   0    I       I       I   1 1 I       I       I       I       I       I       I   76
3.80000000E+01   0    I       I       I   1 1 I       I       I       I       I       I       I   77
3.85000000E+01   0    I       I       I 1   I       I       I       I       I       I       I   78
3.90000000E+01   0    I       I       I   1 I       I       I       I       I       I       I   79
3.95000000E+01   0    I       I       I       I       I       I       I       I       I       I   80
4.00000000E+01   0--------------------------------+-------+----1--+-------+-------+-------+-------I   81
4.05000000E+01   0    I       I       I       I       I   1   I       I       I       I       I   82
4.10000000E+01   0    I       I       I       I       I 1   I       I       I       I       I   83
4.15000000E+01   0    I       I       I       I1    I       I       I       I       I       I   84
4.20000000E+01   0    I       I       I       I   1 1 I       I       I       I       I       I   85
4.25000000E+01   0    I       I       I       I   1   I       I       I       I       I       I   86
4.30000000E+01   0    I       I       I       I 1   I       I       I       I       I       I   87
4.35000000E+01   0    I       I       I       I 1   I       I       I       I       I       I   88
4.40000000E+01   0    I       I       I   1   I       I       I       I       I       I       I   89
4.45000000E+01   0    I       I       I   1   I       I       I       I       I       I       I   90
4.50000000E+01   0--------------------------------+-------1-------+-------+-------+-------+-------I   91
4.55000000E+01   0    I       I       I       I   1 1 I       I       I       I       I       I   92
4.60000000E+01   0    I       I       I       I   1 1 I       I       I       I       I       I   93
4.65000000E+01   0    I       I       I       I   1 1 1 I       I       I       I       I       I   94
4.70000000E+01   0    I       I       I       I   1   I       I       I       I       I       I   95
4.75000000E+01   0    I       I       I       I   1 1 I       I       I       I       I       I   96
4.80000000E+01   0    I       I       I       I   1 1 I       I       I       I       I       I   97
4.85000000E+01   0    I       I       I       I   1I    I       I       I       I       I       I   98
4.90000000E+01   0    I       I       I       I   1I    I       I       I       I       I       I   99
4.95000000E+01   0    I       I       I       I 1   I       I       I       I       I       I   100
5.00000000E+01   0--------------------------------+-------1-------+-------+-------+-------+-------I   101
                 +    +       +       +       +       +       +       +       +       +       +
              0.      2.00E-01  4.00E-01  6.00E-01  8.00E-01  1.00E+00  1.20E+00  1.40E+00  1.60E+00  1.80E+00  2.00E+00
```

PLOTTER SYMBOL - 1
VARIABLE NAME - Y

Fig. 4-2. (c)

MORE ADVANCED FEATURES OF DARE P

4-8. Simulation-Study Control: The Logic Block. * The DARE P FORTRAN control program for multirun simulation studies is called the **logic block.** The DARE P logic block may contain any valid FORTRAN statement except type declarations FUNCTION or SUBROUTINE.

Note that all variables in a derivative block are automatically placed in COMMON by the DARE translator. Hence COMMON statements, if any, in the logic block must be used only to link variables local to the logic block to the FORTRAN or table blocks.

The special logic-block statements for simulation control are those described in Secs. 3-12 and 3-13, viz.,

INPUT *list*	OUTPUT *list*
CALL RUN	CALL RESET
CALL STROF	CALL STRON

The DARE P CALL STORE and CALL SAVE statements are slightly different from those in the DARE/ELEVEN system and will be described in Sec. 4-9.

NOTE: The DARE P subroutine RESET resets *only state variables* prior to CALL RUN. Hence initial values of *defined variables* cannot be read before a run is started.

4-9. Data Storage Files. In a batch-processing environment, observation of the simulation while it is in progress is not usually feasible, and so four files (usually disk files) have been provided for temporary storage of run-time data (Table 4-3).

Special subroutine calls conveniently control data storage in these files, eliminating the need for FORTRAN input/output statements in the logic block.

Unless STROF has been called, **time histories of all state and defined variables are stored in the TIME file.** Two other output-data files can be used with multiple runs.

1. The DARE P statement

CALL SAVE

can replace CALL SAVE statements for individual variables (Sec. 3-13); time histories of all state and defined variables are saved in successively numbered files called SAVEFI, where $I = 1, 2, \ldots$. Note that CALL SAVE is used before CALL RUN; this differs from DARE/ELEVEN (Sec. 3-13).

*See also Secs. 3-11 to 3-15.

2. The DARE P statement

CALL STORE

saves the values, at the time of this call, of all variables in the **OUTPUT** list *and also* the values of all state variables and defined variables as entries in a file called **CROSS**. Another output-data file called **STASH** may be used to store results of a simulation for subsequent output to magnetic tape or punched cards. This permits comparisons with a later simulation. The use of appropriate control cards also permits outputting of the final object code of the simulation problem, so that additional runs can be made later without recompilation.

4-10. Tabulated Functions. DARE P permits entry of tabulated-function data (with one argument or two arguments) in the manner of Sec. 3-8 in **table blocks**. The following rules must be observed:

1. The first card of each table must be

$T

column 2

2. Comment cards, starting with an asterisk in column 1, may be used throughout the block.
3. For one-dimensional tables, the next noncomment line must contain the *name* followed by a *comma* and the *number of data points*.
4. Successive lines must contain a *value* of the *independent variable* followed by a *comma* followed by the *value of* the *dependent* variable at that point, e.g.,

```
$T
*
* A ONE-DIMENSIONAL TABLE
*
    FIRST, 5
    0.0,1.0
    1.1,2.7
    1.5,2.9
    2.8,−3.0
    4.0,−11.3
```

A call to the table could be of the form

Y = FIRST(3.4)

Note that entries should be with the smallest values of the *independent* variable first, and then increasing values in order.

5. If the argument exceeds the range of the table points, the value at the end point of the table is used; e.g., for the above case the value of the function would be 1.0 for all negative values of the argument and −11.3 for all values of the argument greater than 4.0.

6. The *two-dimensional-table* specification begins with the name of the function and the number of breakpoints for both independent variables.

7. Function points are arranged in an array where the *first* independent variable varies with the rows and the second with the columns.

8. In a two-dimensional table, the *first line* consists of *breakpoints for* the second *independent variable*. The next lines consist of a breakpoint for the first independent variable followed by a comma and the corresponding function values, separated by commas. As in a one-dimensional table, neither of the independent variables need be spaced uniformly, although they must be sequential. Lines on a table may be continued over card boundaries by inserting a $ in column 1 of each continuation card. Data may be in columns 2 through 72. An example follows:

```
$T
*
*  A TWO-DIMENSIONAL TABLE
        TWODIM,3,5,
*
*  THE FOLLOWING LISTS BREAKPOINTS OF THE SECOND
*  INDEPENDENT VARIABLE.
        0.0,1.0,2.0,3.0,4.0
*
*  NEXT COMES THE BREAKPOINTS FOR THE FIRST
   INDEPENDENT VARIABLE FOLLOWED BY THE FUNCTION
   VALUES.
*       0.0,0.0,0.1,0.5,
$  0.3,4.0
        1.0,0.1,0.4,1.0,0.8,0.0
        10.0,0.0,6.0,10.0,1.0,0.1
```

4-11. Library Functions and FORTRAN Block. DARE P derivative blocks and logic blocks can freely employ the usual **FORTRAN library functions,** listed in Table 3-1 for a typical FORTRAN system, and the special DARE library functions listed in Table 3-2. These include, in particular, functions representing limiter and sampler operations useful in control-system simulation. In addition, DARE P has a **time-delay generator** suitable for use with both fixed-step and variable-step integration routines (see also Sec. 3-9).

Special FORTRAN subprograms for use with procedural sections or logic block may be entered in the DARE P **FORTRAN block**. The characters $F in columns 2 and 3 cause all card images following, until the next block or the end of the simulation description, to be transferred directly to the translator output file for subsequent FORTRAN compilation. All legal FORTRAN IV is permissible. There may be any number of FORTRAN function blocks with any number of subprograms per block.

Example 4-2: Analysis of a Third-Order Servo. This example illustrates the use of the logic block and data files. Figure 4-3 shows the block diagram of a simple third-order servo system with plant differential equation

$$\frac{d^3X}{dT^3} + \frac{d^2X}{dT^2} + \frac{dX}{dT} = V \qquad (T \geq 0) \tag{4-2}$$

or Laplace transform transfer function

$$\frac{X(s)}{V(s)} = \frac{1}{s(s^2 + s + 1)} \tag{4-3}$$

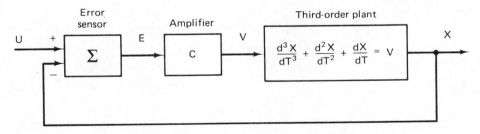

Fig. 4-3. Block diagram of a third-order control system.

An error amplifier, with gain C, is used to implement closed-loop control, tending to make the plant output X follow the system input U, i.e.,

$$V = C(U - X) \tag{4-4}$$

Figure 4-4 shows a DARE P program which finds the step response for five values of C and plots them all on the same graph; finally, it finds the ramp response for one value of C. Note how the logic block is used to sequence the runs, with a CALL SAVE prior to each CALL RUN, except the last, where the TIME file is used to store the solution for the ramp response. Note that output messages are included in the logic block to remind the user later about what values of C correspond to a given run. Note also the output commands used.

```
DARE PORTABLE (VERSION 1.2)

UNIVERSITY OF ARIZONA


            $D1
            *       SERVO SYSTEM ANALYSIS
            *       PLANT
            *       C IS GAIN CONSTANT
                    X1.=X2
                    X2.=X3
                    X3.=-X2-X3+C*E
            *       FORM ERROR
                    E=U-X1
            *       GENERAL RAMP OR STEP INPUT
                    U=C1+C2*T
            $L
                    DO 100 I=1,5
                    CALL RESET
                    CALL SAVE
                    PRINT 200, I,C
            200     FORMAT(1X,* GAIN CONSTANT FOR RUN *,I1,* IS *,E10.3)
                    CALL RUN
                    C=C+0.05
            100     CONTINUE
                    C=0.35
                    PRINT 300,C
            300     FORMAT(* GAIN CONSTANT IS *,E10.3)
            *       RAMP INPUT
                    C1=0.0
                    C2=1.0
                    CALL RESET
                    CALL RUN
    END
                    TMAX=20.,C=0.2,C1=1.0,C2=0.0
    END
            PLOTXS(1,2,3,4,5)X1
            PLOT,X1
    END
```

Fig. 4-4. (a)

Fig. 4-4. Multiple-run study of third-order control system. (a) DARE P problem deck (note use of logic block); (b) messages output during run-time overlay; (c) PLOTXS display of saved solutions for step response; (d) plot of ramp response of final run.

```
    GAIN CONSTANT FOR RUN 1 IS    .200E+00
    RUNGE-KUTTA-MERSON METHOD USED
    GAIN CONSTANT FOR RUN 2 IS    .250E+00
    RUNGE-KUTTA-MERSON METHOD USED
    GAIN CONSTANT FOR RUN 3 IS    .300E+00
    RUNGE-KUTTA-MERSON METHOD USED
    GAIN CONSTANT FOR RUN 4 IS    .350E+00
    RUNGE-KUTTA-MERSON METHOD USED
    GAIN CONSTANT FOR RUN 5 IS    .400E+00
    RUNGE-KUTTA-MERSON METHOD USED
    GAIN CONSTANT IS    .350E+00
    RUNGE-KUTTA-MERSON METHOD USED
```

Fig. 4-4. (b)

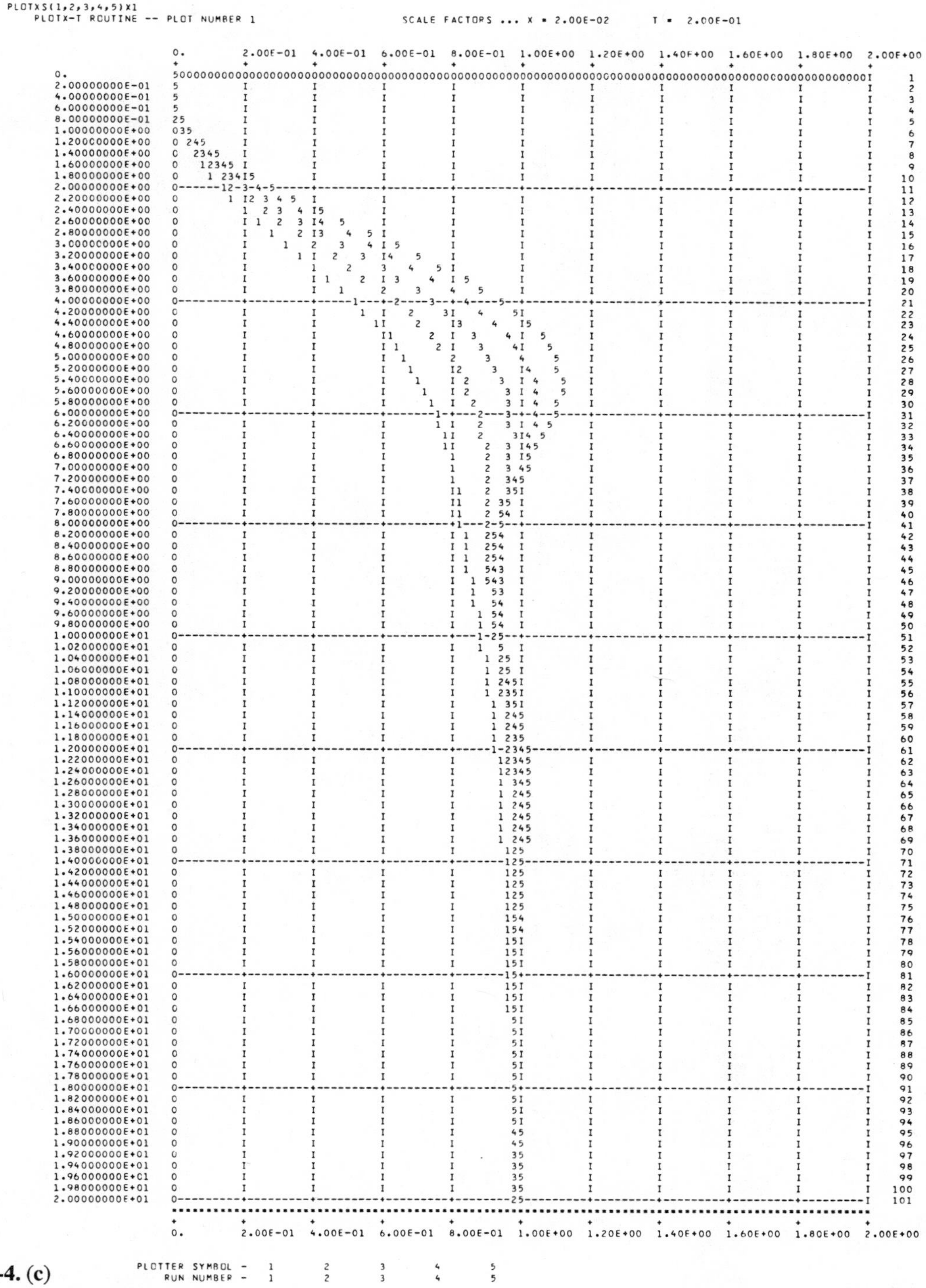

```
PLOTXS(1,2,3,4,5)X1
    PLOTX-T ROUTINE -- PLOT NUMBER 1                      SCALE FACTORS ... X = 2.00E-02     T = 2.00E-01

              0.      2.00E-01  4.00E-01  6.00E-01  8.00E-01  1.00E+00  1.20E+00  1.40E+00  1.60E+00  1.80E+00  2.00E+00
              +         +         +         +         +         +         +         +         +         +         +
   0.         5000000000000000000000000000000000000000000000000000000000000000000000000000000000000000000000000000I    1
2.00000000E-01 5          I         I         I         I         I         I         I         I         I     I    2
4.00000000E-01 5          I         I         I         I         I         I         I         I         I     I    3
6.00000000E-01 5          I         I         I         I         I         I         I         I         I     I    4
8.00000000E-01 25         I         I         I         I         I         I         I         I         I     I    5
1.00000000E+00 035        I         I         I         I         I         I         I         I         I     I    6
1.20000000E+00 0 245      I         I         I         I         I         I         I         I         I     I    7
1.40000000E+00 0  2345    I         I         I         I         I         I         I         I         I     I    8
1.60000000E+00 0  12345 I I         I         I         I         I         I         I         I         I     I    9
1.80000000E+00 0   1 23415 I        I         I         I         I         I         I         I         I     I   10
2.00000000E+00 0------12-3-4-5----------------+---------+---------+---------+---------+---------+---------+-----I   11
2.20000000E+00 0    1 12 3 4  5    I         I         I         I         I         I         I         I     I   12
2.40000000E+00 0     1  2 3   4 I5  I         I         I         I         I         I         I         I     I   13
2.60000000E+00 0     I 1  2   3 I4  5 I       I         I         I         I         I         I         I     I   14
2.80000000E+00 0      1  2   3   4 5I  I       I         I         I         I         I         I         I     I   15
3.00000000E+00 0       I 1   2 I3   4 5 I     I         I         I         I         I         I         I     I   16
3.20000000E+00 0        1 1  2   3 I4   5  I   I         I         I         I         I         I         I     I   17
3.40000000E+00 0        I 1   2    3   4 5 I  I         I         I         I         I         I         I     I   18
3.60000000E+00 0        I I 1   2  I 3   4 I 5 I        I         I         I         I         I         I     I   19
3.80000000E+00 0        I   I 1   2   3    4   5  I     I         I         I         I         I         I     I   20
4.00000000E+00 0--------+----------1--+-2----3--+-4---5----+---------+---------+---------+---------+---------I   21
4.20000000E+00 0        I          1   I 1  2   3I   4    5I       I         I         I         I         I     I   22
4.40000000E+00 0        I          I  1I  2    I3   4   I5  I       I         I         I         I         I     I   23
4.60000000E+00 0        I          I  1I   2   I3    4 I 5  I       I         I         I         I         I     I   24
4.80000000E+00 0        I          I   I 1   2  I3    4I   5  I      I         I         I         I         I     I   25
5.00000000E+00 0        I          I   I 1    2    3    4     5   I   I         I         I         I         I     I   26
5.20000000E+00 0        I          I   I  1    I2   3   I4    5 I   I         I         I         I         I     I   27
5.40000000E+00 0        I          I   I    1   I 2   3  I4   5   I   I         I         I         I         I     I   28
5.60000000E+00 0        I          I   I    1   I 2   3 I4  5    I   I         I         I         I         I     I   29
5.80000000E+00 0        I          I   I     1   I 2   3 I4  5   I   I         I         I         I         I     I   30
6.00000000E+00 0--------+----------+---------1-+--2---3--I-4---5----+---------+---------+---------+---------I   31
6.20000000E+00 0        I          I   I     1 1    2    3I4  5 I     I         I         I         I         I     I   32
6.40000000E+00 0        I          I   I     1I     2    3I4 5 I     I         I         I         I         I     I   33
6.60000000E+00 0        I          I   I     1I     2    3 I45 I     I         I         I         I         I     I   34
6.80000000E+00 0        I          I   I      1      2    3 I5  I     I         I         I         I         I     I   35
7.00000000E+00 0        I          I   I      1      2    3 45  I     I         I         I         I         I     I   36
7.20000000E+00 0        I          I   I      1      2    345  I     I         I         I         I         I     I   37
7.40000000E+00 0        I          I   I      11     2    35I  I     I         I         I         I         I     I   38
7.60000000E+00 0        I          I   I      11     2 35 I     I         I         I         I         I         I     I   39
7.80000000E+00 0        I          I   I      11     2 54 I     I         I         I         I         I         I     I   40
8.00000000E+00 0--------+----------+---------+------+-1---2-5---+---------+---------+---------+---------+-----I   41
8.20000000E+00 0        I          I   I      I 1 1  254  I     I         I         I         I         I     I   42
8.40000000E+00 0        I          I   I      I 1 1  254  I     I         I         I         I         I     I   43
8.60000000E+00 0        I          I   I      I 1 1  254  I     I         I         I         I         I     I   44
8.80000000E+00 0        I          I   I      I 1 1  543 I     I         I         I         I         I     I   45
9.00000000E+00 0        I          I   I      I 1 1 543 I     I         I         I         I         I     I   46
9.20000000E+00 0        I          I   I      I 1 1 53 I     I         I         I         I         I         I     I   47
9.40000000E+00 0        I          I   I      I 1 1 54 I     I         I         I         I         I         I     I   48
9.60000000E+00 0        I          I   I      I 1 54 I     I         I         I         I         I         I     I   49
9.80000000E+00 0        I          I   I      I 1 54 I     I         I         I         I         I         I     I   50
1.00000000E+01 0--------+----------+---------+------+---1-25--+---------+---------+---------+---------+-------I   51
1.02000000E+01 0        I          I   I      I 1  5 I     I         I         I         I         I         I     I   52
1.04000000E+01 0        I          I   I      I 1 25 I     I         I         I         I         I         I     I   53
1.06000000E+01 0        I          I   I      I 1 25 I     I         I         I         I         I         I     I   54
1.08000000E+01 0        I          I   I      I 1 245I     I         I         I         I         I         I     I   55
1.10000000E+01 0        I          I   I      I 1 235I     I         I         I         I         I         I     I   56
1.12000000E+01 0        I          I   I      I 1 35I     I         I         I         I         I         I     I   57
1.14000000E+01 0        I          I   I      I 1 245 I     I         I         I         I         I         I     I   58
1.16000000E+01 0        I          I   I      I 1 245 I     I         I         I         I         I         I     I   59
1.18000000E+01 0        I          I   I      I 1 235 I     I         I         I         I         I         I     I   60
1.20000000E+01 0--------+----------+---------+------+-1-2345--+---------+---------+---------+---------+-------I   61
1.22000000E+01 0        I          I   I      I  12345 I     I         I         I         I         I         I     I   62
1.24000000E+01 0        I          I   I      I 12345 I     I         I         I         I         I         I     I   63
1.26000000E+01 0        I          I   I      I 1 345 I     I         I         I         I         I         I     I   64
1.28000000E+01 0        I          I   I      I 1 245 I     I         I         I         I         I         I     I   65
1.30000000E+01 0        I          I   I      I 1 245 I     I         I         I         I         I         I     I   66
1.32000000E+01 0        I          I   I      I 1 245 I     I         I         I         I         I         I     I   67
1.34000000E+01 0        I          I   I      I 1 245 I     I         I         I         I         I         I     I   68
1.36000000E+01 0        I          I   I      I 1 245 I     I         I         I         I         I         I     I   69
1.38000000E+01 0        I          I   I      I    125I     I         I         I         I         I         I     I   70
1.40000000E+01 0--------+----------+---------+------+---125---+---------+---------+---------+---------+-------I   71
1.42000000E+01 0        I          I   I      I    125 I     I         I         I         I         I         I     I   72
1.44000000E+01 0        I          I   I      I    125 I     I         I         I         I         I         I     I   73
1.46000000E+01 0        I          I   I      I    125 I     I         I         I         I         I         I     I   74
1.48000000E+01 0        I          I   I      I    125 I     I         I         I         I         I         I     I   75
1.50000000E+01 0        I          I   I      I    154 I     I         I         I         I         I         I     I   76
1.52000000E+01 0        I          I   I      I    154 I     I         I         I         I         I         I     I   77
1.54000000E+01 0        I          I   I      I    151I     I         I         I         I         I         I     I   78
1.56000000E+01 0        I          I   I      I    151 I     I         I         I         I         I         I     I   79
1.58000000E+01 0        I          I   I      I    151 I     I         I         I         I         I         I     I   80
1.60000000E+01 0--------+----------+---------+------+---15----+---------+---------+---------+---------+-------I   81
1.62000000E+01 0        I          I   I      I    151 I     I         I         I         I         I         I     I   82
1.64000000E+01 0        I          I   I      I    151 I     I         I         I         I         I         I     I   83
1.66000000E+01 0        I          I   I      I    151 I     I         I         I         I         I         I     I   84
1.68000000E+01 0        I          I   I      I    51 I     I         I         I         I         I         I     I   85
1.70000000E+01 0        I          I   I      I    51 I     I         I         I         I         I         I     I   86
1.72000000E+01 0        I          I   I      I    51 I     I         I         I         I         I         I     I   87
1.74000000E+01 0        I          I   I      I    51 I     I         I         I         I         I         I     I   88
1.76000000E+01 0        I          I   I      I    51 I     I         I         I         I         I         I     I   89
1.78000000E+01 0        I          I   I      I    51 I     I         I         I         I         I         I     I   90
1.80000000E+01 0--------+----------+---------+------+---5-----+---------+---------+---------+---------+-------I   91
1.82000000E+01 0        I          I   I      I    51 I     I         I         I         I         I         I     I   92
1.84000000E+01 0        I          I   I      I    51 I     I         I         I         I         I         I     I   93
1.86000000E+01 0        I          I   I      I    51 I     I         I         I         I         I         I     I   94
1.88000000E+01 0        I          I   I      I    45 I     I         I         I         I         I         I     I   95
1.90000000E+01 0        I          I   I      I    45 I     I         I         I         I         I         I     I   96
1.92000000E+01 0        I          I   I      I    35 I     I         I         I         I         I         I     I   97
1.94000000E+01 0        I          I   I      I    35 I     I         I         I         I         I         I     I   98
1.96000000E+01 0        I          I   I      I    35 I     I         I         I         I         I         I     I   99
1.98000000E+01 0        I          I   I      I    35 I     I         I         I         I         I         I     I  100
2.00000000E+01 0--------+----------+---------+------+---25----+---------+---------+---------+---------+-------I  101

              .............................................................................................
              +         +         +         +         +         +         +         +         +         +         +
              0.      2.00E-01  4.00E-01  6.00E-01  8.00E-01  1.00E+00  1.20E+00  1.40E+00  1.60E+00  1.80E+00  2.00E+00
```

Fig. 4-4. (c)

```
        PLOTTER SYMBOL -  1      2      3      4      5
        RUN NUMBER     -  1      2      3      4      5
```

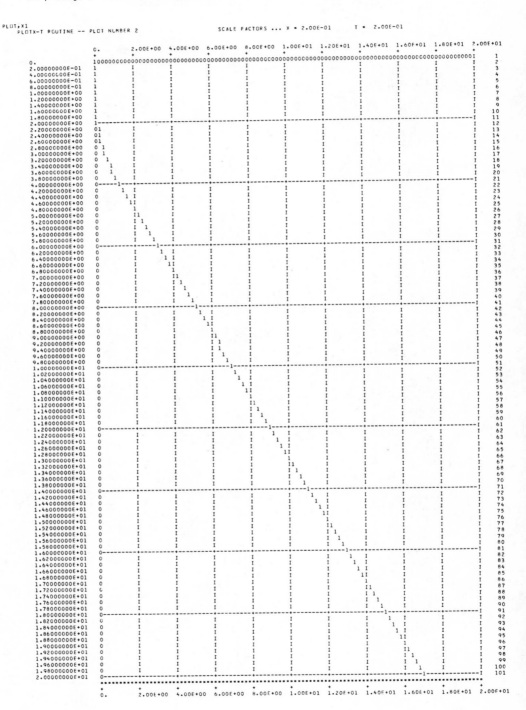

Fig. 4-4. (d)

```
PLOTTER SYMBOL  - 1
VARIABLE NAME   - X1
```

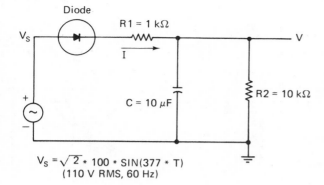

$V_S = \sqrt{2} * 100 * SIN(377 * T)$
(110 V RMS, 60 Hz)

Fig. 4-5. Circuit diagram of simple half-wave rectifier.

Example 4-3: Diode Rectifier. This example illustrates the use of a *procedural section* in a DARE P derivative block. Figure 4-5 shows a simple half-wave diode-rectifier circuit. Depending on the relative values of V_s and V, the diode is assumed to either conduct perfectly ($V_s \geq V$) or be an open circuit ($V_s < V$). We are interested in time plots of the output voltage V and the diode current I. Figure 4-6 shows a DARE P simulation. Note the use of a procedural block to account for the diode state. Complex system nonlinearities may often be handled in this way, through the use of piecewise-linear approximations.

```
DARE PORTABLE (VERSION 1.2)

UNIVERSITY OF ARIZONA


            $D1
            PROCED F=V,VP,W,T1,T2,SSG
            VS= VP*SIN(W*T)
            IF(VS.GT.V) F= -(V/T1)+(SSG/T1)*VS
            IF(VS.LE.V) F= -V/T2
            ENDPRO
            V.=F
            FI=C*F+V/R2
END
            TMAX=0.0666667
            R1=1000.,R2=1.0E+04,C=1.0E-05
            VP=155.,     W=377.
            SSG= P2/(P1+P2)
            RE=R1*SSG
            T1=RE*C
            T2=R2*C
END
        LIST,V,FI
        PLOT,V
        PLOT,FI
END
```

Fig. 4-6. (a)

Fig. 4-6. Analysis of rectifier circuit. (a) DARE P problem deck with procedural block to describe diode; (b) listing of output voltage and diode current: (c) plot of output voltage; (d) plot of diode current.

```
LIST,V,FI

   RUN NUMBER   1

    TIME            V             FI
0.              0.            0.
6.66667E-04     1.26066E+00   3.72872E-02
1.33333E-03     4.84398E+00   6.98295E-02
2.00000E-03     1.03550E+01   9.57519E-02
2.66667E-03     1.72895E+01   1.13583E-01
3.33334E-03     2.50652E+01   1.22350E-01
4.00000E-03     3.30571E+01   1.21637E-01
4.66667E-03     4.06364E+01   1.11617E-01
5.33334E-03     4.72092E+01   9.30358E-02
6.00000E-03     5.22530E+01   6.71712E-02
6.66667E-03     5.53493E+01   3.57496E-02
7.33334E-03     5.62090E+01   8.40688E-04
8.00000E-03     5.58448E+01   2.77556E
8.66667E-03     5.54738E+01   0.
9.33334E-03     5.51052E+01   2.-
1.00000E-02     5.47390E+01
1.06667E-02     5.43753E+01
1.13333E-02     5.40140F+
1.20000E-02     5.3655'
1.26667E-02     5.3-
1.33333E-02
1.40000
```

Fig. 4-6. (b)

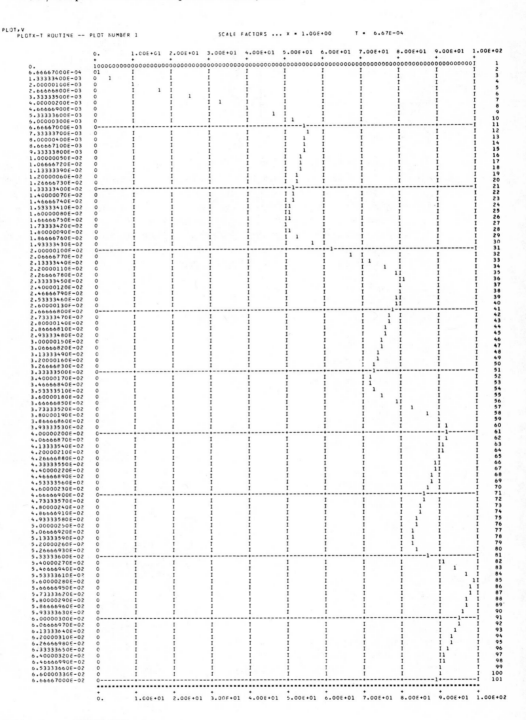

Fig. 4-6. (c)

PLOTTER SYMBOL — 1
VARIABLE NAME — V

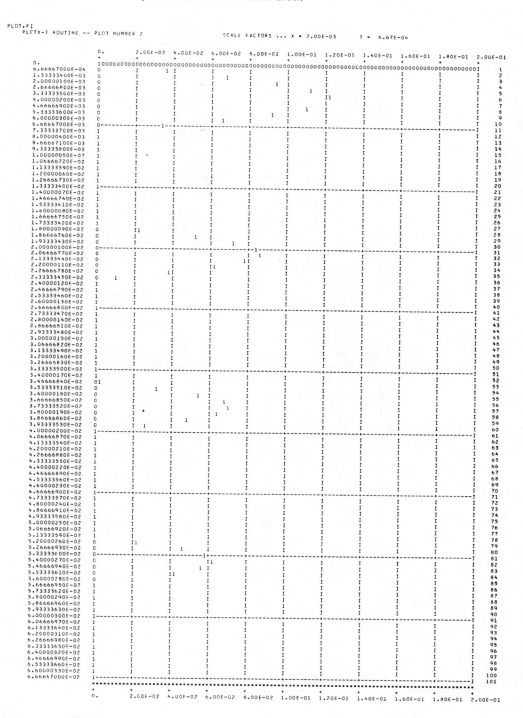

Fig. 4-6. (d)

```
PLOTTER SYMBOL - 1
VARIABLE NAME - FI
```

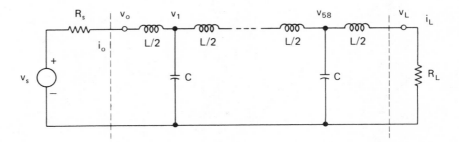

Fig. 4-7. Circuit diagram of a lumped-parameter model of a transmission line.

Example 4-4: Analysis of a 99th-Order Transmission-Line Model. Figure 4-7 shows a 99th-order inductance-capacitance delay-line circuit, which could be considered as a lumped-parameter model of a distributed transmission line. Figure 4-8 shows the DARE P coding to simulate this high-order system. The iterative structure of the system is apparent; here, a REPEAT operator for iteratively repeating the basic equations with stepped indexing would be a useful feature to be added to the language (Sec. 3-18.b).

Figure 4-8(b) shows the step response at nodes $V20$ and $V35$. Note that two-point Runge-Kutta integration was used, with $DT = 0.001$. The entire job, including translation, took 12.0 sec of CPU time on a CDC 6400; of this, 5.5 sec were needed for the simulation run. New values of capacitance and inductance could be tried by merely changing the parameters C and A. The reader may agree that this is a far easier task than setting several dozen potentiometers on an analog computer.

Example 4-5: The Pilot-Ejection Benchmark Problem. A widely used benchmark problem used to test simulation systems, the pilot-ejection problem[1,5] involves a procedural block, function generation, a special run-termination condition, and cross plotting of multiple-run results.

The purpose of the pilot-ejection simulation is to determine combinations of aircraft velocity and altitude (air density) which will enable an ejected pilot to miss his aircraft's vertical stabilizer; high aircraft velocity and high drag (low altitude) will prevent successful ejection. Referring to Fig. 4-9, the aircraft travels in the X direction; the trajectory coordinates X, Y are relative to the aircraft. The ejection-seat rails lean backward at an angle THETAE from the vertical. The seat has an exit velocity VE and disengages from the rails when $Y = Y_1$. The system equations are

$$X' = V \cos (\text{THETA}) - VA$$
$$Y' = V \sin (\text{THETA})$$
$$V' = 0.0 \qquad\qquad\quad \text{for } 0 \leq Y < Y_1$$
$$\quad = -D/M - G \sin (\text{THETA}) \quad \text{for } Y \geq Y_1$$
$$\text{THETA}' = 0.0 \qquad\qquad\quad \text{for } 0 \leq Y \leq Y_1$$
$$\quad = -(G \cos (\text{THETA}))/V \quad \text{for } Y \geq Y_1$$
$$D = (\text{RHO1} * \text{CD} * V)/2$$

```
DARE PORTABLE (VERSION 1.2)

UNIVERSITY OF ARIZONA


        $D1
    * DERIVATIVE BLOCK NO. 1
    *
    * TRANSMISSION LINE PROBLEM
    *
    * LINE TERMINATION
    *
          VL=CL*RL
    *
    * END OF TRANSMISSION LINE
    *
          CL.=2*(V58-VL)/A
          V58.=(C58-CL)/C
          C58.=(V57-V58)/A
          V57.=(C57-C58)/C
          C57.=(V56-V57)/A
          V56.=(C56-C57)/C
          C56.=(V55-V56)/A
          V55.=(C55-C56)/C
          C55.=(V54-V55)/A
          V54.=(C54-C55)/C
          C54.=(V53-V54)/A
          V53.=(C53-C54)/C
          C53.=(V52-V53)/A
          V52.=(C52-C53)/C
          C52.=(V51-V52)/A
          V51.=(C51-C52)/C
          C51.=(V50-V51)/'
          V50.=(C50-C5`  .A
          C50.=(V49   .d)/C
          V49.=(`   -V17)/A
          C4`   .16-C17)/C
           .o.=(V15-V16)/A
          V15.=(C15-C16)/C
          C15.=(V14-V15)/A
          V14.=(C14-C15)/C
          C14.=(V13-V14)/A
          V13.=(C13-C14)/C
          C13.=(V12-V13)/A
          V12.=(C12-C13)/C
          C12.=(V11-V12)/A
          V11.=(C11-C12)/C
          C11.=(V10-V11)/A
          V10.=(C10-C11)/C
          C10.=2*(V0-V10)/A
    *
    * START OF TRANSMISSION LINE
    *
    * SOURCE
          V0=VS-C10*R0
    *
    *
     $M4
END
          TMAX=0.5,DT=0.001,NPOINT=101,A=0.5,C=2.0E-4,R0=50.,RL=50.,VS=1.
END
     PLOT,V20,V35
END
```

Fig. **4-8.** DARE P simulation of a 99th-order transmission-line model. (a) Problem description shows iterative structure of the model; (b) typical plot of node voltages V20 and V35.

Fig. 4-8. (a)

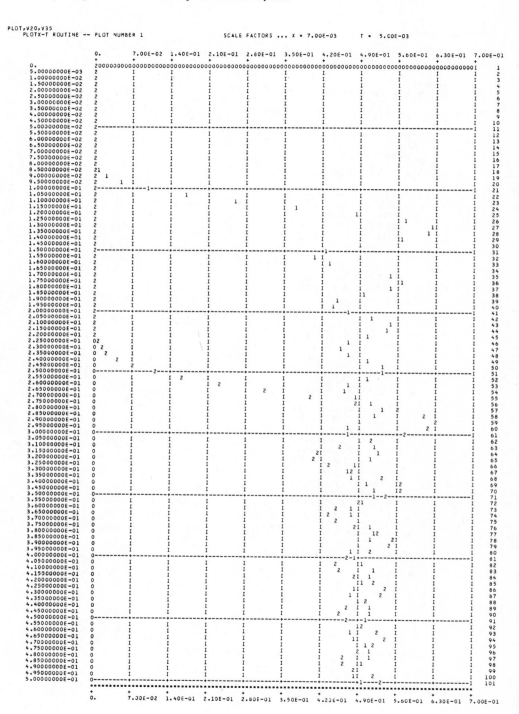

Fig. 4-8. (b)

with the parameters

$$VA = \text{Aircraft velocity}$$
$$M = \text{Mass of pilot plus seat}$$
$$G = \text{Gravitational constant}$$
$$D = \text{Drag force}$$
$$CD = \text{Drag constant}$$
$$H = \text{Aircraft altitude}$$
$$Y_1 = \text{Length of ejection rails}$$
$$VE = \text{Exit velocity}$$
$$THETAE = \text{Exit angle}$$

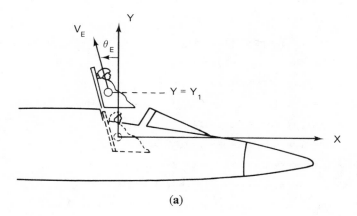

(a)

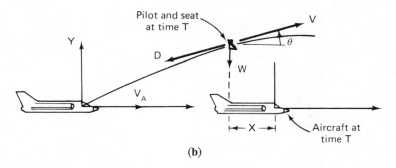

(b)

Fig. 4-9. The pilot-ejection benchmark problem. (a) Phase 1, initial ejection; (b) phase 2, relative trajectory.

The air density RHO1 changes with the aircraft altitude H as given by the DARE table function RHO.

The simulation-control program (logic block) makes successive ejection runs, starting with VA = 900 ft/sec and H = 0. An ejection run terminates when the simulated pilot reaches the X-coordinate value of the vertical stabilizer (X = −30 ft). The logic-block program will increment H until the simulated pilot misses the

```
$D1
*
* PILOT EJECTION PROBLEM
*
      PROCED YGEY1=Y,Y1
      YGEY1 = 1.0
      IF (Y .LT. Y1) YGEY1 = 0.0
      ENDPRO
*
      X. = V * COS(THETA) - VA
      Y. = V * SIN(THETA)
      V. = YGEY1 * (-D/M - G*SIN(THETA))
      THETA. = YGEY1 * (G * COS(THETA))/V
      D = RHO1 * 0.5 * CD *V*V
*
      TERMINATE X + 30.0
*
 $L
*
* PILOT EJECTION STUDY LOGIC BLOCK
*
      OUTPUT H,SAVEVA
      INPUT VE,THETAE
      CALL SECOND(T1)
      CALL STROF
      H = 0.0
*
* CONVERT THEAT TO RADIANS
*
      THETA = THETA/57.2957795
*
* CALCULATE INITIAL PILOT VELOCITY
*
      VESINE = VE * SIN(THETA)
      VECOS = VE * COS(THETA)
 100  V = SQRT((VA - VESINE) ** 2 + (VECOS) ** 2)
*
* CALCULATE INITIAL PILOT ANGLE
*
      THETA = ATAN(VECOS/(VA - VESINE))
      SAVEV = V
      SAVETH = THETA
 200  RHO1 = RHO(H) * 10.0
      CALL RUN
      IF(Y .GT. 20.0) GO TO 300
      CALL RESET
      H = H + 500.0
      V = SAVEV
      THETA = SAVETH
      GO TO 200
*
* SUCCESSFUL SIMULATION - SAVE VA IN SAVEVA AND
* WRITE TO THE CROSS FILE.
*
 300  SAVEVA = VA
      CALL STORE
      CALL RESET
      VA = VA + 50.0
      IF(VA .LE. 900.0) GO TO 100
      CALL SECOND(T2)
      TIME=T2-T1
      PRINT 3000,TIME
3000  FORMAT(1X,E15.6,* SECONDS OF CPU TIME*)
 $T1
```

Fig. 4-10. (a)

```
                    RHO,12
               0.0,      2.377E-3
               1E3,      2.308E-3
               2E3,      2.241E-3
               4E3,      2.117E-3
               6E3,      1.987E-3
              10E3,      1.755E-3
              15E3,      1.497E-3
              20E3,      1.267E-3
              30E3,      0.891E-3
              40E3,      0.587E-3
              50E3,      0.364E-3
              60E3,      0.2238E-3
               $M4
E ND
                    TMAX=2.0
                    NPOINT=2
                    DT=0.01
             VE = 40.0,M = 7,VA = 100.0,  Y1 =  4.0,  THETA =  15.0
                    CD=1.0
E ND
                 *PILOT  EJECTION  SIMULATION
                 LIST(CROSS)SAVEVA,H
                 PLOTXY(CROSS)SAVEVA,H
E ND
```

Fig. 4-10. (a) (continued)

Fig. 4-10. DARE P version of the pilot-ejection problem. The logic block
controls the simulation runs and develops information about safe ejection
in the CROSS file. (a) Problem description; (b) listing of CROSS file; (c)
plot of CROSS file.

```
                                    PILOT  EJECTION  SIMULATION
     LIST(CROSS)SAVEVA,H

            RUN            SAVEVA            H
        1.00000E+00    1.00000E+02     0.
        2.00000E+00    1.50000E+02     0.
        3.00000E+00    2.00000E+02     0.
        4.00000E+00    2.50000E+02     0.
        5.00000E+00    3.00000E+02     0.
        6.00000E+00    3.50000E+02     0.
        7.00000E+00    4.00000E+02     0.
        2.30000E+01    4.50000E+02     7.50000E+03
        3.60000E+01    5.00000E+02     1.35000E+04
        5.00000E+01    5.50000E+02     2.00000E+04
        6.00000E+01    6.00000E+02     2.45000E+04
        7.00000E+01    6.50000E+02     2.90000E+04
        7.90000E+01    7.00000E+02     3.30000E+04
        8.70000E+01    7.50000E+02     3.65000E+04
        9.20000E+01    8.00000E+02     3.85000E+04
        9.90000E+01    8.50000E+02     4.15000E+04
        1.06000E+02    9.00000E+02     4.45000E+04
```

Fig. 4-10. (b)

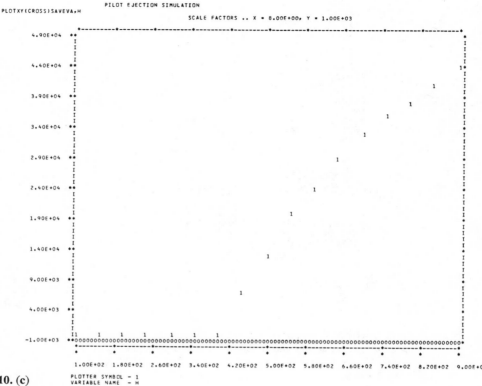

Fig. 4-10. (c)

vertical stabilizer (Y > 20 ft) at the end of the run. Then, VA and H are stored (in the CROSS file) for a cross plot, and VA is incremented so that we can find the smallest safe altitude for the next-higher velocity value. This program continues until suitable velocity and altitude limits are reached; the result will be a cross plot [H versus VA; Fig. 4-10(c)] separating safe and unsafe VA, H combinations.

Figure 4-10 shows the complete DARE P program, with comments. Note the use of CALL STROF to suppress time-consuming time-history storage; time histories of individual runs are not of much interest in this study. The additional output command

GRAPH(CROSS)SAVEA,H

would produce a Calcomp cross plot, if desired.

Note that, although we ask for no output from the individual solutions, fine time resolution is required to locate precisely when the trajectory passes the tail. We have found that *DT* must be no larger than 0.01 for this purpose. Second-order Runge-Kutta integration seems to work well on this problem. The solution shown here required 18.8 CPU sec on a CDC 6400 to produce 106 ejections. Program translation, compilation, and loading required 8.8 sec, and the remaining 10.0 sec were used for the actual simulation runs.

REFERENCES AND BIBLIOGRAPHY

1. LUCAS, JOHN L., "DARE P, A Portable Simulation System," M.S. thesis, University of Arizona, Tucson, 1974.

2. LUCAS, JOHN L., and J. V. WAIT, "DARE P User's Manual," *CSRL Report 255*, Computer Science Research Laboratory, Department of Electrical Engineering, College of Engineering, University of Arizona, Tucson, Aug. 1974.

3. SCI Software Committee, "The SCI Continuous System Simulation Language (CSSL)", *Simulation*, Dec. 1967.

4. CLARKE, D., and J. V. WAIT, "DARE P User's Manual," *CSRL Report 299*, Computer Science Research Laboratory, Department of Electrical Engineering, University of Arizona, Tucson, Aug. 1976. This manual is frequently revised to reflect corrections and additions of new language features.

5. CLARKE, D., and J. V. WAIT, "DARE P Implementation Guide," *CSRL Report 300*, Computer Science Research Laboratory, Department of Electrical Engineering, University of Arizona, Tucson, Aug. 1976.

5

Interactive Simulation with Minicomputers

INTRODUCTION

An **interactive simulation system** permits the experimenter to enter and edit programs and data on a keyboard and to see solution plots and other output as they are computed. He can then modify parameters and model *on line* on the basis of his earlier results and can try his new ideas *immediately* in a new run or multirun sequence. This type of intimate rapport between the experimenter and his "live mathematical model" can be very effective in producing meaningful results, insight, and new ideas.

Interactive simulation is at its best with cathode-ray-tube displays for both problem entry and solution display. A time-shared large computer can be used, but there will be much input/output. The communications and administrative overhead costs (and the loss of local autonomy) involved in a large time-sharing system can be objectionable, especially for time-critical simulations controlling real-world equipment. A stand-alone simulation system using a modern high-performance minicomputer (or a multimicroprocessor system; Sec. 6-10) will, then, be preferable for many simulation laboratories; they must support local computer displays, printers, etc. , in any case. Local simulation minicomputers can and should be time-shared with at least a slow background program such as program development, report editing, etc.

In this chapter we shall list **requirements for effective interactive simulation** and describe **a complete interactive system**. DARE/ELEVEN is based on five years' experience with earlier interactive DARE systems and is unique in that it permits simulation programming *both* in an equation-oriented language and in a block-diagram language designed for extra-fast execution and very convenient control of real-world equipment. Both languages can be used for different parts of *the same* simulation, much as both analog and digital computation is combined in a hybrid computer.

Interactive simulation with block-diagram languages and real-time simulation techniques is treated in Chapter 6, in which interactive simulation systems other then DARE/ELEVEN are also listed and discussed.

AN INTERACTIVE MINICOMPUTER SYSTEM

5-1. Requirements for Interactive Simulation. A practical interactive simulation system requires, first of all, **quick access** for each interactive operation (i.e., minimal waiting time). We also must have convenient facilities for

1. Program entry and modification (editing) and **reasonably fast translation** of programs into object code.
2. Entry and modification of parameters and initial conditions and **selection of integration routines** before and between runs, without retranslation.
3. Graphic display and **cathode-ray-tube- (CRT-) terminal listings** of solutions as well as **hard-copy output. Run-time displays** during the actual solution permit undesirable solutions to be aborted quickly and are psychologically reassuring for the operator.
4. Printout of programs, comments, data, and results for report preparation.
5. Interactive file manipulation: storage, retrieval, and recombination of programs, parts of programs, and data.

An interactive simulation system can use a minicomputer or time-share a larger machine.[1] In fact, even a minicomputer simulation system ought to permit at least slow "background" programs to time-share the computer, since interactive simulation users often spend substantial periods of time looking at their displays and contemplating intermediate results. The DARE/ELEVEN system[2] described here is an advanced interactive minicomputer system which will run on inexpensive Digital Equipment Corporation PDP-11/40s with 28K memory and a system disk in the single-user or foreground/background mode. DARE/ELEVEN could be adapted to time-sharing on the larger PDP-11/45, 50, and 70 models.

5-2. Simple Interactive System Operation

a. Program Entry and Editing. DARE/ELEVEN is started by the operating-system keyboard command*

---

*Command lines are terminated by a typing RETURN (carriage-return/line-feed key).

R(UN)   DARE

i.e. first character R or RUN

which loads a **DARE editor** configured for the keyboard terminal used. This can be simply a **teleprinter** or, preferably, an **alphanumeric cathode-ray-tube display/keyboard**. The alphanumeric display may or may not be combined with the **graphic CRT display** used to display solutions (Fig. 5-1). With CRT displays, the system printer (teleprinter or line printer) will be used only when we actually require hard copy.

The DARE editor is initially in **command mode** and announces this fact by the displayed or printed message

DARE/ELEVEN EDITOR: COMMAND MODE

In this mode (see also Sec. 5-3), the system accepts keyboard commands to **open** (address), **fetch, save,** and **translate named programs** (files) until a file is *opened for editing*. To permit later recovery of our program, we begin by entering a six-character **problem-identification code** (**PIC**), say

PIC = KORN01

To enter a simple new program consisting only of an equation-language derivative block (Sec. 3-1), we type next

OPEN   E1

The editor responds with

DARE/ELEVEN EDITOR: EDIT MODE

and will now accept **editing** commands (**edit mode;** Sec. 5-3). In particular, the keyboard command

I(NSERT)

places the editor in its **text mode**. In this mode, typing no longer produces commands but **text** (program and comments), which will be stored in a **text buffer** in memory. We can advance to a new line by typing the RETURN (carriage-return/line-feed) key. The editor program will "mark" the current input character or line with a number (**pointer address**) for editing (Sec. 5-3).

When our program is ready, the keyboard sequence

LINE FEED, EXIT
COMPILE

or (preferably) a single control-character key closes our file and initiates program translation.

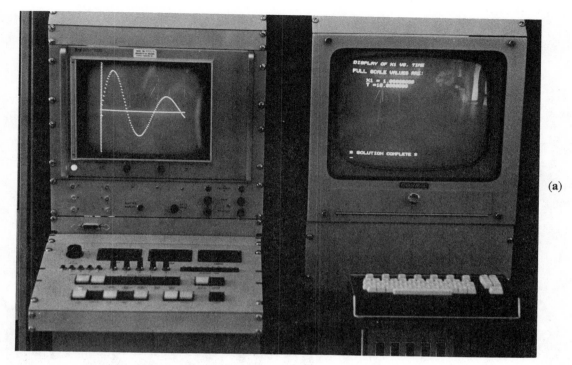

Fig. 5-1. (a) An early interactive DARE system with separate alphanumeric and graphic CRT displays. Programs and data are entered and edited with the CRT-keyboard display on the right, which also displays error messages and labels and scales for the graphic display. A special console keyboard underneath the graphic display has lighted keys for the most important system commands (RESET, RUN, TRANSLATE, PRINT PROGRAM, etc.), has five sense switches for run-time program changes, and also permits manual dial setting of some parameters.[3] (b) A DARE/ELEVEN interactive simulation system using the Digital Equipment Corporation VT-11 graphics package for both alphanumeric and graphic displays. System cost is about $43,000, with a PDP-11/40, 28K memory, full graphics, and floating-point firmware.

(a)

(b)

Fig. 5-1. (c) A DARE/ELEVEN installation using a separate alphanumeric CRT keyboard (TV-raster display). The display is shown in the editor EDIT mode (Sec. 5-2) after the Van der Pol equation program of Example 2-3 has been entered (University of Arizona).

(c)

b. Translation, run-time system, and data entry. The DARE translator, followed by the FORTRAN compiler and/or the assembler and then by the linker and loader (Secs. 3-4 and 6-3), runs as a sequence of automatic overlays. The entire translation and loading process takes 30 to 50 seconds for simple equation-language problems.

The run-time system announces itself with the message

DRTS: COMMAND MODE

and will accept keyboard commands to **enter data** (parameters and initial values), to **select an integration method**, to **call the output program**, and to **recall the editor**. With a *new* problem, **DARE first automatically prompts the user to enter numerical**

values for all needed data-file items (i.e., initial values, system and problem parameters, and logic-file INPUT-list items, if any). The system displays or prints, say,

$$DT = \qquad TMAX =$$
$$X = \qquad XDOT = \qquad ALFA =$$

and the user must supply all numbers before the problem can run. The resulting data file is now in the computer memory for use in the current simulation and becomes part of the problem record on the disk if the user types DATA. If a data file already exists, the keyboard command DATA will display it. Data files may also be entered, edited, *and transferred to other DARE programs* with the DARE editor, like other DARE files (Sec. 5-3).

Typing the name of an individual data-file item will display its value. *To modify data items*, one simply types

$$name = value$$

as often as required; the system accepts real variables and integers, *as appropriate*, and will remind us when we try to enter an inappropriate data type (Fig. 5-2).

Fig. 5-2. A run-time data-file display. A data value is entered or changed by typing, say,

$$TH = 3.5$$

in the *command line* at the bottom of the display and then typing the RETURN key.[3]

We can then **make a simulation run** (or a multirun study, if one has been programmed) by typing

RUN

There will usually be a **run-time display**, so that we can see how the simulation is progressing. To abort a run, type control-C to **reinitialize** the run-time system. We can then modify parameters and initial values for new runs, return to the editor for program modifications, or call the output system.

c. Output operations. With the system in the run-time command mode, the DARE *output program* is loaded by the keyboard command

DOUT

If an **output file** (**output block**; Sec. 3-5) was preprogrammed, each of its output commands (displays, plots, listings) will be executed. Afterwards (or instead of any preprogrammed output), the system will execute any valid typed output command listed in Sec. 3-5 (**conversational-output system**; see also Figs. 5-7, 5-8, and 6-3). To return to the run-time command mode, type DRTS.

5-3. Interactive System Operation: Refinements

a. DARE default strategy. *The simple interactive simulation technique described in Sec. 5-2 is all that needs to be learned for simple simulations.* For advanced simulation users, though, DARE/ELEVEN offers even more sophisticated language features than DARE P, for it is possible to include assembly-language sections and complicated real-time input/output, as well as FORTRAN, in simulation programs. DARE/ELEVEN also permits many interactive operations useful for editing, storage, and combination of programs; for report preparation; and for testing of different integration routines. All these advanced features are conveniently "transparent" to elementary DARE users; the system will automatically default to the simplest practical language feature, command interpretation, or integration routine (see also Sec. 3-21).

b. Editing with teleprinters and CRT keyboards. DARE/ELEVEN can work with only a teleprinter as the system keyboard/display (note that such printers can even produce coarse solution plots, Fig. 4-6). We are then restricted to a **teleprinter editor**, which can only insert, not edit, typed text in the text mode (Sec. 5-2.a). To do any editing, we must return to *edit mode* by typing a LINE FEED and use **keyboard editing commands** (Table 5-1).[2] The effects of editing cannot be seen without a print command after editing. Worse, we must *blindly* move the pointer to the line we wish to edit with a line-counting or string-finding command (Table 5-1); it will be wise to print the line before editing to make sure we have the right line. When the line is found, it is edited by a *string-replacement command*, say,

C(HANGE)/THIMK/THINK

DARE/ELEVEN avoids character-counting editing commands (e.g., "move pointer 13 spaces and delete 4 characters"), since they consistently cause errors due to miscounting.

A CRT keyboard can be used with the simple teleprinter editor to speed editing, but **really convenient interactive editing becomes possible if we have a special CRT editor program**.[3] Text is simply typed onto the CRT screen, and the current-location

TABLE 5-1. DARE/ELEVEN Editor Commands

(a) Edit-Mode Commands for CRT and Teleprinter Editors

I (NSERT)	*Go to text mode.*
T (OP)	Move pointer to *top* of file.
B (OTTOM)	Move pointer to *bottom* of file.
n	Move pointer *forward n lines* (or bottom).
−n	Move pointer *back n lines* (or top).
P (RINT)*n*	*Print the next n lines* (pointer stays put).
L(IST)	*List the file*, starting with current line.
D(ELETE)*n*	*Delete n* lines, starting with current line (pointer points to following line; error message if bottom is exceeded).
G(ET) *string*	*Get* (search text for first occurrence of) *string*, starting at current line. If found, pointer goes to *string* line; and to error message if not found. Teleprinter editor also *prints* line.
C(HANGE)/*string1*/*string2*	Search text for first occurrence of *string1*, starting at current line. If found, replace *string1* with *string2* and move pointer to this line; error message if not found. Teleprinter editor also *prints* line. If *string2* is empty, *delete string1*.
EX(IT)	The current file is *closed* and *output* to system disk. *System now accepts file-manipulation commands.*

(b) Edit-Mode Commands Needed Only for Teleprinter Editor

PRINT	*Print the current line.*
ADVANCE	*Advance pointer to next line*, and print this line.
DELETE	*Delete the current line* (pointer goes to next line).

(c) File-Manipulation Commands

SM = *device code*	Select *storage medium*.
PIC = *code*	Set six-character *problem-identification code* (PIC).
AFL	Display or print currently *active file list*.
OPEN *filename*	*Open* file for input or editing; add filename to AFL.
DELETE *filename*	*Delete* file from AFL *only*, not from system disk.
KILL *filename*	*Delete* file from AFL *and* storage medium.
KILL ALL	*Delete* all files in AFL from system disk; clear AFL.
NEW	*Clear AFL;* ready to start new problem.
SAVE	*Save* all files in AFL, with AFL and PIC on current storage medium.
INPUT	Read all files under current PIC from current storage medium to system disk; overwrites any files entered earlier under this PIC.
RD *filename*	*Read* file from current storage medium to system disk under current PIC, AFL.
RD *filename* = *code*	—Same for file with PIC = code.
WRITE *filename*	Write file from system disk to current storage medium under current PIC.
WRITE *filename* = *code*	—Same, but store under PIC = code.
RUN	Return to *run-time system* (Sec. 5-2.b) *without retranslation*. (Only) DISPLAY and STORE commands may be edited.

TABLE 5-1. continued

EXIT	Return to *operating system*. Do not forget to SAVE files.
COMPILE/*switch*	*Translate* current AFL files.
	Switches produce listings:
TRN	Translator output
FTN	FORTRAN error lines
MAC	Assembly listing
LKR	Loader map and symbol table

The switch FAST trades fast assembly for slower execution. *Multiple* switches can be used.

LIST *filename*	*List* file on system printer.
PR	*Print* all files in the AFL.
HELP	Display or print a *command summary*.

pointer appears as a blinking **cursor**. The most important editing operations are now done in *text mode* with *special keys*:

> MOVE CURSOR: FORWARD, BACK, UP, DOWN
> DELETE CHARACTER preceding the cursor
> DELETE LINE preceding the cursor
> INSERT LINE ahead of the cursor

Typing any character will *insert* it ahead of the cursor; we can, in particular, insert blank spaces.* As the cursor moves, the text "scrolls" up or down on the CRT screen, so that 10 to 20 lines near the cursor are visible; *all editing changes are immediately evident.*

In addition to the special-key editing operations in the *text mode*, we may still use keyboard editing commands in the *edit mode*, particularly commands to find, delete, or replace typed text strings (Table 5-1). The CRT editor will display (echo) typed commands in a **command line** or lines underneath the displayed text.

> *c. Saving, Retrieving, and Combining Programs.* Table 5-1(c) lists the DARE/ ELEVEN **file-manipulation commands** used in the editor command mode (Sec. 5-2.a). After specifying a **problem-identification code** (PIC; Sec. 5-2.a), the user opens and creates or edits each DARE program section as a separate program file. A DARE/ELEVEN program needs at least one derivative file and can comprise any of the following:

E1, E2	equation-language derivative files (Sec. 3-15)
B1, B2	block-diagram-language derivative files (Sec. 6-2)

*Some CRT terminals replace character insertion by *overtyping* and permit insertion only of blank spaces, which can then be overtyped.[3]

LO	FORTRAN simulation-control file (logic block; Sec. 3-12)
OB	output-block file (Sec. 3-5)
T1, T2, . . .	function-table files (Secs. 3-8 and 6-6)
F1, F2, . . .	FORTRAN function or subroutine files (Secs. 3-9, 3-10)
S1, S2, . . .	assembly-language subroutine files (Sec. 6-3)
MA	macro-definition file (Sec. 6-3)
DF	problem data file (Sec. 5-2b; note that the data file can be manipulated by the editor)

The program-section files opened and closed under a given problem-identification code are automatically combined into a **problem master file**, i.e., a complete DARE program, which can be translated as shown in Sec. 5-2. The command SAVE saves this combined program and creates a list of the files used (**active file list, AFL** for this problem-identification code). The file-manipulating commands of Table 5-1(c) will retrieve or delete complete programs including data files or individual program files; note that *one may combine, say, a derivative block from a new program with a logic block* (*e.g., an optimization routine*) *from another problem.* The command AFL will display or print the current active file list.

Closed files go on the system disk. In addition, DARE/ELEVEN has storage and retrieval commands for other storage media selected by the command

$$SM = device\ code$$

Thus, a user could save his program on magnetic tape, on paper tape, or on a separate disk or flexible disk.

User files will be marked with *user identification codes* by the operating system, which may also list the names of files belonging to individual users (this is an operating-system function, not a DARE/ELEVEN function).

d. Report Generation. The LIST filename and PRINT commands will list *programs*, with *comments*, for report preparation. Comment text may contain lowercase type, if desired. Output programs can prepare suitable hard copy of simulation *results*.

5-4. Interactive Multirun Simulation. SHOW and DIDDLE.* In multirun simulation studies controlled by a logic block, a DARE/ELEVEN user can keep track of parameter and variable values for the current run by including the FORTRAN statement

$$CALL\ SHOW\ (name1,\ name2,\ . . .)$$

The DARE system will then display or print the current values of *name1, name2, . . . ,* preferably on a CRT display.

*See also Secs. 3-11 to 3-14.

With suitable accessory hardware, a user can *interactively change parameter values* between simulation runs by the FORTRAN statement

CALL DIDDLE *(name1, name2, . . .)*

which will modify the named variables through manually operated dials or joysticks [Figs. 5-1(a) and 5-3].

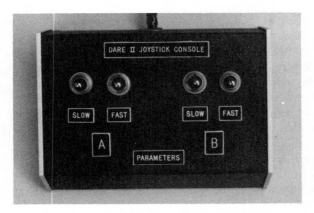

Fig. 5-3. Simple spring-return switches serve as data-entry joysticks by incrementing or decrementing counters in the computer memory (University of Arizona).

Note that SHOW and DIDDLE are called *between* simulation runs. DARE variable-step integration routines (Appendix A) can also display current values of integration step and local truncation error *during* individual runs (Fig. 5-4). Other interactive input/output operations *during* individual runs would have to be programmed in FORTRAN procedural blocks or FORTRAN files or in block-diagram language (Sec. 6-2). It is also possible to employ suitably programmed *sense switches* to modify derivative blocks and/or the logic block while solutions are running.

5-5. Miscellaneous Options, Debugging Facilities, and Hardware. Table 5-2 lists DARE/ELEVEN **run-time keyboard commands** (see also Sec. 5-2.b). In particular, the commands IR(ULE)/*n*, CL(EAR)/*n*, and RE(LINK) permit the user to **select integration rules** for each derivative block from the system library. If the user does not activate any specific integration rule, the system will default to second-order Runge-Kutta integration (Appendix A). The user can also *substitute his own integration routines* and, in fact, his own simulation *system routines* for routines in the system library by writing new routines in FORTRAN or assembly-language subroutine files, as discussed in Sec. 3-20.

Such new routines become part of the active-file-list program under the user's problem-identification code. They can be made a permanent part of the system library only by the system manager.

DARE/ELEVEN displays or prints **diagnostic error messages** to identify programming errors at the translator, compiler/assembler, linker, and data-entry levels.

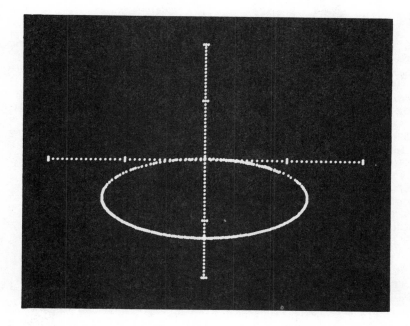

Fig. 5-4. Interactive system display for the satellite-orbit problem of Example 2-4, with display message indicating that the variable integration step has just doubled to DT = 6400 sec.

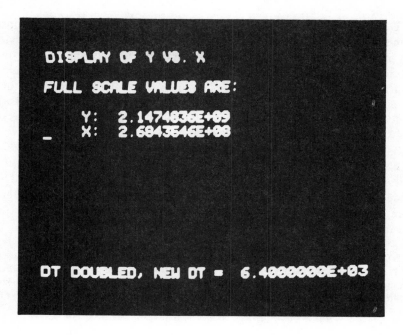

TABLE 5-2. DARE/ELEVEN Run-Time System Commands*

RU(N)	*Run* simulation program (single run or multiple runs).
DA(TA)	Display or list current problem *data file*.
name	Display or print current value of quantity *name* in data file; error message if not found.
name = value	Set quantity *name* to the specified *value*.
DO(UT)	Execute *output program*, if any; wait for typed output commands.
DE(DT)	Return to *editor*.
control-C	*Reinitialize* the run-time system for another run.
ST(ORE)-OFF	Disable disk storage.†
DI(SPLAY)-OFF	Disable run-time display.
ST(ORE)-ON	Reenable disk storage.†
DI(SPLAY)-ON	Reenable run-time display.
IR(ULE)/*n*	Relink to load *integration rule n*.
CL(EAR)/*n*	Remove integration rule *n*.
RE(LINK)	Relink existing object programs and any active integration rules.

*See also Secs. 5-2.b and 5-4.
†These commands will be overridden by the logic-block statements CALL STRON and CALL STROF (Sec. 3-13).

The COMPILE command can be modified by typed "switch" entries (Table 5-1) to produce *translator and assembler output listings* and *load maps* for problem debugging. In addition, DARE/ELEVEN runs under a regular disk operating system whose debugging program (breakpoint insertion, memory dumps) is, thus, available to the user.

DARE/ELEVEN will work with only a teleprinter for keyboard entries and primitive solution plotting; the newer Digital Equipment Corporation teleprinters can prepare 128-column as well as 80-column printer plots and permit the use of lowercase type in comment text. But **a good interactive computer system needs a CRT keyboard** (Sec. 5-3b), and a good interactive simulation system ought to have a **graphic CRT display**.

Reference 5 is an excellent review of interactive display technology and software. The VT–11 graphics system for the PDP–11 [Fig. 5-1(b)] produces vectors (lines) and alphanumeric characters and can double as an alphanumeric CRT display. Much simpler CRT displays will do for interactive simulation. In particular, storage-tube displays and TV-scan graph displays do not require the time and hardware needed to refresh other CRT displays 50 to 60 times per second,* but unrefreshed storage-tube displays cannot generate the *moving* run-time displays produced by fast multirun DARE/ELEVEN simulations.

*60-Hz screen refreshing "steals" 15,000 to 40,000 memory cycles (0.01 to 0.03 second) per displayed curve during each second of computation. Disk storage of solution time histories takes a comparable amount of time. For this reason, DARE/ELEVEN has facilities for suppressing run-time displays and/or disk storage of solutions when they are not needed (Sec. 5-4 and Table 5-2).

High-quality *hard-copy solution output* from DARE systems has been obtained with printers [Fig. 4-6(c)], strip-chart recorders [Fig. 6-3(d)], servo recorders, and digital step-motor recorders [Fig. 4-8(b)]. Most of the solution graphs illustrating this book, though, were obtained directly from DARE CRT displays by means of a hand-held Polaroid camera.

DARE/ELEVEN run-time displays are not restricted to graph plotting. Procedural blocks (Sec. 3-10.b) may access PDP-11 graphics software and can produce moving pictures (animation), e.g., for simulation of moving instrument displays.

The DARE I system shown in Fig. 5-1(a)[3] incorporated a special keyboard (simulation console) with lighted tablet switches for the most important DARE system commands, a very convenient feature.

5-6. Examples

Example 5-1: Simple Flight Simulation. Aircraft and space-vehicle simulation for engineering design and training is perhaps the most important application of continuous-system simulation; simulation here replaces flight experiments, which are expensive, dangerous, and/or not yet possible. References 6 and 7 review aerospace-vehicle dynamics. For clarity's sake, we restrict ourselves to a very simple example illustrating aircraft motion in the pitch plane only. Referring to Fig. 5-5, we have the state equations for the *aircraft velocity V*, the *flight-path angle θ*, and the *pitch angle φ₁*,

$$\frac{dV}{dT} = -G \sin \theta + \frac{\text{THRUST} \cos \gamma_1 - \text{DRAG}}{\text{MASS}} \tag{5-1}$$

$$\frac{d\theta}{dT} = \frac{1}{V}\left(-G \cos \theta + \frac{\text{THRUST} \sin \gamma_1 + \text{LIFT}}{\text{MASS}}\right) \tag{5-2}$$

$$\frac{d\varphi_1}{dT} = \dot{\varphi}_1 \tag{5-3}$$

$$\frac{d\dot{\varphi}_1}{dT} = \frac{\text{AERODYNAMIC MOMENT}}{\text{MOMENT OF INERTIA}} \tag{5-4}$$

where G is the acceleration of gravity and

$$\gamma_1 = \varphi_1 - \theta \tag{5-5}$$

is the pitch *angle of attack* of our aircraft. Trajectory computation would require two additional state equations,

$$\frac{dX}{dT} = V \cos \theta, \qquad \frac{dY}{dT} = V \sin \theta \tag{5-6}$$

Wind-tunnel data give DRAG, LIFT, and AERODYNAMIC MOMENT as functions of the velocity V, the angle of attack γ_1, the aircraft altitude Y, and the *elevator deflection δ*; in other respects, detailed flight simulation based on Eqs. (5-1) to (5-6) is straightforward.

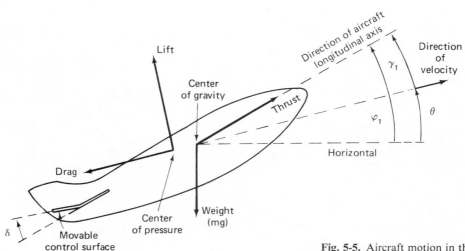

Fig. 5-5. Aircraft motion in the pitch plane.

To simplify our example further, we restrict our simulation to *small perturbations*

$$\varphi_1 = \varphi - \varphi_0, \qquad \gamma_1 = \gamma - \gamma_0 \tag{5-7}$$

from straight and level flight at constant velocity $V = V_0$, with $\theta = \theta_0 = 0$, $\dot{\varphi}_1 = 0$. This is of practical interest in studies of aircraft *stability*[6] and autopilot design, where responses of φ, θ, and γ to small initial pitch angles $\varphi(0)$ and to small elevator deflections δ are supposed to remain small.

In the case of small perturbations, we can substitute Eq. (5-7) into Eqs. (5-2) to (5-5) and replace their right-hand sides by first-order Taylor expansions. Neglecting small terms, we obtain the *linearized flight equations*

$$\frac{d\theta}{dT} = \frac{1}{V_0 \text{MASS}} (L_\gamma \gamma + L_\delta \delta)$$

$$\frac{d\varphi}{dT} = \dot{\varphi}$$

$$\frac{d\dot{\varphi}}{dT} = \frac{M_\gamma \gamma + M_\delta \delta + M_{\dot{\varphi}} \dot{\varphi}}{\text{MOMENT OF INERTIA}} \tag{5-8}$$

$$\gamma = \varphi - \theta$$

where the aerodynamic derivatives L_γ, L_δ, M_γ, M_δ, and $M_{\dot{\varphi}}$ are obtainable from wind-tunnel data. Figures 5-6 and 5-7 illustrate such a linearized flight simulation for a propeller-driven aircraft with aerodynamic derivatives, mass, pitch, moment of inertia, and velocity such that

$$\frac{d\theta}{dT} = \gamma - 0.1\delta$$

$$\frac{d\varphi}{dT} = \dot{\varphi}, \qquad \frac{d\dot{\varphi}}{dT} = -10\gamma + 10\delta - 0.5\dot{\varphi} \tag{5-9}$$

Our simple model shows typical aircraft behavior (see also Sec. 6-8).

```
*  DERIVATIVE BLOCK:

*  SIMPLIFIED FLIGHT EQUATIONS IN THE
*      PITCH PLANE
*
            THET'=GAM−0.1*DEL
            PHI'=PDOT
            PDOT'=−10.*GAM+10.*DEL−0.5*PDOT
            GAM=PHI−THET
*
*  ELEVATOR FORCING FUNCTION
*
            DEL=COMPR (SIN(C*T))
*
*  ALTERNATIVE PROGRAM INTRODUCES A
*      SIMPLIFIED AUTOPILOT DESCRIBED BY
*
*           DEL'=−2.*DEL−40.*PHI−D*PDOT
*
*  RUN-TIME DISPLAY
            DISPLAY PHI, THET,T

*  OUTPUT BLOCK:

            DISPLAY(S)DELT,PHI,THET,T

*  DATA:

DT   = 6.0E-02
TMAX = 1.0E+01
THET =
PHI  =
PDOT =
C = 0.6
```

(a)

Fig. 5-6. Simplified flight-equation program (a) and part of interactive display (b). The square-wave change in the elevator angle δ was generated by using the function COMPR(SIN(C*T)), which is, respectively, equal to 1, 0, and −1 when sin CT is positive, zero, and negative (Table 3-2).

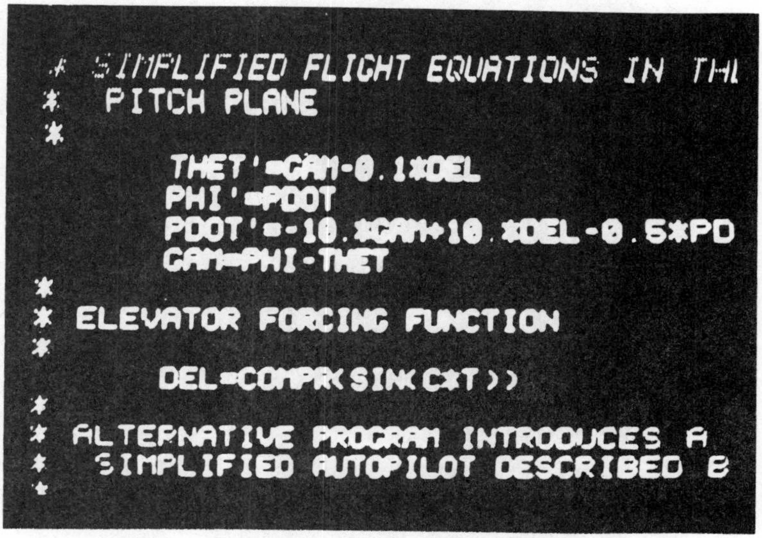

(b)

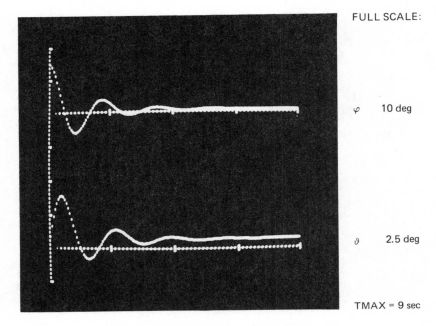

FULL SCALE:

φ 10 deg

ϑ 2.5 deg

TMAX = 9 sec

Fig. 5-7. (a) Transients of the pitch angle φ and the flight-path angle θ after an initial pitch perturbation $\varphi(0)$, with $\delta = 0$. Note weather-cock stability. (b) Response of the pitch angle φ and the flight-path angle θ to elevator deflections δ.

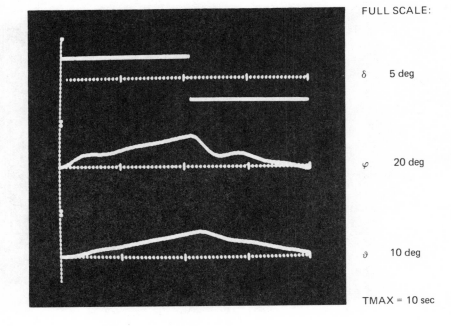

FULL SCALE:

δ 5 deg

φ 20 deg

ϑ 10 deg

TMAX = 10 sec

Example 5-2: Simulation of an Autopilot-Controlled Aircraft. While the natural weathercock stability (negative M_y due to horizontal stabilizer surfaces) tends to keep our aircraft in straight and level flight, perturbations due to gusts or initial pitch errors can be greatly reduced by a *feedback control system* (*autopilot*) which senses the pitching motion with altitude and rate gyros and then counteracts changes of φ and $\dot{\varphi}$ with opposing elevator deflections δ.

Once again, it is possible to model the autopilot gyros, elevator servo, and elevator-surface dynamics in any desired detail. In Fig. 5-8, we have represented the autopilot operation by the simple linear model

$$\frac{d\delta}{dT} = -\frac{\delta}{T_0} - G_1\varphi - D\dot{\varphi} \tag{5-10}$$

where T_0 is an *autopilot time constant* summarizing autopilot open-loop response speed, G_1 is the *autopilot gain*, and D is a *damping coefficient*. Figure 5-8 illustrates the effect of different damping-coefficient values with $T_0 = 0.5$ sec and $G_1 = 40$ sec^{-1}.

REFERENCES AND BIBLIOGRAPHY

1. Aus, H., and G. A. Korn, "The Future of On-Line Continuous-System Simulation," *Proc. FJCC*, 1971.

2. Martinez, R., "A Semi-portable Simulation System Using Both Fixed and Floating Point Derivative Blocks," Ph.D. thesis, The University of Arizona, Tucson, 1975; see also *Proc. DECUS Fall Symposium, San Diego*, 1974.

3. Goltz, J. R., "The DARE I On-Line Continuous-System Simulation Language," Ph.D. thesis, The University of Arizona, Tucson, 1970; see also *Proc. SWIEEECO*, Dallas, 1970.

4. Korn, G. A., *Minicomputers for Engineers and Scientists*, McGraw-Hill, New York, 1973.

5. Newman, W. M., and R. F. Sproull, *Principles of Interactive Computer Graphics*, McGraw-Hill, New York, 1973.

6. Huskey, H. D., and G. A. Korn, *Computer Handbook*, McGraw-Hill, New York, 1961.

7. Bekey, G. A., and W. J. Karplus, *Hybrid Computation*, Wiley, New York, 1968.

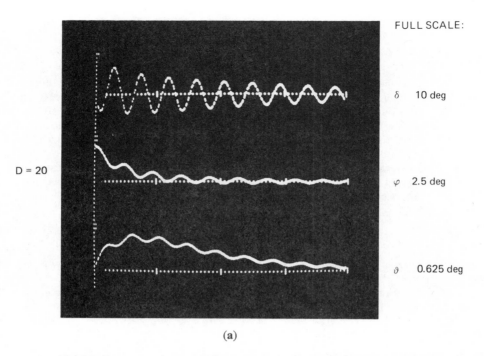

D = 20

δ 10 deg

φ 2.5 deg

ϑ 0.625 deg

(a)

Fig. 5-8. Response of an autopilot-controlled aircraft to an initial perturbation of the pitch angle for three values of rate-gyro-feedback gain D. As with other control systems, there is a trade-off between smooth (nonoscillatory) response and speed of error corrections. Each display was automatically scaled for maximum resolution.

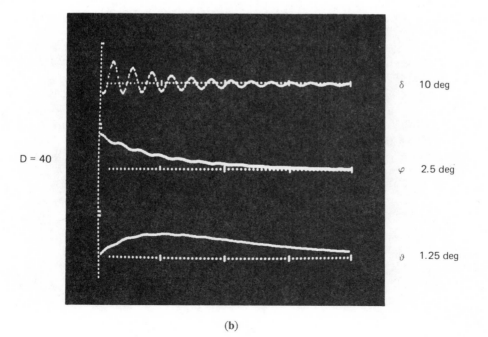

D = 40

δ 10 deg

φ 2.5 deg

ϑ 1.25 deg

(b)

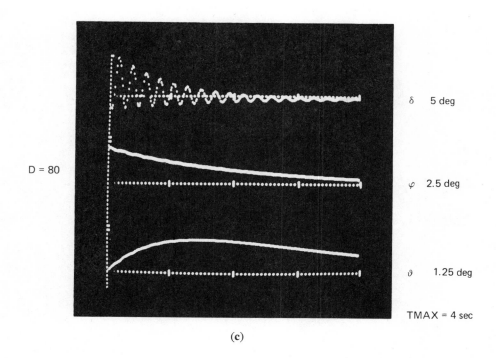

D = 80

δ 5 deg

φ 2.5 deg

ϑ 1.25 deg

TMAX = 4 sec

(c)

6

High-Performance
Simulation Techniques

INTRODUCTION AND SURVEY

After discussing extra-convenient **equation languages** in Chapters 3 to 5, we now make two seeming steps backwards. We introduce a **block-diagram simulation language**, whose statements specify elementary operations of an analog-computer-like block diagram and translate directly into computer instructions or microinstructions (Secs. 6-2 to 6-4). And we even return to a **fixed-point data representation**, which necessitates problem scaling (Sec. 6-5; see also Sec. 1-8). *Both steps complicate problem preparation but can buy a dramatic (10- to 100-fold) improvement in the computing speed of small minicomputer simulation systems.*

Such speed improvements permit a $50,000 minicomputer to match the simulation performance of a CDC 6400 (Sec. 6-14) and are mandatory for real-time minicomputer simulation of complex aerospace vehicles or for multirun simulation studies running faster than real time. *A good block-diagram simulation executes as efficiently as good machine-language code and still does not require assembly-language or microcode programming.* DARE/ELEVEN, moreover, can *combine* simulation-program segments written in floating-point equation language with block-diagram program segments representing "fast" system components, much as a hybrid computer combines digital and analog computations (Sec. 6-9). DARE block-diagram programs are especially powerful for controlling real-time equipment associated with a simulation and have proved even more useful for *nonsimulation* applications of mini/microcomputers (instrumentation, fast data processing; Sec. 6-7).

We want to emphasize, though, that **we recommend block-diagram simulation only where the resulting minicomputer performance improvement is really needed** or where many "production" simulation runs will pay for the greater programming effort. Block-diagram simulation makes little sense for larger computers with good multipass FORTRAN compilers and fast floating-point hardware. In Sec. 6-14 we shall present some performance comparisons.

In Secs. 6-11a and 6-11b we shall survey other *minicomputer simulation languages*, and in Sec. 6-10 we shall discuss *parallel* operation of *multiple microprocessors*, which is needed for fast digital simulation of larger systems. In Secs. 6-12 to 6-14 we shall discuss the comparative performance of various equation-language and block-diagram simulation systems, including some test-problem results.

A BLOCK-DIAGRAM LANGUAGE
FOR FAST MINICOMPUTATION

6-1. Two Ways To Improve Minicomputer Speed. The convenient equation-oriented simulation-language systems discussed in Chapters 3 to 5 run nicely on quite inexpensive minicomputers. Nevertheless, simulation speed (and thus the possibility of real-time or fast-time simulation) is reduced with increasing problem size. Analog computers can simply add extra parallel computing elements, and this is a possibility for digital simulation as well (Sec. 6-10), but with a given minicomputer system we must look elsewhere for performance improvements.

CSSL-type simulation languages (Chapters 3 to 5) translate into FORTRAN. Most minicomputer FORTRAN compilers are fairly simple two-pass compilers designed to minimize memory requirements rather than execution time, which may exceed that of equivalent assembly-language programs by a (very problem-dependent) factor of 4 to 10.* **A block-diagram simulation language** translating directly into assembly language (or, better, into microprograms; Sec. 6-3) can recover essentially all of this speed advantage at some sacrifice in programming convenience.

The second step needed to squeeze the highest possible computing speed out of an existing minicomputer is rather more painful than block-diagram programming: We must give up the convenient scale-factor-free floating-point data representation and **scale simulation variables into fixed-point form** (preferably into fractions between -1 and $+1$), just as for analog simulation (Sec. 6-5). The reason for this is evident from a comparison of minicomputer fixed-point and floating-point addition times:

---

*By contrast, assembly-language programming might buy at most a 2:1 speed advantage compared to the efficient multipass compiler of a large digital computer. Large minis, with five-pass compilers, will be somewhere in between, but few reliable statistics exist.

Floating-point subroutine (no hardware)   40–250 microseconds (μsec)
Floating-point microprogram   10–40 μsec
Separate floating-point-arithmetic   5–12 μsec
  processor
Fixed-point, memory to register   0.6–3 μsec

Multiplication times show a similar relationship. Note that the two-word floating-point representation (24-bit mantissa) will be somewhat more accurate than the 16-bit fixed-point fraction, but fixed-point computation can speed up simulations by a factor of 10 to 20 on many computers.* This can decide whether, say, real-time flight simulation can be done at all with a given machine.

6-2. Block-Diagram Programming. Figure 6-1 illustrates a DARE block-diagram program for the simple differential equation

$$\frac{dX}{dT} = -AX + \sin\frac{\pi}{2}T \tag{6-1}$$

Note that either floating-point or fixed-point data can be used, although we shall usually combine fixed-point arithmetic with block-diagram programming to get more speed.

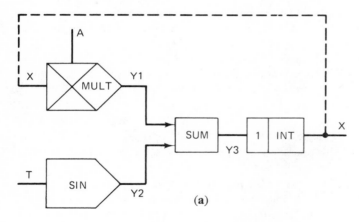

(a)

```
MULT  Y1, X, A
SIN   Y2, T
SUM   Y3, Y1, Y2
INT   X, Y3, 1
```

(b)

Fig. 6-1. Block diagram (a) and program (b) for the differential equation

$$\frac{dx}{dT} = -AX + \sin\frac{\pi}{2}T$$

*The addition-speed advantage is about 10 : 1 for the Digital Equipment Corporation PDP-11/40 with microprogrammed floating-point arithmetic. More elaborate minicomputers with separate floating-point arithmetic processors are also more likely to have improved multipass FORTRAN compilers, so that block-diagram simulation may not be needed.

The simulation software must initialize state variables, compute derivatives, and perform integration steps exactly as in the case of an equation-language program (Chapter 2 and Sec. 3-4). Since we have no compiler, we cannot compile *expressions* like the state derivative on the right of Eq. (6-1). We shall, instead, relate variables and parameters through a set of standard **block-diagram operations** (addition, multiplication, function generation, etc.; see also Table 6-1) which are combined in a **block diagram** to produce each state derivative to be integrated.

Table 6-1. Block-diagram Operators*

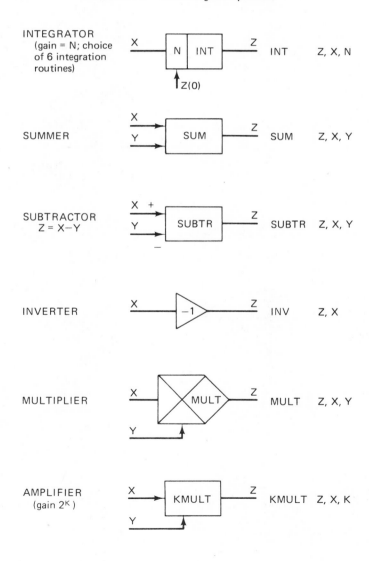

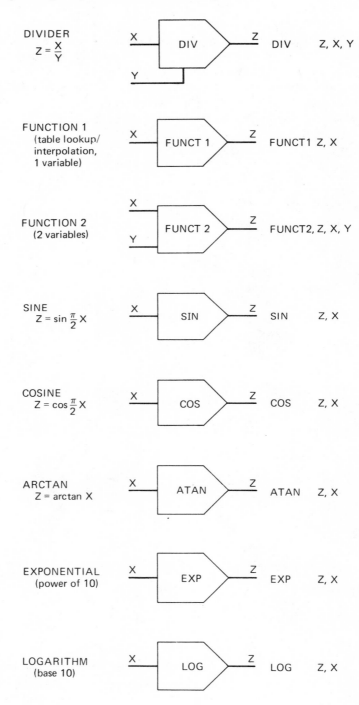

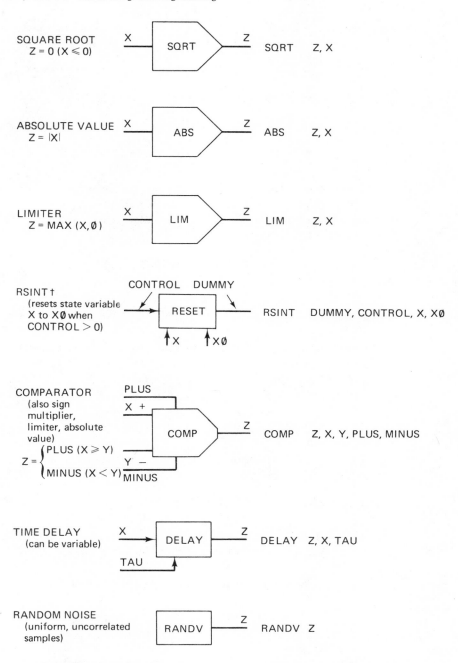

SQUARE ROOT $Z = 0 \ (X \leqslant 0)$	SQRT Z, X
ABSOLUTE VALUE $Z = |X|$	ABS Z, X
LIMITER $Z = \text{MAX} \ (X, \emptyset)$	LIM Z, X
RSINT † (resets state variable X to X∅ when CONTROL > 0)	RSINT DUMMY, CONTROL, X, X∅
COMPARATOR (also sign multiplier, limiter, absolute value) $Z = \begin{cases} \text{PLUS } (X \geqslant Y) \\ \text{MINUS } (X < Y) \end{cases}$	COMP Z, X, Y, PLUS, MINUS
TIME DELAY (can be variable)	DELAY Z, X, TAU
RANDOM NOISE (uniform, uncorrelated samples)	RANDV Z

---

* Additional operators can be created by the user.

† DUMMY output is required by DARE block-diagram translator (all blocks must have an output).

Referring to the block diagram of Fig. 6-1, we introduce defined variables $Y1$, $Y2, \ldots$ as *block outputs* and program Eq. (6-1) as follows:

$$Y1 = A * X \qquad \text{represented by } \mathsf{MULT\ Y1,\ X,\ A}$$

$$Y2 = \sin \frac{\pi}{2} T \qquad \text{represented by } \mathsf{SIN\ Y2,\ T}$$

$$Y3 = Y1 + Y2 \qquad \text{represented by } \mathsf{SUM\ Y3,\ Y1,\ Y2}$$

$$X = \int Y3\, dT \qquad \text{represented by } \mathsf{INT\ X,\ Y3,\ 1}$$

The sequence of **block-operator statements** on the right uniquely represents the block diagram of Fig. 6-1 to the digital computer and constitutes our block-diagram-language program (**block derivative file**; see also Sec. 3-1) for Eq. (6-1). We add a **run-time-display statement** like

DISPLAY X, T

just as in Sec. 3-5.

6-3. Block-Diagram Translation[1-3]*

a. Block operators as macros, subroutines, and microprograms. The DARE/ELEVEN editor (Sec. 5-2) permits entry and editing of a *block* derivative file, labeled B1 or B2, just as with an *equation* derivative file E1 or E2. Each block-operator statement, say,

SUM Y3, Y1, Y2

is a **macro call**,[27] which will be expanded into a corresponding sequence of assembly-language instructions. For fixed-point computation, this instruction sequence might be

LOAD ACCUMULATOR WITH CONTENTS OF MEMORY LOCATION Y1
ADD CONTENTS OF MEMORY LOCATION Y2
BRANCH TO ERROR ROUTINE IF FIXED-POINT SUM OVERLOADS
STORE RESULTS IN MEMORY LOCATION Y3

The *overload-error routine* would terminate the computer run and display the message

OVERLOAD OF VARIABLE Y3

as soon as $|Y3|$ exceeded unity. A library of such macro expansions is stored with the system software, so that **the user need not know assembly language. Knowledge-**

*See also Sec. 3-4.

able users can, however, create and enter their own macro-block operators by writing macro definitions, in assembly language, into a **macro-definition file** in their program. It is, thus, possible to create very powerful and fast operators, including input/output operators, for special purposes.

To save memory, complicated macro operators used repeatedly in user programs can include **subroutines**, so that a portion of code can be used over and over. *With user-microprogrammable minicomputers,[27] another significant improvement in computing speed may be obtained by letting each macro call a microprogram, i.e., a subroutine made up of microinstructions stored in a fast control memory* (see also Sec. 6-7).[2,3,26]

b. Block-diagram sorting and code optimization. As with any routine generating successive defined variables (Sec. 3-2), **block-operator statements must be sorted into procedural order** such that every block output is computed before it is needed as a block input. As with defined-variable equations, block diagrams must not contain **algebraic loops**, i.e., loops which do not comprise an integrator (Fig. 6-2).

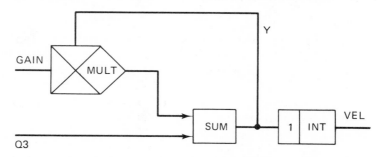

Fig. 6-2. A block diagram containing an algebraic loop, which prevents correct sorting into procedural order.

DARE/ELEVEN users may enter block-operator macros in arbitrary sequence. The DARE translator sorts them automatically into procedural order, rejects programs with algebraic loops, and also optimizes the code so as to minimize the time required for memory references.

The optimizing translator sorts the block operators so that all intermediate-result block outputs which are needed only once (and are not to be output) are stored on a pushdown stack in memory; this avoids two-word memory-reference instructions in 16-bit minicomputers. In addition, when a block macro ends with the instruction

STORE ACCUMULATOR IN MEMORY LOCATION P

and the following macro starts with

LOAD ACCUMULATOR WITH CONTENTS OF MEMORY LOCATION P

such *redundant store/fetch pairs are automatically cancelled.* **DARE/ELEVEN block-diagram programs, therefore, match the efficiency of well-written assembly-language programs.**

 c. Assembly, loading, and run-time system. After the DARE translator, the manufacturer-supplied *macro assembler* expands the sorted block-operator macros and translates them into object code. Additional system-program overlays *compile* FORTRAN program segments, if any (Secs. 6-4 and 6-9), and *link* program segments for loading, as described in Sec. 3-4. **The interactive run-time system then lets the user supply parameters, initial conditions, and integration method**, exactly as described in Sec. 5-2.b, for equation programs. With fixed-point block diagrams, initial values will be **fixed-point fractions between -1 and $+1$**, while **parameters can be either fractions or signed integers.** Integer parameter names should start with I, J, K, L, M, or N, as in FORTRAN.

6-4. Fast Multirun Studies. The FORTRAN Simulation Control Program.[1,18]*

Fixed-point block-diagrams can significantly speed up minicomputer simulation studies requiring many runs, especially in iterative optimization and Monte Carlo studies. DARE/ELEVEN employs the same convenient **FORTRAN simulation-control program (logic block**; Sec. 3-11) for block-diagram derivative files as for equation files. Assembly-language speed is not needed for the control program, which operates only between differential-equation-solving runs.

 The function of the logic-block statements

INPUT *list*	OUTPUT *list*
CALL RUN	CALL RESET
CALL STORE	CALL SAVE (VAR,N)
CALL STROF	CALL STRON

remain exactly the same as with the equation-language programs described in Sec. 3-13. A few additional types of statements may be needed for FORTRAN control of *fixed-point* block-diagram programs.

 1. Fixed-point fractions read into the FORTRAN control program from a block-diagram derivative file must be listed in the statement

   INLIST *list of variables separated by commas*

which causes transformation of the listed variables into REAL (floating-point) variables.

 2. Conversely, REAL variables or parameters read from the FORTRAN

*See also Secs. 3-11 to 3-15.

control program into a fixed-point derivative file must be listed in the statement

OUTLIST *list of variable names separated by commas*

which causes floating- to-fixed-point transformation, with an *overload message* if a variable exceeds unity in absolute value.

When a fixed-point overload occurs in a multirun simulation study, it is usually best to *continue the study but to terminate the guilty run and to mark it for automatic rescaling or so that its results will be disregarded for purposes of optimization or statistics.*

3. The logic-block statement

NO-ABORT

will suppress overload error messages but set a "flag" variable OVLFL greater than zero. FORTRAN IF statements can then modify the control program if OVLFL > 0.

6-5. Scaling Procedure[27] and Examples. Fixed-point block-diagram programs will represent the **problem variables** $x, y, \ldots$ of a given problem by **scaled machine variables**

$$X = (a_x x), \qquad Y = (a_y y) \ldots \qquad (6\text{-}2)$$

$a_x, a_y, \ldots$ are dimensional *scale factors* chosen so that the range (and hence the resolution) of each problem variable is as large as possible without reaching unity (one **machine unit**) in absolute value. It follows that

$$a_x < \frac{1}{\max |x|} \quad \frac{\text{Machine unit}}{\text{Problem unit}} \qquad (6\text{-}3)$$

where $\max |x|$ is the largest absolute value x can attain in the course of a simulation run.

The problem **independent variable** (usually problem **time**) t will be represented by the scaled machine-independent variable (machine time)

$$T = (\alpha_t t) \qquad (6\text{-}4)$$

where the **time-scale factor** α_t again satisfies

$$\alpha_t < \frac{1}{\max t} \quad \frac{\text{Machine unit}}{\text{Time unit}} \qquad (6\text{-}5)$$

so that $0 \leq T < 1$.

For convenience, scale factors are usually chosen to be powers of 2 or 10 (or products of powers of 2 and 10, such as 4000 or $\frac{1}{20}$).

To obtain **scaled machine equations** describing a fixed-point block-diagram program for a given set of problem equations, we simply substitute

$$x = \frac{1}{a_x}X, \qquad y = \frac{1}{a_y}Y \dots$$

$$t = \frac{1}{\alpha_t}T, \qquad \frac{d}{dt} = \alpha_t \frac{d}{dT} \tag{6-6}$$

in the given problem equations. Note that block-diagram programs will require scaling of many intermediate block-output variables. As noted earlier, system *parameters* will be represented either by *scaled-fraction (machine) parameters* or by signed *integers*.

> NOTE: If the independent variable T does not occur explicitly as a block-operator input, a simple way to *decrease* the time-scale factor α_t (i.e., to *speed up* the simulation) by a factor n is to *increase* all integrator gains by the same factor. Note that this will affect the numerical stability of solutions just like an increase of the integration step DT (Appendix A).

While the scaling procedure as such is straightforward, we frequently lack good estimates of the maximum excursions $(\max |x|)$ for all variables (especially for intermediate block outputs), and *rescaling* is often necessary. The need for scaling and rescaling is a significant drawback of fixed-point programming, as of analog computation. **The best way to scale a large block-diagram program is to make a preliminary run with an equivalent floating-point equation-language program,** which is easy to do with DARE/ELEVEN.

In some real-time simulations (e.g., flight training, partial-system tests), *one may wish to continue a simulation run indefinitely*, i.e., $T > 1$ even with fixed-point simulation. In such cases, the DARE statement

CONTINUOUS

in a block-diagram derivative block will suppress run termination at $T = \text{TMAX}$ or $T = 1$, but then T cannot be used as an input to any block-operator. Note that it is still possible to generate and use variables such as $0.5 \sin T$, which remain between -1 and $+1$.

Example 6-1: Van der Pol's Differential Epuation. Van der Pol's differential equation

$$\frac{d^2x}{dt^2} + \alpha(x^2 - 1)\frac{dx}{dt} + x = 0 \tag{6-7}$$

or

$$\frac{dx}{dt} = \dot{x}, \qquad \frac{d\dot{x}}{dt} = \alpha(1 - x^2)\dot{x} - x \tag{6-8}$$

(see also Example 2-3) describes a nonlinear oscillator whose amplitude-dependent damping eventually produces constant-amplitude (limit-cycle) oscillations for any positive α and nonzero initial values of x or $\dot{x}$. For $0 \leq \alpha \leq 1$, it turns out that $x(t)$ and $\dot{x}(t)$ remain less than 4 if this is true for their initial values, so that the scaled quantities

$$x = \frac{x}{4}, \qquad \text{XDOT} = \frac{\dot{x}}{4} \tag{6-9a}$$

will stay within ± 1 machine unit. We substitute Eq. (6-9a) and

$$T = \frac{t}{16} \tag{6-9b}$$

into the given state equations (6-8) to find the *scaled machine equations*

$$\frac{dX}{dT} = 16 * \text{XDOT}$$

$$\frac{d}{dT}\text{XDOT} = 256\left[\text{ALFA}\left(\frac{1}{16} - X^2\right)\text{XDOT} - \frac{1}{16}X\right] \tag{6-10}$$

which are implemented by the block-diagram program of Fig. 6-3. By way of comparison, note than an *equation-language* program would comprise merely two lines, viz., the two state equations (6-8), and would require *no scaling* or *rescaling* if we wanted to make $\alpha > 1$. But execution of the fixed-point block-diagram program on a minicomputer will be *5 to 15 times faster*.

Example 6-2: Cannonball Trajectory. For fast block-diagram simulation of the cannonball trajectory of Example 3-5 (Sec. 3-14), we must scale the given problem equations

$$\frac{dx}{dt} = \dot{x}, \qquad \frac{dy}{dt} = \dot{y}$$

$$\frac{d\dot{x}}{dt} = -\frac{r}{m}v\dot{x}, \qquad \frac{d\dot{y}}{dt} = -\frac{r}{m}v\dot{y} - g \tag{6-11}$$

$$v = \sqrt{\dot{x}^2 + \dot{y}^2}$$

with

$$x(0) = 0, \qquad\qquad \dot{x}(0) = v(0)\cos\theta(0)$$
$$y(0) = 0, \qquad\qquad \dot{y}(0) = v(0)\sin\theta(0)$$
$$v(0) = 900 \text{ ft/sec}, \qquad\qquad g = 32.2 \text{ ft/sec}^2$$
$$r = 4.7 \times 10^{-5} \frac{\text{lb}}{(\text{ft/sec})^2}, \qquad m = 0.621 \text{ slug (20 lb)}$$

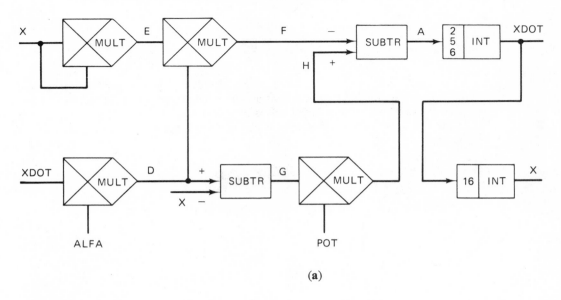

(a)

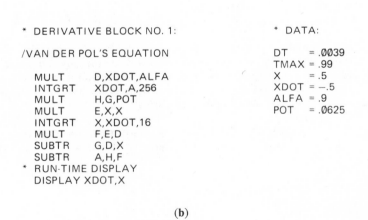

```
* DERIVATIVE BLOCK NO. 1:              * DATA:

/VAN DER POL'S EQUATION                DT    = .0039
                                       TMAX = .99
    MULT      D,XDOT,ALFA              X     = .5
    INTGRT    XDOT,A,256               XDOT = −.5
    MULT      H,G,POT                  ALFA  = .9
    MULT      E,X,X                    POT   = .0625
    INTGRT    X,XDOT,16
    MULT      F,E,D
    SUBTR     G,D,X
    SUBTR     A,H,F
*   RUN-TIME DISPLAY
    DISPLAY XDOT,X
```

(b)

Fig. 6-3. Block diagram (a) and program (b) for Van Der Pol's differential equation in the scaled form (6-10). The symbolic entries #256, #16 fix the parameters in question (here integrator gains), so that fixed parameters need not be entered as data. (c) Displays of X, XDOT versus T, X versus XDOT, and a listing for the program of Fig. 6-3(a) and (b). Full-scale excursions on graphs are one machine unit. (d) A strip-chart-recorder plot of solutions for the program of Fig. 6-3(a) and (b).

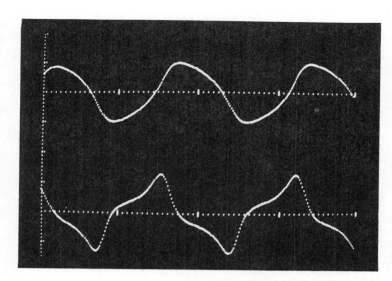

(c)

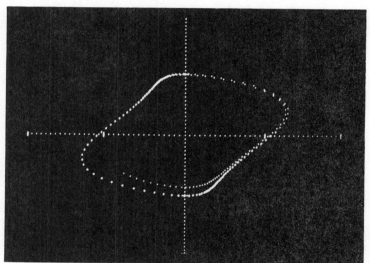

TIME	X	XDOT
0.00300	0.31863	0.37624
0.05097	0.42729	-0.05346
0.09896	0.31492	-0.22294
0.15092	0.03764	-0.48437
0.19889	-0.39790	-0.43483
0.24686	-0.48326	0.09188
0.29884	-0.34668	0.22551
0.34681	-0.10796	0.43082
0.39478	0.33092	0.56987
0.44675	0.49449	-0.07184
0.49473	0.38194	-0.20268
0.54270	0.17269	-0.36919

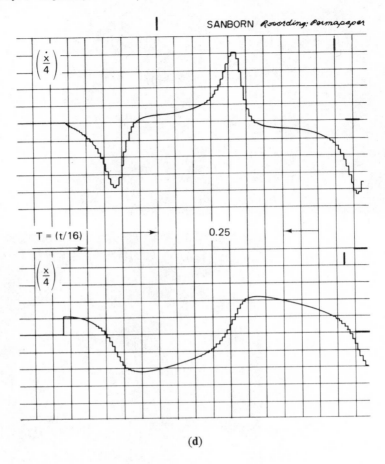

SANBORN *Recording: Permapaper*

$$\left(\frac{\dot{x}}{4}\right)$$

T = (t/16)   0.25

$$\left(\frac{x}{4}\right)$$

(d)

For 15 deg $< \theta(0) <$ 30 deg, if we stop the simulation on impact ($y = 0$), we find, either from energy considerations (solve analytically with $r = 0$) or from a preliminary floating-point simulation run, that

$$t < 25 \text{ sec}, \qquad x < 20{,}000 \text{ ft} \qquad y < 6{,}000 \text{ ft}$$
$$v < 900 \text{ ft/sec}, \qquad \dot{x} < 900 \text{ ft/sec}, \qquad |\dot{y}| < 900 \text{ ft/sec}$$

Hence we can use the machine variables

$$T = \frac{t}{40}, \qquad X = \frac{x}{20{,}000}, \qquad Y = \frac{y}{10{,}000}$$

$$V = \frac{v}{1000}, \qquad \text{XDOT} = \frac{\dot{x}}{1000}, \qquad \text{YDOT} = \frac{\dot{y}}{1000}$$

to find the scaled machine equations

$$\frac{dX}{dT} = 2 * \text{XDOT}, \qquad \frac{dY}{dT} = 4 * \text{YDOT}$$

$$\frac{d}{dT}\text{XDOT} = -R * V * \text{XDOT}$$

$$\frac{d}{dT}\text{YDOT} = -R * V * \text{YDOT} - 0.04g \qquad (6\text{-}12)$$

$$V = \sqrt{\text{XDOT}^2 + \text{YDOT}^2}$$

with $R = 40,000\dfrac{r}{m} = 0.303$

which are implemented by the block-diagram program of Fig. 6-4.

Example 6-3: Monte Carlo Study of a Correlation Detector. In the block-diagram program of Figs. 6-5 and 6-6, a sinusoidal *signal*

$$\text{SIG} = 0.9 * \cos(40T) \qquad (6\text{-}13)$$

is generated as the solution of the differential equation

$$\frac{d^2}{dT^2}\text{SIG} = -1600 * \text{SIG} \qquad (6\text{-}14)$$

SIG is mixed with a random or pseudorandom signal ANOIS obtained by passing a noise-generator output (Sec. 3-9b) R through a one-integrator low-pass filter to form the detector input SN:

$$\frac{d}{dT}\text{ANOIS} = \frac{\text{BW}}{256}(\text{ATT} * R - \text{ANOIS}) \qquad (6\text{-}15)$$

$$\text{SN} = \text{AA} * \text{SIG} + \text{ANOIS} \qquad (6\text{-}16)$$

The parameter BW sets the noise bandwidth, and 0.9 AA/ATT is a measure of signal-to-noise ratio. The correlation detector uses a priori knowledge of the signal to generate the test statistic

$$\text{CORR} = \text{GAIN} \int_0^{\text{TMAX}} \text{SN} * \text{SIG} \, dT \qquad (6\text{-}17)$$

The comparator output

$$\text{TEST} = \text{CORR} - \text{CR} \qquad (6\text{-}18)$$

will be positive if the test statistic CORR exceeds a *threshold* CR; this registers a *detection* if a signal is present or a *false alarm* if AA = SIG = 0 (noise only).

The FORTRAN logic block of Fig. 6-6(b) makes N detection runs, counts the number NDET of detections, and displays the accumulated relative frequency $P = \text{NDET/NRUN}$ of detections (signal present) or false alarms (noise only). P could also be plotted against the signal-to-noise ratio, the noise bandwidth, or the detector threshold.

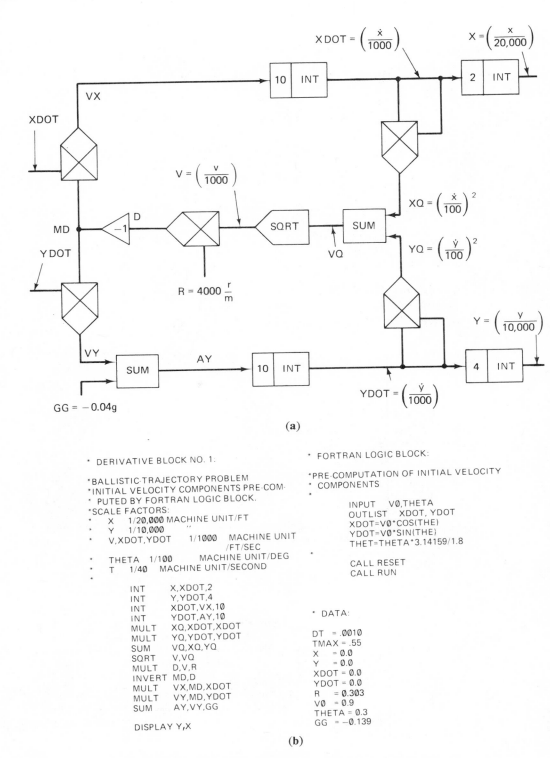

Fig. 6-4. Block diagram (a) and program (b) for the ballistic-trajectory problem of Example 6-2. The FORTRAN logic block precomputes the initial velocity components XDOT, YDOT before simulation run.

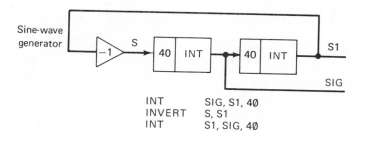

```
INT      SIG, S1, 40
INVERT   S, S1
INT      S1, SIG, 40
```

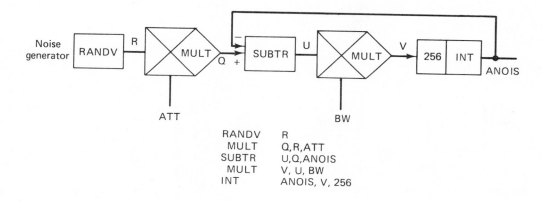

```
RANDV    R
MULT     Q,R,ATT
SUBTR    U,Q,ANOIS
MULT     V, U, BW
INT      ANOIS, V, 256
```

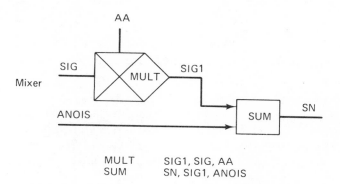

```
MULT     SIG1, SIG, AA
SUM      SN, SIG1, ANOIS
```

Fig. 6-5. Generation and mixing of a sine-wave signal SIG and low-pass filtered noise ANOIS for detection experiments. The noise-generator block produces noise samples uniformly distributed between -1 and $+1$ each time the derivative routine is called and may be implemented by a pseudorandom-noise routine or by sampling a real noise generator.

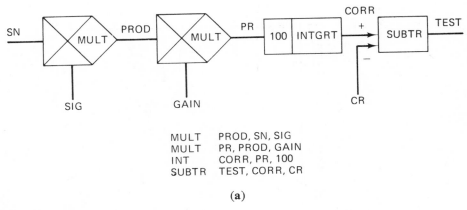

```
MULT    PROD, SN, SIG
MULT    PR, PROD, GAIN
INT     CORR, PR, 100
SUBTR   TEST, CORR, CR
```

(a)

```
*     FORTRAN LOGIC BLOCK
*
*     MANUALLY ENTERED SAMPLE SIZE
      INPUT N
*     INPUT FROM DERIVATIVE FILE
      INLIST TEST
*     KILL DISK STORAGE TO SPEED COMPUTATION
      CALL STROF
*     INITIALIZE COUNTS AND RUN
      NRUN = 0
      NDET = 0
12    NRUN = NRUN+1
      CALL RESET
      CALL RUN
      IF (TEST) 14,14,13
13    NDET = NDET+1
14    P = NDET/NRUN
      CALL SHOW (NRUN,NDET,P)
*     STOP WHEN NRUN>N, STORE LAST RUN
      IF (NRUN−N+1) 12,15,16
15    CALL STRON
      GO TO 12
16    CONTINUE
```

(b)

Fig. 6-6. Block-diagram program for a correlation detector (a) and a FORTRAN logic block which takes statistics for a Monte Carlo detection study (b).

HIGH-SPEED AND REAL-TIME SIMULATION

6-6. Some Useful Block Operators. The DARE block operators listed in Table 6-1 emulate an elaborate (and expensive) analog computer including multiple **function generators.** Fixed-point function-table lookup/interpolation is especially fast when uniform breakpoint spacing is employed (see also Sec. 3-8). This technique also quickly produces **square roots, logarithms, exponentials**, and **trigonometric functions.** *One-argument function generation requires only 20 to 30 microseconds with a PDP-11/40 and less than 8 microseconds with a user-microprogrammable minicomputer.*[4,5,27]

It is easy to add new block operators for special applications. The **Schmitt-trigger block** TRIGG, with the hysteresis-type input/output transfer characteristic of Fig. 6-7(a), is especially useful in the signal-generator program of Fig. 6-7(b), which emulates an analog *triangle/square-wave generator.*

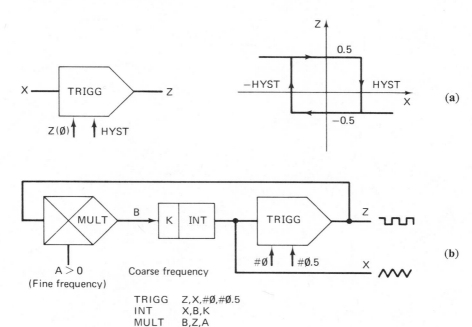

TRIGG   Z,X,#Ø,#Ø.5
INT   X,B,K
MULT   B,Z,A

Fig. 6-7. Schmitt-trigger input/output transfer characteristic with hysteresis (a), and digital generation of accurate square-wave and triangle-wave signals through regenerative Schmitt-trigger feedback around an integrator [(b) and (c)]. This signal generator can be frequency-modulated by a variable A. ZO is a given initial condition for Z (needed if |Z| < HYST).

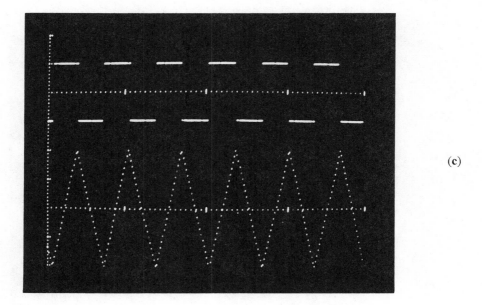

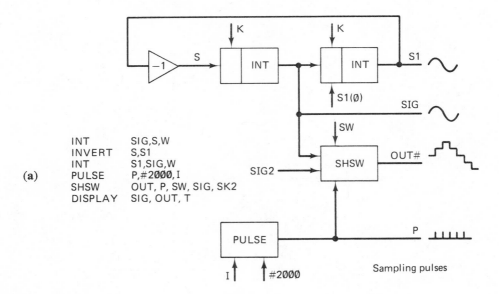

(a)

```
INT      SIG,S,W
INVERT   S,S1
INT      S1,SIG,W
PULSE    P,#2000,I
SHSW     OUT, P, SW, SIG, SK2
DISPLAY  SIG, OUT, T
```

Fig. 6-8. A *sine-wave generator* produces

$$SIG = SIG(0) \sin KT$$

as a solution of the harmonic-oscillator equation

$$\frac{d^2}{dT^2} SIG = -K^2 SIG$$

The *sample-hold switch* SHSW samples the sine wave at times determined by the pulse generator PULSE.

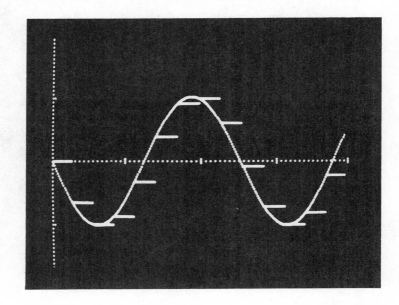

(b)

In Fig. 6-8(a), the output SAMPL of the **pulse generator** PULSE is *positive* at the start of the 1st, Ith, $2I$th, ..., and NIth DT interval. The pulse variable SAMPLE is *negative* between positive pulses and *zero* after the Nth pulse to signal the end of the pulse train at $T = NI$. With SW ≥ 0, the **sample-hold switch** SHSW samples the sinusoidal signal SIG with each positive pulse and holds the sample-hold output OUT after each pulse [Fig. 6-8(b)]. This is useful for simulations of sampled-data systems (see also Secs. 6-9 and 6-18).

With SW < 0, the sample-hold circuit would sample an alternative input signal, SIG 2, instead of SIG. SHSW thus serves as a *single-pole-double-throw switch* as well as a sample-hold.

Logic variables such as SAMPL and SW in Fig. 6-8 can be related by special block operators emulating **logic gates, flip-flops,** and **counters** for simulation of digital subsystems, e.g., in control-system simulation.

To store an *N-sample time history* of a simulation variable for use in a subsequent run, the **function-memory operator** WRITE is driven by a control operator called ARRAY, which generates N sampling commands IDT time units apart (exactly like PULSE) and also reserves a suitable N-word array in memory. The memory operator READ similarly reads a time history stored during an earlier run. WRITE and READ are turned on and off by switch variables set by the logic-block program, which can also enter *initial conditions* into the storage array before the first run. Very sophisticated iterative function optimization can be implemented in this manner (see also Sec. 6-7).

6-7. Block Operators for Real-Time Input/Output

a. Real-time operations. **When the real equipment or human operators are to be part of a simulation experiment, we must synchronize the time variable T with real time.** We can do this easily (for either equation or block-diagram simulation programs) by making the RUN routine (Sec. 2-1) interrogate a sense line connected to a real time clock before every DT step; the program can proceed to the next step only after a suitable clock interval has elapsed.*

Block-diagram languages can have **real-time block operators** to read **analog-to-digital converters, sense lines (flags)** which inform the program that some voltage outside the computer is on, and various **instruments.** Other block operators can control **logic levels, relays, electronic switches,** and **digital-to-analog converters** in the real world. For real-time synchronization, one of these block operators can sense a real-time clock, so that there is no need to modify the RUN routine for this purpose (Fig. 6-9).

Real-time simulations with real instruments, control systems, or human operators interacting with a simulated system or environment are of great practical importance for **partial-system tests, operator training,** and **crew-station design** (see also Sec. 6-8).

---

*There is no need to program clock *interrupts* (except possibly in a time-sharing system), since the program has to wait for the clock in any case.

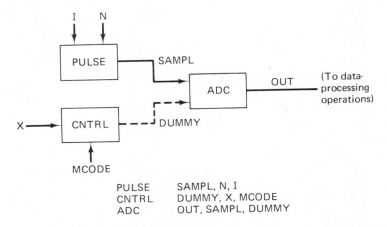

PULSE   SAMPL, N, I
CNTRL   DUMMY, X, MCODE
ADC   OUT, SAMPL, DUMMY

Fig. 6-9. A simple DARE real-time data-input program. The block operator CNTRL starts a real-time experiment (and, in particular, starts a real-time clock) by setting the integer MCODE into a *control register* when the input variable X = 0; typically X = T, so the experiment starts when the computer run starts. PULSE tells ADC to read the analog-to-digital converter output after every Ith computer-time increment *DT*. But successive actual conversions are started by the real-time clock at a somewhat slower rate, and the ADC block simply stops the digital program until each conversion is completed. This synchronizes the simulation program with real time. The ADC output is passed on for further block-operator processing. Note that the DUMMY output of CNTRL is not a run-time variable but forces the DARE translator to order block-operators correctly so that ADC follows CNTRL (procedural flow of real-time control).

b. Instrumentation applications and random-process measurements. DARE block-diagram programs for input/output, interface control, and data processing execute as efficiently as good assembly-language code; still, the user need not learn assembly language. It turns out that **DARE block-diagram-language systems, with their convenient interactive multirun programs and simple output commands, are ideally suited for nonsimulation applications in instrumentation and control.** In fact, such applications will be *more* important than simulation with block-diagram languages (which we would recommend only when their higher execution speed is really needed).

DARE control of real experiments is described in References 2, 5, 22 to 25, and 28. As an example, consider the signal-processing system of Fig. 6-5. Instead of generating samples of the sine wave SIG and the noise waveform R in the digital computer, we can readily obtain these samples from real signal and noise generators through two analog-to-digital converters ADC1 and ADC2 (Fig. 6-10). The program of Fig. 6-5 would then implement digital filtering (smoothing) of real noise. Practical sampling rates obtainable in such experiments can be as high as 2000 samples per second, depending on the number of converters and the amount of processing. To handle higher sampling rates, one may employ a direct-memory-access interface[27] to read arrays of samples into memory and then write successive samples from each array into a DARE program at a slower rate.[2,22,23]

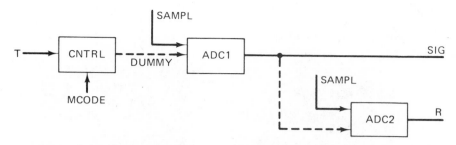

Fig. 6-10. Block diagram illustrating the "flow of control" in DARE real-time operations. CNTRL operates a control-register interface which turns on an experiment involving a sine-wave generator and a noise generator at T = 0 (see also Fig. 6-9). The dummy connections (dashed lines) ensure that analog-to-digital converter ADC1 is read before ADC2; note that the ADC1 output SIG, a real digital variable, is also used as a dummy variable for sequencing. SAMPL can be a pulse as in Fig. 6-9, or if SAMPL = 0.1, both converters will be read at every derivative call.

Special DARE block operators have been used to perform **on-line measurements of probability densities (amplitude-distribution estimation), correlation functions, and Fourier transforms** of real or simulated random time functions (Fig. 6-11).[2,3,25] Special operators for **periodic-signal enhancement through function averaging** have also been developed.[2,27] Reference 25 describes control of a wide variety of fast analog-computer experiments by DARE block-diagram programs. **DARE real-time block-diagram programs are equally useful for interactive minicomputer-controlled experimentation and for dedicated mini/microcomputer instrumentation and control systems.**[28] A simplified DARE language system (MICRODARE) has been developed especially for small mini/microcomputer instrumentation systems without a disk operating system (i.e., with paper-tape or cassette programming only; see also Sec. 6-11).[19,28]

Fig. 6-11. DARE displays of the block-diagram programs (a) and of waveform and probability-density estimates [(b) and (c)] for the sine-wave-plus-noise example of Fig. 6-5. In this instance, the sine wave was generated digitally as in Fig. 6-5, and the noise-generator block RANDV read a real noise generator 400 times per second.

(a)

(b)

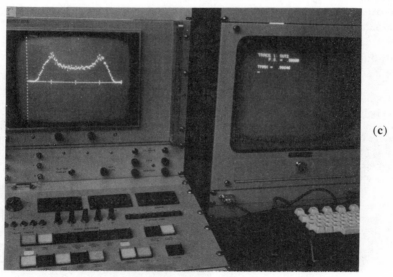

(c)

6-8. Real-Time Flight Simulation. As noted in Sec. 5-6, aerospace-vehicle flight simulation is one of the most important applications of continuous-system simulation. Again, equation-language programming in the manner of Sec. 5-6 is most convenient for engineering-design purposes. **The higher execution speed of block-diagram programs, however, makes it possible to use inexpensive (and easily interfaced) minicomputers for real-time partial-system tests, such as tilt-table tests of autopilot components and realistic flight training.** DARE/ELEVEN block-diagram programs are, in fact, especially suitable for programming dedicated flight-trainer computers and work nicely in faster-than-real-time flight-simulation studies.

DARE/ELEVEN block-diagram programs will easily implement realistic three-dimensional flight equations and engine-performance equations for multiengined aircraft in real time. To avoid discussion of a complicated model, though, Fig. 6-12

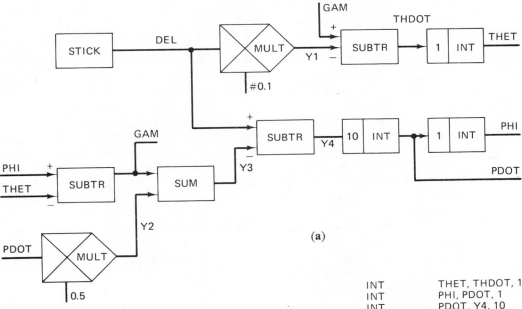

(a)

INT	THET, THDOT, 1
INT	PHI, PDOT, 1
INT	PDOT, Y4, 10
SUBTR	THDOT, GAM, Y1
MULT	Y1, DEL, #0.1
STICK	DEL
SUBTR	Y4, DEL, Y3
SUM	Y3, GAM, Y2
SUBTR	GAM, PHI, THET
MULT	Y2, PDOT, #0.5
DISPLAY	THET, PHI, T

(b)

Fig. 6-12. Block-diagram program for real-time flight simulation. The real-time block operator STICK outputs the elevator angle DEL 1000 times per second and permits the program to continue only after each millisecond interval has passed. This program implements only the simple linearized pitch-plane flight equations of Sec. 5-6 and is so fast that the computer is mostly idle, waiting for STICK. Real-time simulation of very elaborate nonlinear, three-dimensional flight equations plus engine equations is easily possible with a PDP-11/40.

shows only a very simple example, viz., the linearized pitch-plane flight simulation of Sec. 5-6. Referring to Sec. 5-6, our block diagram implements the flight equations (5-9),

$$\frac{d\theta}{dt} = \gamma - 0.1\delta$$

$$\frac{d\varphi}{dt} = \dot{\varphi}, \qquad \frac{d\dot{\varphi}}{dt} = -10\gamma + 10\delta - 0.5\dot{\varphi} \qquad (6-19)$$

$$\gamma = \varphi - \theta$$

where θ is the flight-path angle, φ the pitch angle, and γ the angle of attack. The elevator deflection δ is supplied by the block operator STICK, which reads δ once per time increment *DT*, in real time, from a real *joystick* through a shaft encoder or analog-to-digital converter. The pitch angle φ can be inverted and displayed on a cathode-ray oscilloscope, which thus simulates an *aircraft artificial horizon*. Even with our simple model, the pitch-angle indication will respond with realistic delays to the joystick motion, and the model is easily modified to simulate the pitch response of different types of aircraft.

6-9. Simulation with Combined Equation and Block-Diagram Program Segments.[19]

DARE/ELEVEN will accommodate four different derivative-file programs representing subsystems to be simulated. These subsystems may be simulated concurrently, or they may alternate in segmented simulation studies (Sec. 3-15). To permit efficient simulation of subsystems with different "bandwidths" or frequency responses, individual derivative blocks may utilize different integration routines. **It is, moreover, possible to program one or two of the derivative files in fast-executing fixed-point block-diagram language, while the rest of the program is written in the more convenient floating-point equation language.** This new technique can speed up critical portions of a simulation and will also simplify real-time-interface programming.

Transition between fixed-point and floating-point variables is easily accomplished by special FLOAT and FIX block operators in the block-diagram derivative files. Reference 19 shows a simple example. The use of different integration routines (and possibly also different integration intervals DT) in different derivative files still requires much research.

6-10. A Parallel-Microprocessor System.

For faster interactive simulation, the larger 16-bit computers ("mega-minis" with hardware floating-point arithmetic, e.g., DEC PDP-11/45, 50, and 70; Varian 74; Data General Eclipse; and Modcomp IV) will give excellent results, and small 32-bit systems (Interdata 8/32, Systems 32) should match the simulation performance of a CDC 6400 (Secs. 6-12 and 6-14). Nevertheless, the run execution time of any single-processor digital machine necessarily increases with problem size. **Faster digital solution of large simulation problems will require multiple parallel processors.**

Figure 6-13 suggests an inexpensive multiprocessor system employing a PDP-11/40 as a **control processor** to implement DARE/ELEVEN-type software and input/output and 1 to 16 microprogrammed bipolar microprocessors as fast **arithmetic processors.**[26] The latter are interrupt-driven slaves of the control processor. Each microprocessor has a fast **two-port semiconductor memory**, which is loaded with a derivative-file program and an integration-step routine through the control-processor bus interface. The control-processor bus can also transfer data words between arithmetic-processor memories and between these two-port memories and the disk.

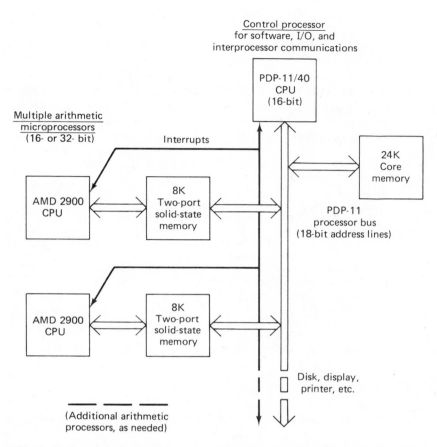

Control processor
for software, I/O, and
interprocessor communications

PDP-11/40
CPU
(16-bit)

Multiple arithmetic
microprocessors
(16- or 32- bit)

Interrupts

24K
Core
memory

AMD 2900
CPU

8K
Two-port
solid-state
memory

PDP-11
processor bus
(18-bit address lines)

AMD 2900
CPU

8K
Two-port
solid-state
memory

Disk, display,
printer, etc.

(Additional arithmetic
processors, as needed)

Fig. 6-13. A simple multimicroprocessor system for fast simulation of large systems. The PDP-11/40 *control processor* handles the DARE software, input/output, and data transfers between 2 to 16 *arithmetic processors*. The last are very fast microprogrammed bipolar microprocessors with two-port solid-state memories.

In operation, the sole function of each arithmetic processor is to integrate a subset of the system equations for one derivative call at a time to produce 5 to 50 updated state-variable and defined-variable values. As the various parallel processors finish their integration-routine steps, they interrupt the control processor, which now transfers the variables needed by other processors for the next step and then restarts the arithmetic processors with an interrupt signal. At specified communication levels (Sec. 3-5a), the control processor also moves selected variables to the graphic display for a run-time display and to its own memory and/or to the disk for postrun displays and data-processing operations.

Control programs for iterative and statistical multirun simulation studies are typically performed by the control processor alone, since their operations are needed only once per differential-equation-solving run. Both equation- and block-diagram-language segments can be implemented and possibly combined as in

DARE/ELEVEN. But there is little need for resorting to fixed-point arithmetic, for *very fast 32-bit floating-point arithmetic processors can be built quite inexpensively from bit-sliced bipolar microprocessor chips*. Each such processor, matching the arithmetic speed of a CDC 6400, should cost well under $2000, with 8K words of 300-nanosecond memory adding another $1500 [see also Table 6-2(c)]. Thus, a complete simulation system with 12 arithmetic processors should cost less than $100,000, including disk, display, and printer.

TABLE 6-2. Estimated Computation Speeds for a Medium-Sized Aerospace-Vehicle Simulation

Assumed are 100 additions, 140 multiplications, 8 tabulated functions of one variable, 10 sines or cosines, and 12 integrations. Second-order Runge-Kutta integration (two complete derivative evaluations per *DT* step) is assumed in order to accommodate discontinuous control inputs. Computation speed is described in terms of the fastest sine-wave output at 25 *DT* steps per sine-wave period.

(a) Floating-point, equation-oriented, simulation systems (allowing for some compiler inefficiencies in minicomputer systems)

PDP-11/40, FP firmware, core memory	0.8 to 1 Hz
PDP-11/45, FP hardware, bipolar memory	2 to 3 Hz
CDC 6400[26]; Systems Engr. 32	5 to 8 Hz
CDC 6600	15 to 25 Hz

(b) Fixed-point, block-diagram simulation systems with optimizing translator

PDP-11/40, core memory	4 to 6 Hz
PDP-11/45, bipolar memory	7 to 13 Hz
Interdata 85, solid-state memory, special microprogram[5]	17 to 24 Hz

(c) Multimicroprocessor system (PDP-11/40 and 4 AMD 2900, 200-nsec memory)

Equation language	15 to 25 Hz
Floating-point block-diagram language	30 to 60 Hz
Fixed-point block-diagram language	45 to 85 Hz

Since the arithmetic processors must exchange intermediate results between integration steps, **efficient multiprocessor operation requires clever partitioning of program segments among processors** so that

1. Different arithmetic processors require approximately equal execution times per integration step, and

2. Fewer problem variables need be passed between processors.

The first requirement is the more important one, for it requires at most 5 microseconds to pass one 32-bit floating-point variable, while a typical integration step takes between 2 and 50 milliseconds. Different problem-partitioning schemes could be tried interactively, or an automatic optimization method might be developed. In any case, **continuous-system simulation is an especially suitable multiprocessor application, because each processor can do a relatively large task before needing data from another processor.**

COMPARATIVE PERFORMANCE OF DIFFERENT SIMULATION-LANGUAGE SYSTEMS

6-11. Minicomputer Simulation-Language Systems

a. Equation-language systems. In addition to the DARE systems developed for the Digital Equipment Corporation PDP-9* and PDP-11 minicomputers, two new equation-language systems permit interactive simulation with minicomputers. Both are designed to *interpret or compile one equation statement at a time* rather than translate complete programs. *This permits very fast retranslation after model changes*, although less code optimization is possible.

BEDSOCS, designed at the University of Bradford,[17] is a true CSSL-specification language (Sec. 3-16) which translates into BASIC[27] rather than into FORTRAN. Written for Hewlett-Packard 21XX minicomputers with a simple storage oscilloscope display, BEDSOCS utilizes a simple paper-tape-loaded translator and the BASIC interpreter, so that *no disk operating system is required.* More elaborate BEDSOCS systems run on minicomputer BASIC time-sharing systems and could also utilize *compiled* BASIC.

SIMEX, written for a DEC PDP-9 (or PDP-15) at Washington State University,[18] is entirely different. Unlike CSSL-type languages, SIMEX is not translated

TABLE 6-3. Some Examples of Measured Digital-Simulation Performance
(all for floating-point, equation-oriented CSSL systems)

---

1. Six-degree-of-freedom VTOL aircraft study (Xerox Data Systems Sigma 7 Computer, SL-1 language)[30]

> 40 integrations, with *three different integration routines*
> 308 equations
> 26 one-variable functions
> 15 two-variable functions
> 18 trigonometric functions

This simulation was carried out in *real time*. The smallest system time constants were between 10 and 30 msec. The highest frequency components observed are estimated above 10 Hz.

2. Pilot-ejection study (Sec. 4-11)

> Fourth-order trajectory problem, 4 trigonometric functions,
> procedural block
> CDC 6400, DARE P   0.14 sec/trajectory run
>   (RK2 integration)

3. Delay-line problem (Sec. 4-11)

> 99 integrations, 100 multiplications, 99 subtractions
> CDC 6400, DARE P   0.8 sec for 800 DT steps
>   (RK2 integration)

---

*The DARE I and II interactive simulation systems are written for a PDP-9 with a special display console, so that the software would have to be modified to run on ordinary PDP-9s or PDP-15s.[1-3]

into a host language but employs its own one-line-at-a-time compiler. *Fixed-point* code is produced, but an *automatic scaling scheme* keeps the various equations scaled correctly once proper system-variable scale factors have been entered. The execution speed of this fixed-point equation-language system almost (but not quite) matches that of a block-diagram system with optimized code (Table 6-4). SIMEX permits real-time operations and can run a 300-equation system with 24K words of core.[18] Like BEDSOCS, SIMEX does not need a disk operating system, so that computer cost is very low.

SIESTA, written at the Technical University of West Berlin,[14] is interesting in that *floating-point equations are translated into block-operator statements*, which are then translated into machine language. There is also a version which accepts input in the form of block-operator symbols and interconnections drawn on a graphic-display screen (like MOBSSL; Sec. 6-11b). SIESTA was written for the now-obsolete SDS 930 Computer but could be readily adapted to other machines, since the translator was written in FORTRAN II.

b. Block-diagram systems. **Block CSMP**, a floating-point block-diagram simulation system, was probably the first system that permitted interactive digital simulation. Originally developed for the IBM 1620 and 1130 computers,[12-13] Block CSMP, whose software is written in FORTRAN, is fairly easy to adapt to other small computers and is now available for Digital Equipment Corporations PDP-9, PDP-15, and PDP-11. Block-operator statements similar to those in Fig. 6-14 are quickly sorted into procedural order and are interpreted as library routines each time a simulation run is made; model changes are thus very quick. Later versions of Block CSMP can also *compile* a binary version of the simulation program to double execution speed, but this is still quite slow (Table 6-4). MOBSSL is a special form of Block CSMP which permits the user to select and interconnect block-operator symbols by means of a light pen on a graphic-display screen.[15]

ISL (Interactive Simulation Language),[7,16] sold by Interactive Mini Systems, Kennewick, Washington, for many minicomputers, is a simple block-diagram system implementing block operators with machine-language subroutines, so that *fairly large simulations can run in only 8K words of minicomputer memory*. ISL can utilize fixed-point arithmetic, floating-point arithmetic, or, where accuracy can be sacrificed to speed, a simplified two-word, floating-point format with a one-word mantissa (12, 16, or 18 bits) called *Mini-point* (see Table 6-4). Quick model changes are possible, but ISL lacks the capability of sorting block-operator statements into procedural order.

Block CSMP and ISL have a wide variety of block-operators. ISL has facilities for simple multirun iteration but cannot control complex multirun studies with a FORTRAN control program like the DARE logic block. Moreover, Block CSMP and ISL cannot employ symbolic variable names; Fig. 6-14 illustrates their more primitive method for specifying block interconnections in terms of *block numbers*.

MICRODARE, under development at the University of Arizona,[20,28] employs DARE-type block statements translated into subroutines or microprograms

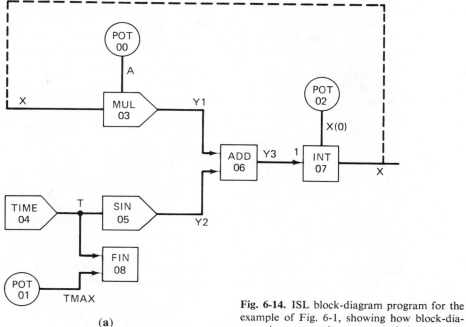

(a)

00	POT	00
01	POT	01
02	POT	02
03	MUL	07, 00
04	TIME	04
05	SIN	04
06	ADD	05, 03
07	INT	02, 06, 1
08	FIN	04, 01
09	END	00

(b)

Fig. 6-14. ISL block-diagram program for the example of Fig. 6-1, showing how block-diagram interconnections are specified. No intuitively suggestive symbolic variables can be used. The Block CSMP language is quite similar. Specifically, POT values are set before simulation. POT 00 sets the coefficient A, POT 01 sets TMAX (the block operator FIN terminates the run when its first input T exceeds its second input), and POT 02 sets the initial integrator output.

"canned" in read-only-memory (ROM) chips. A simple minicomputer BASIC system serves as the operating system and editor and also supplies a DARE-type logic block programmed in BASIC as well as output and display routines. The main purpose of MICRODARE is really not simulation but programming for computer-controlled instrumentation and generation of programs to be loaded into microcomputers. Since most such programs are short enough to be readily hand-sorted into procedural order, MICRODARE's fast translator does not do any sorting. As with Block CSMP and ISL, no disk is required.

6-12. Simulation Performance Studies. Selection criteria for simulation-language systems are **programming convenience** (which is the reason for using a simulation language), **execution speed,** and, especially for interactive simulations requiring frequent model changes, **translation speed.** Computer **memory requirements** are less important, since extra memory is becoming very cheap.

Interactive interpreter and on-line compiler languages such as interpreted Block CSMP and SIMEX translate about as quickly as new programs can be typed, and the same is true for ISL and MICRODARE (Sec. 6-11). But even the powerful CSSL-type simulation languages require only tens of seconds for translation.

Execution speed, vital for real-time simulation and for multirun statistical and optimization studies, depends on the computer hardware and on software efficiency. FORTRAN-based CSSL languages should execute as quickly as FORTRAN, and a good block-diagram program should be faster. Performance prediction is further complicated by the fact that smooth derivative functions permit the use of high-order predictor-corrector integration routines (Appendix A) with relatively large DT steps, while discontinuous forcing functions (typical of many control problems) require Runge-Kutta integration and short steps. A rough measure of "simulation bandwidth" *for a given problem* is the real-time frequency f of the fastest sine wave which can be generated with at least 25 DT steps per sine-wave period, or

$$f = \frac{1}{25 \ (\text{max. real time per } DT \text{ step})} \tag{6-20}$$

The time per DT step can be estimated from the required number of computer operations, the instruction execution time for the machine used, and an educated guess at the software efficiency. Table 6-2 shows the resulting very rough estimates for a typical aerospace problem solved with different simulation languages and computers. More accurate performance comparisons require solution of well-accepted **benchmark problems.** In Secs. 6-13 and 6-14 we shall describe what is, unfortunately, the only well-accepted simulation benchmark problem tried on most current simulation systems. Table 6-3 lists results of a few other documented performance measurements.

6-13. The PHYSBE Blood-Circulation Model (PHYsiological BEnchmark Problem)[6-11]

a. Model description. Figure 6-15 shows a simplified model of human blood circulation. The myriad of different blood vessels have been abstracted into seven compartments, viz., two heart chambers, aorta, vena cava, two lung compartments, and "systemic circulation," which describes body, head, and limbs. In each compartment, the *blood volume* is introduced as a state variable:

$$\frac{d}{dT} \text{VOLUME} = \text{FLOW}_{\text{IN}} - \text{FLOW}_{\text{OUT}} \tag{6-21}$$

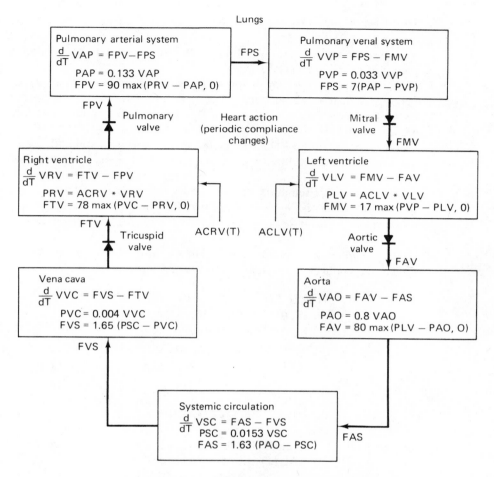

Fig. 6-15. Blood-circulation model for the PHYSBE benchmark problem (based on References 6 and 7).

Flows are driven by *pressures* determined in each department by the linearized elasticity relation

$$\text{PRESSURE} = \frac{1}{\text{COMPLIANCE}} \text{VOLUME} \qquad (6\text{-}22)$$

so that

$$\text{FLOW}_{\text{compartment 1 to 2}} = \text{ADMITTANCE}(\text{PRESSURE}_1 - \text{PRESSURE}_2) \quad (6\text{-}23a)$$

If there is a heart valve between compartments, then only positive flow is possible, i.e.,

$$\text{FLOW}_{\text{compartment 1 to 2}} = \text{ADMITTANCE} * \text{MAX}(\text{PRESSURE}_1 - \text{PRESSURE}_2, 0)$$

$$(6\text{-}23b)$$

Volumes are represented in milliliters, flows in milliliters per second, and blood pressures in millimeters of mercury.

Circulation is driven by the pumping action of the heart, which we represent by making the heart-chamber compliances CRV, CLV (really their reciprocals ACRV, ACLV) periodic functions of the time *T*. The other compliances and admittances are constants.

One can make the PHYSBE model much more realistic and detailed by subdividing the various blood vessels into more compartments and by making some of the relations (6-22) and/or (6-23) nonlinear. Such models have been used for studying various circulatory diseases and weightlessness effects in space flight. In the simple form of Fig. 6-15 the PHYSBE simulation has been very useful as *a benchmark problem for comparing different computer simulation systems* (Sec. 6-14).

b. Equation-language program. A DARE derivative-file program for PHYSBE directly reproduces the system equations of Fig. 6-16(a):

```
* SYSTEM EQUATIONS (RIGHT VENTRICLE)
    VRV   = FTV-FPV
    PRV   = ACRV*VRV
    FTV   = 78*AMAX(PVC-PRV,0.0)
* SYSTEM EQUATIONS (LEFT VENTRICLE)
    VLV   = FMV-FAV
    PLV   = ACLV*VLV
    FMV   = 17*AMAX(PVP-PLV,0.0)
```

and so forth. To simulate the periodic heart action, we first generate a *periodic sawtooth waveform* TAU(T) with the procedural block (Sec. 3-10.b)

```
        PROCED TAU = P
        IF (T.EQ.0.0) K = 0
5       FK = K
        TAU = T/P-FK
        IF (TAU.LT.1.0) GO TO 10
        K = K+1
        GO TO 5
10      CONTINUE
        ENDPRO
```

The periodic coefficients ACRV and ACLV are then generated as *tabulated functions* of TAU (Fig. 6-16), or

$$ACRV = F1T(TAU)$$
$$ACLV = F2T(TAU)$$

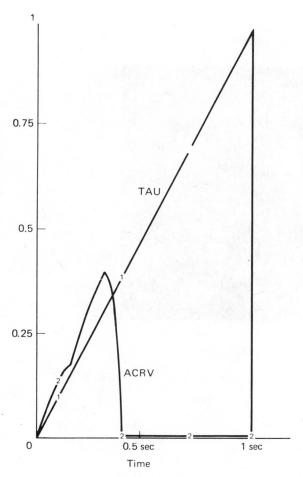

TAU

ACRV

0.5 sec

1 sec

Time

Fig. 6-16. (a) PHYSBE output, showing generation of the periodic function ACRV as a tabulated function of the periodic sawtooth waveform TAU. ACLV is generated in the same manner. (b) and (c) PHYSBE output (Reference 8).

(a)

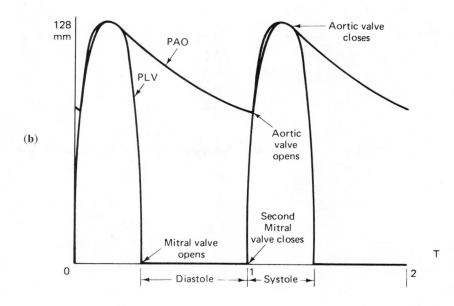

(b)

128 mm

PAO

PLV

Aortic valve closes

Aortic valve opens

Second Mitral valve closes

Mitral valve opens

T

0

Diastole

Systole

1

2

161

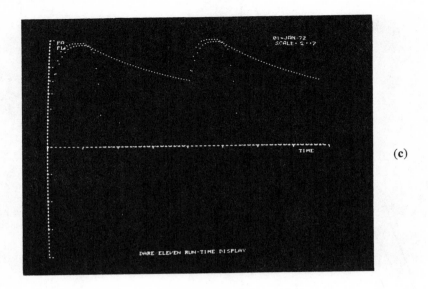

(c)

with the aid of two table blocks (Sec. 3-8):

* TABLE BLOCK NO. 1:	
F1T, 12	
0.0,	0.0033
0.04,	0.05
0.08,	0.1
0.12,	0.15
0.16,	0.17
0.20,	0.24
0.24,	0.30
0.28,	0.36
0.32,	0.4
0.36,	0.3
0.40,	0.0033
1.00,	0.0033

* TABLE BLOCK NO. 2:	
F2T, 12	
0.00,	0.0066
0.04,	0.06
0.08,	1.0
0.12,	1.25
0.16,	1.4
0.20,	1.5
0.28,	1.6
0.32,	1.6
0.36,	1.5
0.36,	1.0
0.40,	0.0066
1.0,	0.0066

Volumes, pressures, and flows will become periodic after an initial transient, which can be minimized by initial conditions approximating the start of a steady-state period:

$$VRV = 150 \text{ ml} \quad VLV = 150 \text{ ml}$$
$$VAP = 120 \text{ ml} \quad VAO = 100 \text{ ml}$$
$$VVP = 240 \text{ ml} \quad VSC = 3340 \text{ ml}$$
$$VVC = 500 \text{ ml}$$

The system is fairly stiff (Appendix A), but values of DT ≤ 0.01 give acceptable results with second- and fourth-order Runge-Kutta integration (Fig. 6-16).

   c. Block-diagram program. Figure 6-17 shows a scaled DARE block-diagram program for PHYSBE; a limiter block LIM Y, X has the output

$$Y = \max (X, 0) = \begin{cases} X & (X > 0) \\ 0 & (X \leq 0) \end{cases} \tag{6-24}$$

Instead of implementing a sawtooth oscillator, the program simply runs for one heartbeat period (1 second) and then repeats runs without resetting the integrators. The quantities denoted as PVC, PRV, . . . in Fig. 6-17 are actually scaled quantities a_{PVC} PVC, a_{PRV} PRV, ... The scale factors, determined by a preliminary equation-language run, are numerically equal to

   1/100 for PVC, PRV, PAP, PSC, PVC, DVSC
   1/200 for PVP, PAO, VRV, VAP, VLV, VAO, DVVC
   1/400 for VVP
   $1/10^4$ for all flows except FAV, which has the scale factor $1/2 * 10^4$.

6-14. PHYSBE Performance Comparisons. The PHYSBE benchmark problem is a seventh-order problem (seven state-variable integrations). Typical derivative-block implementations involve

   21 additions or subtractions
   15 multiplications
    4 limiters
    2 function generators (table lookup/interpolation)

which are executed twice for each of 100 second-order Runge-Kutta integration steps per simulated heartbeat (half as many with Euler integration, resulting in lower accuracy). The PHYSBE benchmark problem thus illustrates a fair variety of operations typical of biological and control-system simulations. On the other hand, PHYSBE is not a good test for aerospace simulation performance, which would usually require more trigonometrical functions.

   Table 6-4 compares actual PHYSBE results obtained with several large and small digital computers, using both equation and block-diagram simulation systems. The results would seem to indicate that Block CSMP is obsolete. The fixed-point DARE block-diagram program and SIMEX run faster on inexpensive minicomputers than the FORTRAN-based systems on IBM 360/65 and CDC 6400. The minicomputers are, however, more prone to roundoff-error accumulation in long simulation runs.

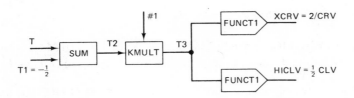

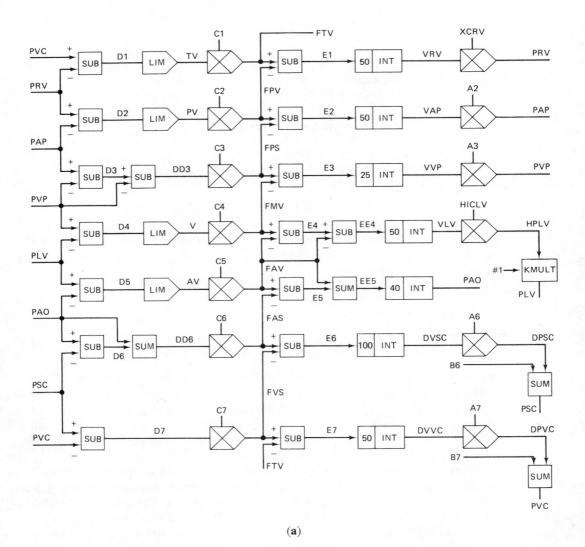

(a)

Fig. 6-17. (a) DARE PHYSBE block-diagram program for one heartbeat. Repeated heartbeats are simulated by repeating runs without CALL RESET. (b) DARE program for the PHYSBE block diagram of Fig. 6-17(a).

* DERIVATIVE BLOCK NO. 1:		* TABLE BLOCK NO. 1:		*DATA:	

```
* DERIVATIVE BLOCK NO. 1:        * TABLE BLOCK NO. 1:        *DATA:

/PHYSBE—————                      CRV,4                      DT = .0040
/                                0.0066                     TMAX = .99
        SUM     T2,T,T1          0.16                       VRV = 0.75
        KMULT   T3,T2,#1         0.32                       VAP = 0.6
        FUNCT   XCRV,T3,CRV      0.45                       VVP = 0.6
        FUNCT   HICLV,T3,CLV     0.625                      VLV = 0.75
  *                              0.78                       PAO = 0.4
        SUBTR   D1,PVC,PRV       0.27                       DVSC = 0.0
        LIM     TV,D1            0.0066                     DVVC = 0.0
        MULT    FTV,TV,C1        0.0066
        SUBTR   E1,FTV,FPV       0.0066
        INTGRT  VRV,E1,G1        0.0066                     A2 = 0.266
        MULT    PRV,VRV,XCRV     0.0066                     C1 = 0.78
  *                              0.0066                     C2 = 0.9
        SUBTR   D2,PRV,PAP       0.0066                     C3 = 0.07
        LIM     PV,D2            0.0066                     A3 = 0.066
        MULT    FPV,PV,C2        0.0066                     C4 = 0.34
        SUBTR   E2,FPV,FPS       0.0066                     C7 = 0.0165
        INGRT   VAP,E2,G2                                   C5 = 0.8
        MULT    PAP,VAP,A2                                  C6 = 0.0163
  *                                                         A7 = 0.008
        SUBTR   D3,PAP,PVP       *TABLE BLOCK No. 2:        A6 = 0.0153
        SUBTR   DD3,D3,PVP                                  T1 = −0.5
        MULT    FPS,DD3,C3       CLV,4                      B6 = 0.512
        SUBTR   E3,FPS,FMV       0.0033                     B7 = 0.02
        INTGRT  VVP,E3,G3        0.41
        MULT    PVP,VVP,A3       0.63
  *                              0.73
        SUBTR   D4,PVP,PLV       0.8
        LIM     MV,D4            0.76
        MULT    FMV,MV,C4        0.25
        SUBTR   E4,FMV,FAV       0.0033
        SUBTR   EE4,E4,FAV       0.0033
        INTGRT  VLV,EE4,G4       0.0033
        MULT    HPLV,VLV,HICLV   0.0033
        KMULT   PLV,HPLV,#1      0.0033
  *                              0.0033
        SUBTR   D5,PLV,PAO       0.0033
        LIM     AV,D5            0.0033
        MULT    FAV,AV,C5        0.0033
        SUBTR   E5,FAV,FAS       0.0033
        SUM     EE5,E5,FAV
        INTGRT  PAO,EE5,G5
  *
        SUBTR   D6,PAO,PSC
        SUM     DD6,D6,PAO
        MULT    FAS,DD6,C6
        SUBTR   E6,FAS,FVS
        INTGRT  DVSC,E6,G6
        MULT    DPSC,DVSC,A6
        SUM     PSC,DPSC,B6
  *
        SUBTR   D7,PSC,PVC
        MULT    FVS,D7,C7
        SUBTR   E7,FVS,FTV
        INTGRT  DVVC,E7,G7
        MULT    DPVC,DVVC,A7
        SUM     PVC,DPVC,B7
  *
        STORE   PLV,PAO,XCRU,HICLV,PVP
        DISPLAY PLV,PAO,T
```

Fig. 6-17. (b)

TABLE 6-4. Comparison of PHYSBE Benchmark Problem Execution Times for One Heartbeat (1-sec real time; 0.01-sec integration step)[7-11]

(a) Batch-Processed, Equation-Oriented, Floating-Point Languages, Large Computers			
System	*Computer*	*Integration Routine*	*Execution Time (sec)*
FORTRAN	CDC 3600	Not known	2
CSMP III	IBM 360/50	Not known	1.46
	IBM 360/65	Not known	0.42
DARE P	CDC 6400	Runge-Kutta 2	0.16
		Runge-Kutta-Merson (0.001 rel. error)	0.91
RSSL	CDC 6600	Runge-Kutta 2	0.056

(b) Interactive, Equation-Oriented, Floating-Point Language, Minicomputers			
DARE/ELEVEN	DEC PDP-11/40		
	Floating-point software (DOS)	Runge-Kutta 2	6.5
	Floating-point firmware (RT-11)	Runge-Kutta 2	3.6
	DEC PDP-11/45		
	Core memory, floating-point software (DOS)	Runge-Kutta 2	4.5
	Bipolar memory, floating-point hardware	Runge-Kutta 2	<1.2*

(c) Interactive, Block-Diagram, Floating-Point Languages, Minicomputers			
Block CSMP	IBM 1130		
	Interpreter mode	Runge-Kutta 2	40
	Compiler mode	Runge-Kutta 2	20
	DEC PDP-11/45	Not known	14.6
	FP software only		
ISL-11†	DEC PDP-11/20	Euler	1.4
	DEC PDP-11/45	Runge-Kutta 2	2.8
	FP software only	Euler	0.6

(d) Interactive, Block-Diagram, Fixed-Point Languages, Minicomputers (with hardware multiplication)			
DARE II	DEC PDP-9	Runge-Kutta 2	0.2
DARE/ELEVEN	DEC PDP-11/40	Runge-Kutta 2	0.19
	DEC PDP-11/45	Runge-Kutta 2	0.06*
	bipolar memory		

(e) Interactive, Equation-Oriented, Fixed-Point Language with Semiautomatic Scaling, Minicomputers (with hardware multiplication)			
SIMEX	DEC PDP-9	Euler	0.19
	DEC PDP-15	Euler	0.15*

*Estimated.

†ISL used *Mini-point* (fast, low-resolution floating-point software with a 16-bit mantissa) for derivative computation and also made a nonadaptive step-size change to DT = 0.03 sec, based on a preliminary trial run. Other minicomputer floating-point systems used a 24-bit mantissa for derivative computation.

REFERENCES AND BIBLIOGRAPHY

DARE Block-Diagram Systems

1. LIEBERT, T. A., "The DARE II On-Line Simulation System," *Proc. Summer Simulation Conference, Denver*, 1970; also *Ann. AICA*, Jan. 1972.

2. KORN, G. A., "Ultra-Fast Minicomputation with a Simple Microprogrammed Block-Diagram Language," *Proc. SWIEECO, Houston*, 1973; also *Trans. ASEE/COED*, March 1974.

3. KORN, G. A., "Recent Computer-System Developments and Continuous-System Simulation," *Proc. 7th AICA Conference, Prague*, 1973; also *Ann. ACIA*, April 1974.

4. AUS, H. M., and G. A. KORN, "Table-Lookup/Interpolation Function Generation for Fixed-Point Digital and Hybrid Computers," *IEEETC*, Aug. 1969.

5. CONLEY, S., "Comparison of Block-Diagram-Language Routines Microprogrammed on Four Different Minicomputers," *CSRL Report No. 259*, University of Arizona, Tucson, Oct. 1974.

The PHYSBE Benchmark Problem

6. MCLEOD, J., "PHYSBE, A Physiological Simulation Benchmark Experiment," *Simulation*, Dec. 1966.

7. BENHAM, R. D., "ISL-8 and ISL-15 Study of PHYSBE," *Simulation*, April and Aug. 1972; see also "ISL-11 Study of PHYSBE," *Proc. DECUS Symposium*, Fall 1974, Digital Equipment Corp., Maynard, Mass., 1974.

8. KORN, G. A., J. MCLEOD, and J. V. WAIT, "DARE/PHYSBE," *Simulation*, Nov. 1970.

9. KORN, G. A., "Language Comparisons for the PHYSBE Benchmark Problem," *Simulation*, May 1973.

10. MITCHELL, E. E. L., "PHYSBE in the Raytheon Scientific Simulation Language (RSSL)," *Simulation*, March 1974.

11. FRANKLIN, M. A., and B. A. FRELEK, "Continuous-System Simulation on Four Digital Computers," *Simulation*, Aug. 1974.

Miscellaneous Simulation Languages

12. BRENNAN, R. D., and H. SANO, "PACTOLUS—A Digital Simulator Program for the IBM 1620," *Proc. FJCC*, 1964.

13. BRENNAN, R. D., and M. Y. SILBERBERG, "Two Continuous-System Modeling Programs," *IBM Systems J.*, April 1967.

14. RECHENBERG, P., "Simulationssysteme für Digitalrechner," Doctoral thesis, Technical University, West Berlin, 1969.

15. MILLER, D. S., and M. J. MERRITT, "MOBSSL-UAF," *Proc. FJCC*, 1969.

16. BENHAM, R. D., "Interactive Simulation Language-8 (ISL-8)," *Simulation*, March 1971 (see also Reference 7).

17. BROWN, G., "Multi-User Simulation via a Small Digital Computer," *Proc. 7th AICA Conference, Prague*, 1973.

18. WORTH, G. A., "SIMEX—Simulation Executive and Compiler," *Proc. SCSC*, 1974.

19. MARTINEZ, R., "A Semi-portable Simulation System Using Both Fixed and Floating Point Derivative Blocks," PH.D. thesis, University of Arizona, Tucson, 1975; see also *Proc. DECUS Fall Symposium, San Diego*, 1974.

20. CONLEY, S., "MICRODARE/BASIC," Ph.D. dissertation, University of Arizona, Tucson, 1977.

DARE Real-Time Applications

21. KORN, G. A., "New Methods for Hybrid and Digital Simulation," *Proc. 6th AICA Conference, Munich*, 1970.

22. SPINHIRNE, J., "PDP-9/Transient-Recorder Interface and of its Use with the DARE II Operating System," *CSRL Report No. 251*, University of Arizona, Tucson, Nov. 1973.

23. KREBAUM, K., "Use of the DARE II Language/Operating System for Testing Real-World Devices, Interface Test Programs," *CSRL Report No. 247*, University of Arizona, Tucson, Oct. 1973.

24. KREBAUM, K., and D. SCHNABEL, "EKG Transfer Programs," *CSRL Report No. 256*, University of Arizona, Tucson, Oct. 1973.

25. KORN, G. A., and O. PALUSINSKI, "Ultra-Fast Hybrid Analog-Digital Computation with Convenient Simulation-Language Software," *Trans.* IMACS, Vol. XVIII, No. 1, January 1976.

Multiprocessor Systems and Microprocessors

26. KORN, G. A., "Back to Parallel Computation: Proposal for a Completely New On-Line Simulation Using Standard Minicomputers for Low-Cost Multiprocessing," *Simulation*, Aug. 1972; see also *Best Computer Papers of 1972*, Auerbach, Philadelphia, 1973.

27. KORN, G. A., *Minicomputers for Engineers and Scientists*, McGraw-Hill, New York, 1973.

28. KORN, G. A., "A Study of Simplified Microcomputer Programming," *CSRL Report No. 264*, University of Arizona, Tucson, Sept. 1974.

29. KORN, G. A., and T. M. KORN, *Electronic Analog and Hybrid Computers*, 2nd ed., McGraw-Hill, New York, 1972.

Miscellaneous

30. SCHRAM, D., and J. BOREN, "A Real-Time 6-Degree-of-Freedom Aircraft Simulation with SL-1," *Proc. SCSC*, 1970.

A

Integration Routines

A-1. Introduction. At least as far back as Euler's time (late eighteenth century), countless individuals have developed schemes for accurate and efficient numerical integration of ordinary differential equations. Here we shall restrict ourselves to a selection of methods which are useful either for a large class of problems or for their pedagogical value in tracing the state of the art. Many references are given; Gear's book,[3] in particular, gives an excellent presentation.

The choice of a particular algorithm is governed by many factors. Certainly **numerical-integration errors** due to numerical approximations and finite word-length (roundoff) effects are important. Overall **computing effort**, in terms of processor seconds, is also important, particularly in real-time simulations and in large multi-run studies. For some installations, **computer memory requirements** limit the use of the more sophisticated integration routines.

A-2. General Form of Numerical-Integration Formulas. In the simulation of continuous-time systems, the primary numerical task is the approximate integration of a vector first-order differential equation

$$\frac{dX}{dT} = X' = G(X, T) \tag{A-1}$$

We want to approximate, for $T = 0, T_1, T_2, \ldots,$

$$X(T_{k+1}) = X(0) + \int_0^{T_{k+1}} G(X, T)\, dt = X(T_k) + \int_{T_k}^{T_{k+1}} G(X, T)\, dt \tag{A-2}$$

by

$$^{k+1}X \approx {}^kX + {}^kQ \tag{A-3}$$

with

$$^kQ \approx \int_{T_k}^{T_{k+1}} G(X, T)\, dt \tag{A-4}$$

Note that ^kX is an **approximation** to the **true solution value** $X(T_k)$; ^kQ, in turn, differs from the true integral.

A-3. Multistep Rules. *Multistep rules* utilize *past* values ^{k-i}X and ^{k-i}G to approximate an updated solution value ^{k+1}X in the form (for equal step-size, DT)

$$^{k+1}X = \sum_{i=0}^{P} A_i^{k-i}X + DT \sum_{i=-1}^{P} B_i^{k-i}G \tag{A-5}$$

where

$$^kG = G(^kX, T_k) \tag{A-6}$$

If $B_{-1} = 0$, then the rule will be called an **explicit** or **open rule**, or a **predictor**, since the future value ^{k+1}G is not used. For $B_{-1} \neq 0$, the rule is an **implicit** or **closed rule**, or a **corrector**; note that the right-hand side of Eq. (A-5) now contains the unknown ^{k+1}X. **Multistep methods** store past values of ^kX and ^kG and require a single **derivative call** (computation of the derivative G) per integration step (see also Sec. 1-7).

The coefficients A_i, B_i are selected so as to make the rule (A-5) exact for a polynomial of degree R, viz.,

$$X = C_0 + C_1T + \ldots + C_RT^R \tag{A-7}$$

with a small remainder (error) and a large region of stability (Sec. A-9), plus a choice of coefficients which are simple and minimize roundoff errors.

Table A-1 lists several popular rules of this type called the **Adams-Bashforth predictors** ($B_{-1} = 0$) and the **Adams-Moulton correctors**. In each of these we make $A_0 = 1$ and all other $A_i = 0$; thus

$$\sum_{i=-1}^{P} B_i = 1 \tag{A-8}$$

This approach ensures unity gain for integration of a constant.

A-4. Predictor-Corrector Methods. One often combines a *predictor rule* to estimate ^{k+1}X with a *corrector rule* which improves the estimate and uses the predicted ^{k+1}X to compute ^{k+1}G. Thus with *two* derivative calls per integration step, it may be possible to improve local accuracy and stability. Predictor-corrector methods usually incorporate a strategy to **increase or decrease the integration-step size** DT depending on the difference between predicted and corrected ^{k+1}X values (see below).

A-5. Runge-Kutta Methods. Multistep rules present problems *at the beginning of a solution*, where past values of ^kX are not available, and with *discontinuous derivatives*, where the approximation (A-5) is inaccurate. This usually means that multistep rules have to be started (or restarted) by some form of *single-step, self-starting* algorithm of consistent accuracy.

TABLE A-1. Coefficients for Adams-Bashforth-Moulton Rules, Eq. (A-5)

$$A_0 = 1; \text{ all other } A_i = 0$$

Designation	B_{-1}	B_0	B_1	B_2	B_3	Common Name
P1	0	1	0	0	0	Open or explicit Euler
P2	0	$\frac{3}{2}$	$-\frac{1}{2}$	0	0	Open trapezoidal
P3	0	$\frac{23}{12}$	$-\frac{16}{12}$	$\frac{5}{12}$	0	Adams 3-point predictor
P4	0	$\frac{55}{24}$	$-\frac{59}{24}$	$\frac{37}{24}$	$-\frac{9}{24}$	Adams 4-point predictor
C1	1	0	0	0	0	Closed or implicit Euler
C2	$\frac{1}{2}$	$\frac{1}{2}$	0	0	0	Closed trapezoidal
C3	$\frac{5}{12}$	$\frac{8}{12}$	$-\frac{1}{12}$	0	0	Adams 3-point corrector
C4	$\frac{9}{24}$	$\frac{19}{24}$	$-\frac{5}{24}$	$\frac{1}{24}$	0	Adams 4-point corrector

A self-starting **Runge-Kutta routine of order** N has the form

$$^{k+1}X = {}^kX + \sum_{j=1}^{N} R_i K_i$$

with

$$K_1 = G(^kX, {}^kT)DT \tag{A-9}$$

$$K_i = G\left(^kX + \sum_{j=1}^{i-1} B_{ij}K_j, \; T = {}^kT + DT \sum_{j=1}^{i-1} B_{ij}\right)DT \qquad (i = 2, \dots, N)$$

where the R_i and B_{ij} are selected to fit a polynomial (A-7), with R usually equal to N. In general, the choice of Runge-Kutta coefficients for a given N is not unique; Table A-2 lists coefficients for commonly used Runge-Kutta formulas. Note that open or explicit **Euler integration** (Sec. 1-7) belongs to this class and that **Heun's method** ($N = 2$) is really Euler rule prediction followed by a closed trapezoidal corrector.

TABLE A-2. Coefficients for Runger-Kutta Rules, Eq. (A-9)

Common Name	N	B_{ij}	R_i
Open or explicit Euler	1	All zero	$R_1 = 1$
Improved Polygon	2	$B_{21} = \frac{1}{2}$	$R_1 = 0, \, R_2 = 1$
Modified Euler or Heun's method	2	$B_{21} = 1$	$R_1 = R_2 = \frac{1}{2}$
Third-order Runge-Kutta	3	$B_{21} = \frac{1}{2}$	$R_1 = R_3 = \frac{1}{6}$
		$B_{31} = -1$	$R_2 = \frac{2}{3}$
		$B_{32} = 2$	
Fourth-order Runge-Kutta	4	$B_{21} = \frac{1}{2}$	$R_1 = R_4 = \frac{1}{6}$
		$B_{31} = 0$	$R_2 = R_3 = \frac{1}{3}$
		$B_{32} = \frac{1}{2}$	
		$B_{43} = 1$	

In general, since Runge-Kutta rules are designed to be exact for a polynomial of order N, local numerical approximation errors are of the order

$$\text{Error} \propto DT^{N+1} \frac{d^{N+1}X}{dT^{N+1}} \tag{A-10}$$

A-6. Types of Numerical-Integration Errors. The following discussion summarizes points developed in more detail by Gear.[3] Section A-6c illustrates how the choice of the step size DT can minimize the total error from various sources.

a. Numerical-approximation (truncation) errors. We shall use the terms **numerical-approximation** error or **truncation error** for errors due to the inherent limitations of the integration algorithm; these errors would arise regardless of the digital precision (number of bits in the computer word) used in implementing the algorithm with a computer. With inifinite precision, a given integration scheme would produce a **local** or per-step approximation error

$$^kE = {}^kX - X(T_k) \tag{A-11}$$

for a solution started at T_{k-1}. Often ^kE can be estimated as the solution proceeds. However, a more important quantity is the **total** or **global approximation error**

$$^kE_T = {}^kX - X(T_k) \tag{A-12}$$

for a solution started at $T = 0$. Usually $|{}^kE_T|$ is larger than ^kE and in some cases may grow without bound as T_k increases. Moreover, ^kE_T usually cannot be estimated. *Thus efforts to reduce numerical approximation errors by keeping ^kE within certain bounds may still yield unacceptable total errors.* Usually the per-step numerical-approximation error is reduced by reducing DT, and one can often establish that

$$^kE \propto DT^m$$

so that ^kE can be made quite small by picking a rule where the *exponent of variation m* is high[4,5]; higher-order integration rules usually have a higher value for m.

b. Roundoff errors. In practice, integration algorithms are implemented by computer arithmetic with **finite precision** (finite **word length**, number of bits). This leads to a second class of errors, usually called **roundoff errors.*** **Roundoff errors accumulate and become increasingly serious with increasing integration time TMAX, with integration-rule order N and, unfortunately, with decreasing integration-step size DT**, since a smaller DT means more integration steps for a given TMAX.

---

*Some computer arithmetic units "truncate" or "chop" rather than truly round the portion of, say, a double-precision product not retained in the computation. This is, in particular, true in most two's-complement fixed-point computations. We shall, however, use the term *truncation error* for numerical-approximation errors (Sec. A-6a).

To keep the per-step roundoff error insignificant, we need a resolution of n decimal digits, so that

$$\text{Per-step roundoff error} \approx \frac{1}{2}10^{-n} \ll \underset{i}{\text{MIN}}\{|G_i(X, T_k)|\}DT \qquad \text{(A-13)}$$

where G_i are the elements of the derivative vector in Eq. (A-1). We thus require more digits (or bits) as the local solution rate of change increases and as DT decreases.

Roundoff-error accumulation is not easy to predict accurately. With true rounding, errors may be assumed to be uniformly distributed between plus and minus $\frac{1}{2}10^{-n}$. Thus, for M accumulation steps

$$\text{Total roundoff error (true rounding)} \approx \frac{10^{-n}}{2}\sqrt{\frac{M}{12}} \qquad \text{(A-14a)}$$

where

$$M \approx N\frac{\text{TMAX}}{DT} \qquad \text{(A-14b)}$$

and N is the order of the multistep or Runge-Kutta method used. If the processor used "chops" rather than rounds, we have the crude bound

$$\text{Total roundoff error (chopping)} \approx 10^{-n}M \qquad \text{(A-15)}$$

which is quite a bit worse than (A-14).

c. Roundoff versus numerical-approximation errors: an example. In this section, we shall describe the numerical solution of the second-order linear differential equation

$$\frac{d^2Y}{dT^2} + 2R\frac{dY}{dT} + Y = 0$$

$$Y(0) = 100 \qquad \frac{dY}{dT}\bigg|_0 = 0 \qquad \text{(A-16)}$$

using second- and fourth-order Runge-Kutta rules (Table A-3) on an IBM 7072 with 8 decimal-digit floating-point arithmetic and true rounding.

The equations were solved with several step times DT from 0.001 to 1.0 second and with two values of damping, $R = 0$ (undamped harmonic oscillator) and $R = 0.5$. All runs were made over the range $0 \leq T \leq 13$. Solution values were output for each 0.1 second (except, of course, when $DT > 0.1$), and the error in the value of Y was found by comparison to the analytical solution

$$Y = Ae^{-Rt} * \cos(\omega_d T + \theta)$$

where

$$A = 100/\cos\theta, \qquad \theta = \tan^{-1}(-R/\omega_d), \qquad \omega_d = \sqrt{1 - R^2} \qquad \text{(A-17)}$$

Table A-3 summarizes the results, listing the maximum error occurring during the first 13 seconds of solution and also the error at $T = 12.6$ (just after two cycles for the case $R = 0$). For the case $R = 0.5$, errors were observed near $T = 1.1$ and 4.0 (close to the first extrema).

TABLE A-3. Errors Generated in Solution of Eq. (A-17)

	DT *Step Size* *(sec)*	*Second-Order Runge-Kutta*		*Fourth-Order Runge-Kutta*	
		Max. *Error*	*Error* *at t = 12.6*	*Max.* *Error*	*Error* *at t = 12.6*
$R = 0$	0.001	0.00798	0.00797	0.00797	0.00729
	0.01	0.01832	0.00134	0.00078	0.00078
	0.02	0.07364	0.00197	0.00038	0.00037
	0.05	0.46138	0.00050	0.00021	0.00015
	0.10	1.84962	0.06498	0.00104	0.00013
	0.20	7.46967	0.63649	0.01501	0.00225
	0.50	48.52581	11.43471	0.59470	0.30296
	1.00	315.42655	Blows up	9.48049	Blows up
$R = 0.5$	0.001	0.00105	0.00003	0.00104	0.00003
	0.01	0.00115	0.00003	0.00010	0.00000
	0.02	0.00451	0.00011	0.00005	0.00000
	0.05	0.02869	0.00068	0.00001	0.00000
	0.10	0.11838	0.00285	0.00003	0.00000
	0.20	0.50435	0.01228	0.00107	0.00001
	0.50	3.59918	0.08533	0.01645	0.00001
	1.00	15.97000	0.28289	0.79498	0.03274

The results of Table A-3 show that there is an optimum choice for *DT*, which minimizes the total error due to the combined effects of finite word length and numerical-approximation errors. This optimum choice of *DT* will depend on the *integration rule* and also on the *specific computer* used. For small *DT*, the roundoff error due to finite word-length effects becomes larger, and at larger values of *DT*, the numerical-approximation errors become greater. For example, with $R = 0$, the second-order Runge-Kutta rule gave a minimum peak error of 0.0005 with *DT* = 0.05, and the fourth-order Runge-Kutta gave a minimum peak error of 0.00013 with *DT* = 0.1. Note that solutions generated by the higher-order rule are much less sensitive to the use of a larger step size. Finally, the oscillatory case ($R = 0$) is much more sensitive to increases in the step size. Choice of step size does not strongly influence the peak error generated in the solution of the damped case ($R = 0.5$). Also note that for typical engineering analysis, with 0.1% accuracy, the second-order Runge-Kutta may be used with *DT* = 0.1 (126 steps per cycle), while the fourth-order Runge-Kutta (which has twice the computing effort per step) could be used with *DT* greater than 0.2. Of course, if the solution for the undamped case must be allowed to run for many cycles, then the inherently better stability of the fourth-order method would make it much more desirable. Our example shows that

1. With *smooth derivative functions*, higher-order integration rules may pay off.

2. Although reducing the step size *DT* decreases numerical-integration errors, roundoff errors predominate as *DT* is decreased beyond some optimal point (Fig. A-1).

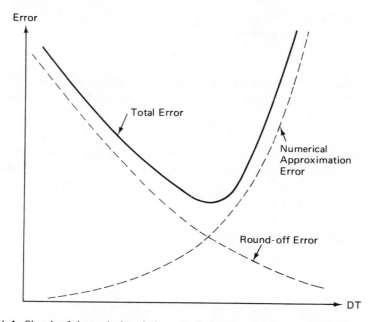

Fig. A-1. Sketch of the typical variation of solution error with step size DT. The solid curve is the total error which might accrue up to a given solution time. The dashed curves show how the error components (roundoff and numerical-approximation errors) individually depend on DT. Note that there is in general an optimum value of DT which reduces the total error to a minimum.

A-7. System Time Constants and Stability. A major reason for problems with numerical integration is that the system to be simulated may have system-response time constants that are short compared to the solution time (this can be true even if the system response is not oscillatory). This may force one to use integration steps *DT* of the order of the smallest time constant, causing not only slow computation but also serious roundoff errors (Sec. A-6).

To be more specific, consider the simple first-order linear equation

$$\frac{dX}{dT} = \lambda X \qquad \text{(A-18)}$$

whose well-known solution is

$$X = X(0)e^{\lambda T} \qquad \text{(A-19)}$$

$|1/\lambda|$ is the *system time constant*; large values of λ are associated with fast transients.

We next consider a vector (column-matrix) linear differential equation

$$\frac{dX}{dT} = AX \tag{A-20}$$

where $X = X(T)$ is an *n*-element column matrix and A is an $n \times n$ matrix. The solution (state vector) is

$$X = X(0)e^{AT} \tag{A-21}$$

which amounts to a linear combination of real and/or complex terms $a_i e^{\lambda_i T}$, where the λ_i are the eigenvalues of the matrix A, or the roots of the characteristic equation

$$\det (A - \lambda I) = 0 \tag{A-22}$$

Here I is the unit (diagonal) matrix. The transient-response speed is related to the **system time constants** $|1/\lambda_i|$. The system (A-18) is **completely stable** (effects of initial-condition changes decay to zero as $T \longrightarrow \infty$) if all eigenvalues λ_i have negative real parts.

A-8. Stiff Systems. For the general nonlinear vector equation

$$\frac{dX}{dT} = G(X, T) \tag{A-23}$$

we similarly speak of **local stability** if the eigenvalues $\lambda_i(X, T)$ of the local **Jacobian matrix**

$$J \equiv \frac{\partial G}{\partial X} \equiv \text{Jac}(G) \tag{A-24}$$

have negative real parts.

A differential-equation system (A-18) or (A-23) will be called **stiff** if the relative range of its local time constants $|1/\lambda_i|$ is large, say larger than 100, for any point (X, T). For example, the system

$$\frac{d^2 X}{dT^2} + 101 \frac{dX}{dT} + 100X = 0 \tag{A-25}$$

is a stiff system with eigenvalues -100 and -1; the solution can contain a "fast" component $a_1 e^{-100T}$ and a "slow" component $a_2 e^{-T}$. Note that the response is nonoscillatory in this case.

A-9. Stability of Integration Rules. Application of numerical-integration rules transforms a given differential-equation system into a system of difference equations. *The latter can be unstable (and thus amplify small numerical errors as the* *solution proceeds) even though the original differential-equation system is completely stable.* Consider open Euler integration applied to the simple differential equation

$$\frac{dX}{dT} = \lambda X \tag{A-26}$$

i.e.,

$$^{k+1}X = {}^{k}X + \lambda^{k}X DT = (1 + \lambda DT)^{k}X \tag{A-27}$$

This difference equation is completely stable only if

$$|1 + \lambda DT| < 1 \tag{A-28}$$

even though the original differential equation (A-26) is completely stable for

$$Re\{\lambda\} < 0 \tag{A-29}$$

Figure A-2 shows the **stability region** determined by Eq. (A-28) for the Euler integration rule ($K = 1$) together with similar plots for various Runge-Kutta rules. Note that although a higher-order rule may provide improved per-step accuracy, the stability regions of the various orders do not differ greatly; as a general rule, one might say that *Runge-Kutta rules can successfully integrate equations of the form* (A-20) *only if all eigenvalues of A satisfy*[12]

$$|\lambda_i| DT < 2\text{–}3 \tag{A-30}$$

Fig. A-2. Stability regions for Runge-Kutta rules of order K. Note that for $K = 1$ we have explicit Euler, with the stability region given by Eq. (A-28). Note that the higher-order rules do not have significantly larger regions of stability but only improved accuracy within the region of stability (Reprinted from Reference 12, with permission of the author.)

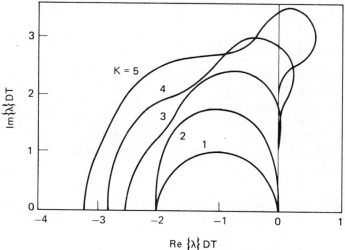

The same restriction holds for nonlinear systems (A-23) if the λ_i are the eigenvalues of the local Jacobian matrix (A-24).

Note carefully that **integration stability can force us to use a painfully small DT even though the transients associated with the larger values λ_i contribute little to our particular solution.**

We are, then, led to seek integration rules with large regions of stability. Dahlquist[11] defined an integration rule as **A-stable** if and only if the numerical solution goes to zero for all DT as $T_k \longrightarrow \infty$ for any asymptotically stable differential-equation system (A-20) (i.e., a system with $Re\{\lambda_i\} < 0$). It can be shown[11] that, of the rules discussed in Secs. A-3 and A-4, *only* the implicit Euler and trapezoidal rules are A-stable; unfortunately, both are implicit and generate relatively large numerical-approximation errors. We shall discuss improved implicit rules in Sec. A-10.

A-10. Implicit (Closed) Integration Rules for Stiff Systems. Since the stiff systems are common in many simulation problems (electric networks, nuclear reactors, blood-flow simulation), **practical digital simulation systems must include at least one stiff-system integration rule.** The most successful rules, though not A-stable, are **implicit methods.** Unfortunately, they require substantial per-step computing effort, but this is often paid for by the possibility of using much larger integration steps.

Implicit rules require solution of a possibly large system of Eq. (A-23) for the vector ^{k+1}X at each step. The typical approach to this problem is to use a form of Newton-Raphson iteration. This involves finding an approximation to the Jacobian of the derivative matrix,

$$J = \frac{\partial G}{\partial X} \tag{A-31}$$

This is usually done by making $n + 1$ calls to the derivative function and finding the local approximations to the elements of J:

$$K_{J_{ij}} \simeq \frac{G_i(^kX + \Delta X_j) - G_i(^kX)}{\Delta X_j}, \qquad j = 1, 2, \ldots, n \tag{A-32}$$

where G_i is the ith element of the nth-order derivative vector. This time-consuming process is obviously only worth doing if DT can be vastly increased, which is indeed the case in many problems. Pope's method was an early successful approach that was popular in several of the large-scale network simulation programs during the mid-1960s. Rosenbrock[13,14] proposed an extension of the Runge-Kutta process to implicit forms. A simple second-order example is

$$K_1 = \left[I - \frac{DT}{2}{}^kJ\right]^{-1}DT^kG \tag{A-32a}$$

$$^{k+1}X = {}^kX + K_1 \tag{A-32b}$$

Calahan[12] presents similar methods. Note that such methods require not only the $n + 1$ call of the derivative function to estimate ^kJ but also the inversion of (possibly large) $n \times n$ matrices at each step. Clearly, a lot of per-step effort is required for a high-ordered set of differential equations. Gear[3,16] has developed his "stiffly stable" strategies, which provide high accuracy for major system eigenvalues of small magnitude and retain stability for relatively unimportant short time constants associated with eigenvalues of large magnitude. Moreover, his methods are variable-order, variable-step strategies. To further reduce average per-step computing effort, Gear recomputes the Jacobian only when tests indicate that the current approximation to J is no longer suitable.

Brayton et al.[17] have also developed an implicit integration scheme which they claim is somewhat faster and which uses sparse-matrix methods to save computing effort. Brandon[20] presents an excellent tutorial discussion of current stiff-system solution methods and presents a new algorithm which takes advantage of the fact that the Jacobian matrix is typically sparse. Although we have not had an opportunity at this writing to test Brandon's method, it appears to be a promising alternative to Gear's approach. His tests indicate that it can handle oscillatory systems well, which is not true of most implicit methods. Gear[16] has also noted that his implicit schemes work not only for ordinary differential equations but for implicit algebraic equations, thus removing the usual requirement for eliminating algebraic loops from the system equations. Indeed, a suitably expanded implicit-integration scheme could eliminate the requirement for sorting system equations.

Shortly before this book went to press, we obtained a copy of the EPISODE package (Byrne and Hindmarsh[21]). This is an extension of Gear's method which they claim is more truly variable-step. Our preliminary tests of EPISODE are quite favorable.

A-11. Numerical Integration with Adaptive Step-Size Changes. Adaptive changes of the integration-step size DT can ensure that at least *local* per-step errors remain within specified bounds as the integration algorithm adapts to local changes in system time constants. Such strategies also save computing effort by allowing larger DT steps for much of the computation.

a. Multistep (*predictor-corrector*) methods. We use a **predictor formula** (Table A-1) to form a first estimate of $^{k+1}X_{\text{PRED}}$. This is then used to compute the predicted derivative vector $^{k+1}G_{\text{PRED}}$ in an **implicit corrector formula** to find an improved solution value $^{k+1}X_{\text{CORR}}$. The corrector can be iterated to improve the estimate (this is only rarely done), or a fraction of

$$^{k+1}X_{\text{PRED}} - {}^{k+1}X_{\text{CORR}} \tag{A-33}$$

may be added to $^{k+1}X_{\text{CORR}}$. A common approach combines the fourth-order Adams predictor P4 with the fourth-order corrector C4 from Table A-1. The **local per-step error** is approximated by

$$^{k+1}E \approx \frac{19}{270} (^{k+1}X_{\text{PRED}} - {}^{k+1}X_{\text{CORR}}) \tag{A-34}$$

Note that only two derivative calls per step are needed.

We now double or halve the integration step DT depending on the error estimate (A-34) (Sec. A-12). One saves appropriate past values of X and G for use when DT is **doubled**. To **halve** DT, though, the new values of X at the smaller spacing must be found through some self-starting algorithm, usually a Runge-Kutta rule. This is cumbersome in problems with *derivative discontinuities*, e.g., due to switching operations.

 b. Variable-step Runge-Kutta methods. To get a local per-step error estimate, one may **simultaneously compute** ^{k+1}X **by Runge-Kutta rules of two different orders and take their difference.** Computation is minimized through a clever choice of Runge-Kutta coefficients such that some intermediate results are common to both Runge-Kutta formulas.[6,9] Table A-4 shows examples of such rules, which are self-starting and are usually a good choice for nonstiff systems. The **Runge-Kutta-Merson rule,** used in many digital simulation systems, is probably inferior to the **Runge-Kutta-Fehlberg 4(5) rule.** Runge-Kutta-Fehlberg 1(2) may be of particular interest for fast integration. The orders of the two Runge-Kutta rules used may also differ by more than 1.

 Chai[8] has developed methods to implement a similar algorithm which uses some information about the *past step* to reduce the number of derivative evaluations, except when the step size is to be changed.

A-12. Step-Size-Change Strategies. As noted in Sec. A-6, the choice of the step size DT will be governed by a compromise among truncation error, roundoff error, and computation effort. In addition, a subset of the *computation times* T_k should coincide with the end points of *communication intervals* (Sec. 3-5) at which simulation output is required.

 Typically, some upper bound on DT satisfies the above requirements, and DT can be reduced by a considerable factor below this bound before roundoff errors significantly increase total computing errors (see Fig. A-1). Unfortunately, it is not always easy to find the best value of DT, and some form of variable-step integration routine is preferable for general-purpose use. This approach usually involves extra per-step computing effort, but the reliability of the results usually warrants this extra effort. For a broad class of practical simulation problems, integral accumulation with at least 36-bit floating-point mantissas (using double-precision accumulation if necessary) makes roundoff errors negligible for step sizes corresponding to a per-step truncation error better than 0.01 %.

TABLE A-4. Coefficients for Special Variable-Step Runge-Kutta Strategies

Method	Coefficients		
	B_{ij}	R_i	S_i
Merson, fourth-order	$B_{21} = 1$	$R_1 = R_5 = \dfrac{1}{6}$	$S_1 = \dfrac{1}{15}$
	$B_{31} = B_{32} = \dfrac{1}{6}$	$R_4 = \dfrac{2}{3}$	$S_3 = \dfrac{-9}{30}$
	$R_{41} = \dfrac{1}{8}, B_{43} = \dfrac{3}{8}$		$S_4 = \dfrac{4}{15}$
	$B_{51} = \dfrac{1}{2}, B_{53} = \dfrac{-3}{2}$		$S_5 = \dfrac{-1}{30}$
	$B_{54} = 2$		
Fehlberg RK4(5), fourth-order	$B_{21} = \dfrac{1}{4}$	$R_1 = \dfrac{16}{135}$	$S_1 = \dfrac{-1}{360}$
	$B_{31} = \dfrac{3}{32}$	$R_3 = \dfrac{6656}{12,825}$	$S_2 = \dfrac{128}{4275}$
	$B_{32} = \dfrac{9}{32}$	$R_4 = \dfrac{28,561}{56,430}$	$S_4 = \dfrac{2197}{75240}$
	$B_{41} = \dfrac{1932}{2197}$	$R_5 = \dfrac{-9}{50}$	$S_5 = \dfrac{-1}{50}$
	$B_{42} = \dfrac{-7200}{2197}$	$R_6 = \dfrac{2}{55}$	$S_6 = \dfrac{-2}{55}$
	$B_{43} = \dfrac{7296}{2197}$		
	$B_{51} = \dfrac{439}{216}$		
	$B_{52} = -8$		
	$B_{53} = \dfrac{3680}{513}$		
	$B_{54} = \dfrac{-845}{4104}$		
	$B_{61} = \dfrac{-8}{27}$		
	$B_{62} = 2$		
	$B_{63} = \dfrac{-3544}{2565}$		
	$B_{64} = \dfrac{1859}{4104}$		
	$B_{65} = \dfrac{-11}{40}$		
Fehlberg RK1(2), second-order	$B_{21} = \dfrac{1}{2}$	$R_1 = R_3 = \dfrac{1}{512}$	$S_1 = \dfrac{1}{512}$
	$B_{31} = \dfrac{1}{256}$	$R_2 = \dfrac{255}{256}$	$S_3 = \dfrac{-1}{512}$
	$B_{32} = \dfrac{255}{256}$		

Coefficients K_i and R_i refer to Eq. (A-9); the error estimate is

$$^kE = \sum_{i=1}^{N} S_i K_i$$

Given the *n per-step truncation-error estimates* $|{}^k E_i|$ obtained from predictor-corrector or Runge-Kutta differences, we, respectively, *halve or double DT* if some specified error measure becomes larger than a specified upper bound EMAX or lower bound EMIN. The error measure used may be

1. The maximum absolute error, $\max_i |{}^k E_i|$.

2. The absolute error $|{}^k E_i|$ in a specified variable of special interest.

3. The *maximum relative error*

$$
{}^k RE = \max_i \left(\frac{{}^k E_i}{|{}^k X_i| + |{}^k X_i - {}^{k-1} X_i| + \delta} \right) \tag{A-35}
$$

where δ is a parameter usually set equal to 1. ${}^k RE$ measures *fractional error* unless some state variable is close to zero. In this case, ${}^k RE$ is more nearly an *absolute-error* measure.

To avoid possible waste of computer time, we specify a *minimum value* DTMIN below which *DT* is no longer halved. We normally also set an *upper bound* DTMAX, typically equal to the communication interval. Finally, to avoid continual halving and doubling of *DT*, most routines prevent *DT* from doubling if it was just halved during the last step, and possibly vice versa.

A-13. Integration-Rule Selection. No one integration rule is best for all purposes. One might begin by asking

1. Are there many derivative-function steps or other discontinuities (e.g., on-off control systems)? This would militate against the use of multistep methods because of the need for frequent restarts.

2. Is the system stiff? If so, can we neglect output of high-frequency solution components? If both are true, special stiff-system routines may be able to use economically large *DT* values.

Our basic goal is to achieve an acceptable limit of error with a near-minimum amount of computing effort. The trade-off between roundoff and numerical-approximation errors is usually not a major factor in our selection if double-precision accumulation of state variables is used. Often we have an upper bound on step size due to the need to output at fairly close communication intervals or due to discontinuities in derivative functions.

In many smooth, well-behaved problems, with no discontinuities in the derivative functions and no stiffness, a second-order Adam's predictor will often work well with one derivative call per step. Runge-Kutta routines are self-starting and provide fair stability; multistep methods have only one or two derivative calls per step and facilitate estimating local error. Shampine et al. report the results of a careful study[19] of many popular multistep and Runge-Kutta methods and conclude that the *fourth-order Runge-Kutta-Fehlberg strategy is often a good choice as a general-purpose integration rule* (see Table A-4). Variable-step rules are generally preferable when there is little a priori knowledge about solutions. On the other hand, fast real-time fixed-point simulation systems may not be able to use variable-step methods.

In general, **interactive simulation systems are especially useful for trying different integration rules and *DT* values on a given problem by comparing computing time and accuracy**; a high-order Runge-Kutta method with small *DT* can often serve as a standard for comparisons.

REFERENCES AND BIBLIOGRAPHY

1. McCracken, D. D., and W. S. Dorn, *Numerical Methods and FORTRAN Programming*, Wiley, New York, 1964.

2. Ralston, A., *A First Course in Numerical Analysis*, McGraw-Hill, New York, 1965.

3. Gear, C. W., *Numerical Initial Value Problems in Ordinary Differential Equations*, Prentice-Hall, Englewood Cliffs, N.J., 1971.

4. Hamming, R. W., *Numerical Methods for Scientists and Engineers*, McGraw-Hill, New York, 1973.

5. Klerer, M., and G. A. Korn, *Digital Computer User's Handbook*, McGraw-Hill, New York, 1967.

6. Merson, R. H., "An Operational Method for the Study of Integration Processes," *Proc. Symp. on Data Processing Weapons Rsch. Estab., Salisbury, South Australia*, 1957.

7. Chai, A. S., and G. H. Burgin, "Comment on Runge-Kutta-Merson Algorithm," *Simulation*, Aug. 1970.

8. Chai, A. S., "Modified Merson's Integration Algorithm Which Saves Two Evaluations at Each Step," *Simulation*, March 1974.

9. Fehlberg, E., "Low-Order Classical Runge-Kutta Formulas with Step-Size Control and Their Application to Some Heat Transfer Problems," *NASA Report TR R-315*, George C. Marchall Space Flight Center, Huntsville, Alabama, April 15, 1969.

10. Schwarz, R. J., and B. Friedland, *Linear Systems*, McGraw-Hill, New York, 1965.

11. Dahlquist, G., "A Special Stability Problem for Linear Multistep Methods," *BIT*, 1963.

12. Calahan, D. A., *Computer-Aided Network Design*, rev. ed., McGraw-Hill, New York, 1972.

13. Rosenbrock, H. A., "Some General Implicit Processes for the Numerical Solution of Differential Equations," *Comp.*, Vol. 5, 1963.

14. Allen, R. H., "Numerically Stable Explicit Integration Techniques Using a Linearized Runge-Kutta Extension," *Report No. 39*, Boeing Scientific Research Laboratories, Information Sciences Laboratory, Seattle, Oct. 1969.

15. SCHICHMAN, H., "Integration System of a Nonlinear Network-Analysis Program," *Trans. IEEE/PGCT*, Vol. CT-17, No. 3, Aug. 1970.

16. GEAR, C. W., "Simultaneous Numerical Solution of Differential-Algebraic Equations," *Trans. IEEE/PGCT*, Vol. CT-18, No. 1, Jan. 1971.

17. BRAYTON, R. K., F. G. GUSTAVSON, and G. D. HACHTEL, "A New Efficient Algorithm for Solving Differential-Algebraic Systems Using Implicit Backward Differentiation Formulas," *Proc. IEEE*, Vol. 60, No. 1, Jan. 1972.

18. POPE, D. A., "An Exponential Method of Numerical Integration of Ordinary Differential Equations," *Comm. ACM*, Vol. 6, No. 8, Aug. 1963.

19. SHAMPINE, L. F., et al., "Solving Non-Stiff Ordinary Differential Equations—the State of the Art," *SIAM Rev.* Vol. 18, No.3, July 1976.

20. BRANDON, D. M., "A New Single-Step Implicit Integration Algorithm with A-Stability and Improved Accuracy," *Simulation*, July 1974.

21. BYRNE, G. D., and A. C. HINDMARSH, "A Polyalgorithm for the Numerical Solution of Ordinary Differential Equations," *ACM Trans. Math. Software*, Vol. 1, No. 1, Jan. 1975.

B

More on the FORTRAN Package

B-1. Portability. We have made an attempt to code the FORTRAN package of Chapter 2 in a manner that will make it easy to adapt it to new systems. To this end, we have used the FTN compiler of the CDC 6400 to check that all code is ANSI standard with some notable exceptions:

> **1.** We have used the non-ANSI input/output statements READ and PRINT *without unit numbers*. Most FORTRAN compilers admit these older "FORTRAN II" statements. Otherwise, the user will discover this on a first compilation; it is easy to convert these statements to two-number FORTRAN IV READ and WRITE commands, with preferred local unit numbers.
> **2.** On systems with *virtual memory*, the user should not attempt to segment or overlay the program; subroutines are assumed to reside in core throughout execution and may need to have temporary storage locations preserved.
> **3.** We use DATA statements to initialize variables in labeled COMMON blocks. Most modern compiler-loader combinations permit this, even though it is not an ANSI standard capability.

We have assumed that character strings, such as titles, can be in *A5 format*. In some short-word-length machines, this may create a problem in the use of INSUB and OUTSUB for specifying and outputting titles, since A5 format may actually involve two or more computer words. In this event, the array TITLE and the associated input format statements in INSUB and output formats in OUTSUB must be changed to fit local requirements.

We have also used *high-precision formats* for listing solution output, e.g., G25.13. Many systems will need this changed.

The user should note that in plotting routines PLOTXT and PLOTXY (Fig. B-3) we have output scale factors in E9.2; a better choice might be 1P9.2, but different FORTRAN compilers seem to treat the P format differently. Local changes may be desirable.

B-2. Required Peripherals. Our subroutine package assumes that the user has a *132-column line printer* for plotting and listing solutions. If an 80-column printer is to be used, the output routines (OUTSUB, PLOTXY, and PLOTXT) will need some minor recoding.

B-3. Interactive Version. We currently have an interactive version of the FORTRAN package running on a DEC-10 via column teletype-format terminals. This was written by D. Freund and may be obtained by writing for Reference 2. The package includes both 80-column and 132-column line-printer plotting routines.

B-4. Subroutines INSUB and RESET.* Figure B-1 provides listings of these data-initialization routines. Their use is described in Sec. 2-7. RESET provides default values for important system variables. The version of INSUB shown is compatible with the general-purpose version of OUTSUB described in Secs. 2-8 and B-5.

B-5. General-Purpose Version of OUTSUB. Figure B-2 provides a listing of the version of OUTSUB described in Sec. 2-8. In addition to the examples in Chapter 2, the following discussion indicates the various output options that may be signaled by data cards via INSUB [Fig. B-1(b)].

No output requests made: If output is desired (OUTPUT=.TRUE.), default is to

> **1.** Listing against time (LISTT) of all the state variables (up to a maximum of four).
> **2.** Plotting against time (PLOTT) of the first two state variables (if there are two; otherwise, plotting of just one against time).
> **3.** Plotting of the first variable against the second. (This is exercised only if there are two variables.)

Explicit requests made:

LISTT	(signal card is always A5, left-justified)
03,02,04,05	(data card is always 5(I2,1X) format)

*See also Sec. 2-8.

```
      SUBROUTINE RESET
C     VERSION 2, DEC. 1970
C     SETS Y"S AND P"S AND MOST SYSVAR TO 0.0
C     SETS TITLE TO V1,V2,V3,V4,BLANK
C     SETS EMAX=0.001,EMIN=0.00001,NPOINT=101,OUTPUT=INIT=.TRUE.
      COMMON/STADER/G
      COMMON/STATEV/Y
      COMMON/UNDVAR/P
      COMMON/OUTVAR/NLIST,NPLOT,NOUT,TITLE,V,IV,ISEL,W
      COMMON/SYSVAR/T,DT,TMAX,TNEXT,DTMAX,DTMIN,EMAX,EMIN,S1,S2,S3,
     1NORDER,NPARAM,NPOINT,K1,K2,K3,INIT,OUTPUT,L1,L2,L3
      DIMENSION TITLE(32),V(10),IV(10),ISEL(25),W(101,4)
      DIMENSION G(20),Y(30),P(20)
      LOGICAL INIT,OUTPUT,L1,L2,L3
      DATA TITLE(1),TITLE(2),TITLE(3),TITLE(4),TITLE(5),TITLE(6),
     1 TITLE(7),TITLE(8),TITLE(9),TITLE(10),TITLE(11),TITLE(12),
     2 TITLE(13),TITLE(14),TITLE(15),TITLE(16),TITLE(17),TITLE(18),
     3 TITLE(19),TITLE(20),TITLE(21),TITLE(22),TITLE(23),TITLE(24),
     4 TITLE(25),TITLE(26),TITLE(27),TITLE(28),TITLE(29),TITLE(30),
     5 TITLE(31),TITLE(32)  /5H     ,5H     ,
     6 5H     ,5H     ,5H     ,5H     ,5H     ,5H     ,
     7 5H     ,5H     ,5H     ,5H     ,5H     ,5H     ,
     8 5H     ,5H     ,5H     ,5H     ,5H     ,5H     ,
     9 5H     ,5H     ,5H     ,5H     ,5H     ,5H     ,
     A 5H     ,5H     ,5H     ,5H     ,5H     ,5H     /
      DATA ISEL(1),ISEL(2),ISEL(3),ISEL(4),ISEL(5)/0,1,2,3,4/
      DATA ISEL(6),ISEL(7),ISEL(8),ISEL(9),ISEL(10)/0,1,2,3,4/
      DATA ISEL(11),ISEL(12),ISEL(13),ISEL(14),ISEL(15)/0,1,2,3,4/
      DATA ISEL(16),ISEL(17),ISEL(18),ISEL(19),ISEL(20)/0,1,2,3,4/
      DATA ISEL(21),ISEL(22),ISEL(23),ISEL(24),ISEL(25)/0,1,2,3,4/
      DO 1 I=1,20
      Y(I)=0.0
      J=I+10
      Y(J)=0.0
    1 P(I)=0.0
      DO 2 I=1,10
      V(I)=0.0
    2 IV(I)=0
      NLIST=0
      NPLOT=0
      NOUT=0
      DT=0.0
      TMAX=0.0
      DTMAX=0.0
      DTMIN=0.0
      S1=0.0
      S2=0.0
      S3=0.0
      K1=0
      K2=0
      K3=0
      L1=.FALSE.
      L2=.FALSE.
      L3=.FALSE.
      EMAX=1.0E-03
      EMIN=1.0E-05
      NPOINT=101
      OUTPUT=.TRUE.
      INIT=.TRUE.
      RETURN
      END
```

Fig. B-1. Initialization subroutines. (a) subroutine RESET.

```
      SUBROUTINE INSUB
C     VERSION 2, DEC. 1970
C     CALL RESET AND THEN SPECIFY NORDER AND NP BEFORE CALLING INSUB
C     USE AN ALPHANUMERIC SIGNAL CARD (FORMAT A5) FOLLOWED BY
C     ASSOCIATED DATA CARDS
C     ITEMS MAY BE PROVIDED IN ANY ORDER
C     NOT ALL ITEMS NEED BE PROVIDED
C     TERMINATE A SET OF DATA WITH A PERIOD AND 4 BLANKS IN COL. 1-5
C     THE SIGNALS AND ASSOCIATED DATA ARE AS FOLLOWS
C     IC             INITIAL CONDITIONS (4E20.13)
C     PARAM          PARAMETERS (4E20.13)
C     DT             (4E20.13)
C     TMAX           (4E20.13)
C     ERROR          EMAX,EMIN,DTMAX,DTMIN (4E20.13)
C     NPOIN          NPOINT (I5)
C     IDENT          IDENTIFICATION (16A5)
C     K              K1,K2,K3 (3I5)
C     L              L1,L2,L3   (3L1)
C     TITLE          SET OF TITLES
C                    FIRST CARD IS 4 10-CHAR. TITLES FOR LISTT
C                    AND 4 10-CHAR. TITLES FOR LISTW
C                    SECOND CARD IS A 40-CHAR. TITLE FOR PLOTT
C                    AND ANOTHER FOR PLOTW
C     LISTT          THE NUMBER OF INDICES AND THE INDICES OF Y(I) TO
C                    BE PRINTED VERSUS T (5(I2,1X))
C     STORE          THE NUMBER OF INDICES AND THE INDICES OF Y(I) TO
C                    BE STORED FOR OUTPUT (5(I2,1X))
C     LISTW          THE NUMBER OF INDICES AND THE INDICES OF W(NOUT,I)
C                    TO BE PRINTED VERSUS TIME
C     PLOTT          THE NUMBER OF INDICES AND THE INDICES OF W(NOUT,I)
C                    TO BE PLOTTED VERSUS TIME (5(I2,1X))
C     PLOTW          THE NUMBER OF INDICES AND THE INDICES OF W(NOUT,I)
C                    TO BE PLOTTED VERSUS THE FIRST INDEX (5(I2,1X))
C     A BLANK SIGNAL WILL STOP EXECUTION WITHIN INSUB
      COMMON/STADER/G
      COMMON/STATEV/Y
      COMMON/UNDVAR/P
      COMMON/OUTVAR/NLIST,NPLOT,NOUT,TITLE,V,IV,ISEL,W
      COMMON/SYSVAR/T,DT,TMAX,TNEXT,DTMAX,DTMIN,EMAX,EMIN,S1,S2,S3,
     1NORDER,NPARAM,NPOINT,K1,K2,K3,INIT,OUTPUT,L1,L2,L3
      DIMENSION TITLE(32),V(10),IV(10),ISEL(25),W(101,4)
      DIMENSION G(20),Y(30),P(20)
      DIMENSION IDENT(16),F(16)
      LOGICAL INIT,OUTPUT,L1,L2,L3
      DATA F(1),F(2),F(3),F(4),F(5),F(6),F(7),F(8),F(9),F(10),F(11),
     1 F(12),F(13),F(14),F(15),F(16)/5HIC   ,5HPARAM,5HDT   ,5HTMAX ,
     2 5HERROR, 5HNPOIN, 5HIDENT, 5HTITLE, 5HK    , 5HL    , 5HLISTT,
     3 5HSTORE, 5HLISTW, 5HPLOTT, 5HPLOTW, 5H.    /
      PRINT 1
1     FORMAT(1H1)
2     READ 3,FLAG
3     FORMAT(A5)
      DO 4 I=1,16
      NTYPE=(I-11)*5
      IF(FLAG.EQ.F(I))GO TO(5,7,8,9,10,12,14,17,19,21,24,24,24,24,24,
```

Fig. B-1. (b) subroutine INSUB.

```
    126),I
  4 CONTINUE
    GO TO 34
  5 READ 6, (Y(I),I=1,NORDER)
  6 FORMAT(4E20.13)
    GO TO 2
  7 READ 6, (P(I),I=1,NPARAM)
    GO TO 2
  8 READ 6,DT
    GO TO 2
  9 READ 6,TMAX
    GO TO 2
 10 READ 6,EMAX,EMIN,DTMAX,DTMIN
    PRINT 11,EMAX,EMIN,DTMAX,DTMIN
 11 FORMAT(/8H EMAX = ,G20.7,8H EMIN = ,G20.7,/9H DTMAX = ,G20.7,
    19H DTMIN = ,G20.7,/)
    GO TO 2
 12 READ 13,NPOINT
 13 FORMAT(3I5)
    GO TO 2
 14 READ 15, IDENT
 15 FORMAT(16A5)
    PRINT 16,IDENT
 16 FORMAT(/1X,16A5/)
    GO TO 2
 17 READ 18, TITLE
 18 FORMAT(16A5)
    GO TO 2
 19 READ 13, K1,K2,K3
    PRINT 20, K1,K2,K3
 20 FORMAT(/6H K1 = ,I5,6H K2 = ,I5,6H K3 = ,I5,/)
    GO TO 2
 21 READ 22,L1,L2,L3
 22 FORMAT(3L1)
    PRINT 23,L1,L2,L3
 23 FORMAT(/6H L1 = ,L1,6H L2 = , L1,6H L3 = ,L1,/)
    GO TO 2
 24 READ 25, ISEL(NTYPE+1),ISEL(NTYPE+2),ISEL(NTYPE+3),
    1ISEL(NTYPE+4),ISEL(NTYPE+5)
 25 FORMAT(5(I2,1X))
    GO TO 2
 26 IF(TMAX.EQ.0.0)GO TO 32
    PRINT 27
 27 FORMAT(19H INITIAL CONDITIONS,/)
    PRINT 28, (I,Y(I),I=1,NORDER)
 28 FORMAT(5X,I2,5X,G25.13)
    PRINT 29
 29 FORMAT(//,11H PARAMETERS,/)
    PRINT 28,(I,P(I),I=1,NPARAM)
    PRINT 30,DT,TMAX
 30 FORMAT( /6H DT = ,G25.13,8H TMAX = ,G25.13 / )
    PRINT 31, NPOINT
 31 FORMAT(/,20H NUMBER OF POINTS = ,I5,/)
    GO TO 36
 32 PRINT 33
 33 FORMAT(9H TMAX = 0,)


    STOP
 34 PRINT 35
 35 FORMAT(20H TERMINATED BY INSUB,)
    STOP
 36 RETURN
    END
```

Fig. B-1. (b) (continued)

```
      SUBROUTINE OUTSUB
C     MODIFIED NOV. 1,1972
C     MODIFIED AUG. 21, 1972
C     VERSION 2, DEC. 1970
      COMMON/STADER/G
      COMMON/STATEV/Y
      COMMON/UNDVAR/P
      COMMON/OUTVAR/NLIST,NPLOT,NOUT,TITLE,V,IV,ISEL,W
      COMMON/SYSVAR/T,DT,TMAX,TNEXT,DTMAX,DTMIN,EMAX,EMIN,S1,S2,S3,
     1NORDER,NPARAM,NPOINT,K1,K2,K3,INIT,OUTPUT,L1,L2,L3
      DIMENSION TITLE(32),V(10),IV(10),ISEL(25),W(101,4)
      DIMENSION G(20),Y(30),P(20),A(4)
      LOGICAL INIT,OUTPUT,L1,L2,L3
      IF(.NOT.INIT)GO TO 1
      COMINT=TNEXT
      IF(NPOINT.GT.101) GO TO 13
      IF(.NOT.((ISEL(1)+ISEL(6)).LE.0))GO TO 1
      ISEL(1)=MINO(NORDER,4)
      ISEL(6)=MINO(NORDER,2)
      ISEL(16)=ISEL(6)
      ISEL(21)=ISEL(6)-1
    1 IF(ISEL(1).LE.0)GO TO 5
C
C     THE FOLLOWING EIGHT STATEMENTS PRINT THE REQUESTED CURRENT
C     VALUES OF THE Y ARRAY.
C
      IF(INIT)PRINT 2,(TITLE(I),I=1,8)
    2 FORMAT(1H1, 12X, 4HTIME, 18X,2A5,15X,2A5,15X,2A5,15X,2A5,//)
      J=ISEL(1)
      DO 3 I=1,J
      K=ISEL(I+1)
    3 A(I)=Y(K)
      PRINT 4,T,(A(I),I=1,J)
    4 FORMAT(1X,5G25.13)
    5 IF(ISEL(6).LE.0)GO TO 7
C
C     THE NEXT FOUR STATEMENTS STORE THE REQUESTED VALUES OF Y
C     IN W (THE STORE FILE).
C
      J=ISEL(6)
      DO 6 I=1,J
      K=ISEL(I+6)
    6 W(NOUT,I)=Y(K)
    7 IF(NPOINT.GT.NOUT)RETURN
      IF(ISEL(11).LE.0)GO TO 10
C
C     THE FOLLOWING NINE STATEMENTS PRINT THE REQUESTED VALUES
C     FROM W.
C
      PRINT 2, (TITLE(I),I=9,16)
      T=0.0
      K=ISEL(11)
      DO 9 I=1,NPOINT
      DO 8 J=1,K
      L=ISEL(J+11)
```

Fig. B-2. Subroutine OUTSUB.

```
    8 A(J)=W(I,L)
      PRINT 4,T,(A(J),J=1,K)
    9 T=T+COMINT
   10 IF(ISEL(16).LE.0)GO TO 12
C
C
C     THE FOLLOWING FIVE STATEMENTS PLOT THE REQUESTED VARIABLES
C     IN W AGAINST TIME.
C
      PRINT 11, (TITLE(I), I=17,24)
   11 FORMAT(1H1, 8X, 8A5)
      J=ISEL(16)
      I=ISEL(17)
      CALL PLOTXT(0.0,COMINT,W(1,I),101,J,NPOINT,0.0,0.0)
   12 IF(ISEL(21).LE.0)RETURN
C
C     THE REST OF THIS SUBROUTINE DOES THE X-Y PLOTS.
C
      PRINT 11, (TITLE(I), I=25,32)
      I=ISEL(21)
      J=ISEL(22)
      K=ISEL(23)
      CALL PLOTXY(W(1,J),W(1,K),101,I,NPOINT,0.0,0.0,0.0,0.0)
      RETURN
   13 PRINT 14
   14 FORMAT(32H NPOINT .GT. 101, JOB TERMINATED )
      STOP
      END
```

Fig. B-2. (continued)

This command requests that three variables be listed against time: specifically, Y(2), Y(4), and Y(5). Note that

LISTT

03,04,02,05

is legal and reserves the positions of Y(2) and Y(4) on the output page.

STORE

03,01,03,06

This command requests that three variables be stored for future plotting or listing: specifically, STORE Y(1), Y(3), and Y(6) as W(I,1), W(I,2), and W(I,3). Note that the variables can be stored in any order. For example,

STORE

03,06,01,03

will store the same variables but will assign Y(6) to W(I,1), Y(1) to W(I,2), and Y(3) to W(I,3).

It is important to remember that in using data cards with signals STORE, LISTT, PLOTT, and PLOTW *the first number is the number of indices to follow*. When using LISTW, PLOTT, and PLOTW, the indices of arrays to be displayed reference the W array, not the original indices on the Y array. For example,

STORE

03,01,04,07   (commas optional)

stores Y(1), Y(4), and Y(7). To plot Y(4) and Y(7) versus time then use

PLOTT

02,02,03

since these were the second and third arrays in the order of storage.

Once variables have been stored, any of the remaining three output commands can be used.

LISTW

02,03,02

This command will list against time the third and second variables stored in the W file.

PLOTT

03,01

This will plot against time three variables from W starting with the first one and proceeding through the third. Note that this statement is implicitly

PLOTT
03,01,02,03

The remaining arguments are implied. Note here that it is not possible to select any variable at random from the W file for **PLOTT** or **PLOTW**. It is only possible to select successive variables from W for plotting by both **PLOTT** and **PLOTW**.

PLOTW
03,01,01   (02,03 implied)

will plot three variables against the variable stored in W(I,1), namely, W(I,1), W(I,2), and W(I,3).

Manipulation of the **STORE** command makes it possible to LISTW, PLOTT, or **PLOTW** any four variables in any combination.

For example, suppose we would like to

1. List against time Y(1), Y(3), Y(4), Y(6), Y(21), and Y(22),
2. Plot against time Y(6) and Y(3), and
3. Plot against Y(4) both Y(6) and Y(21).

The following sets of commands would accomplish these functions:

LISTT
02,01,22
STORE
04,04,03,06,21
LISTW
04,02,01,03,04
PLOTT
02,02   (03 implied)
PLOTW
02,01,03   (04 implied)

Samples of typical output may be seen in Figs. 2-7(e) and (f) and 2-9(e).

B-6. Line-Printer Plotting Routines. These routines are intended to be used with a 132-column line printer (Fig. B-3). Although they are normally used in a self-scaling mode, the user may override self-scaling with his own display range. The calling statements are as follows:

CALL PLOTXT (TO,DT,X,NXDIM,NFUN,NPNT,XMINZ,XMAXZ)

where TO is the starting value of the independent variable,

DT is the increment of the independent variable,

X(NXDIM,NFUN) is an array of values of dependent variables,

NXDIM is the first dimension of X (as declared in the dimension statement for X),

NFUN is the number of functions of the dependent variable to be plotted,

NPNT is the number of points from each function to be plotted (not necessarily NXDIM),

XMINZ, XMAXZ are limits on the dependent variable; they should be set equal for autoscaling.

CALL PLOTXY(X,Y,NYDIM,NFUN,NPNT,MMN,XXMIN,XXMAX,YYMIN,YYMAX)

where X(NYDIM) is the independent variable array,

Y(NYDIM,NFUN) is the array of dependent variables,

NYDIM is the dimension of Y as declared in its dimension statement,

MMN is the rate at which points are displayed; i.e., if MMN = 2, every second point is displayed, etc.; if MMN = 0, PLOTXY determines the rate for the best looking display.

Other variables are the same as defined above.

B-7. A Variable-Step Runge-Kutta-Merson Integration Rule. Figure B-4 shows a version of the Runge-Kutta-Merson variable-step fourth-order integration method. The algorithm is described in Sec. A-11.b and the step-size changing strategy is described in Sec. A-12. Error-control options are described in Sec. 2-9. Figure B-4(a) is the main routine INTEG; Fig. B-4(b) shows a step-size changing routine STEP which could be used as part of other variable-step algorithms with some modification. COMMON block ERR passes error-control information between the two routines. In particular, one would have to change the calculation of TE(J) (just above statement 1 and in statement 10) in accordance with the desired error-estimation equations.

```
      SUBROUTINE PLOTXT(TO,DT,X,NXDIM,M,N,XXMIN,XXMAX)
C
C  PLOT UP TO 7 VARIABLES VERSUS A CONTINUOUS INDEPENDENT VARIABLE.
C  THE LENGTH OF THE GRAPH IS DETERMINED BY THE NUMBER OF INDEPENDENT
C  VARIABLE INCREMENTS.
C        WRITTEN BY D. CLARKE (PLOTER PACKAGE), MOD. BY J.V. WAIT
C        APRIL, 1976
C
C  ARGUMENTS
C     TO -- STARTING VALUE OF INDEPENDENT VARIABLE
C     DT -- THE CONSTANT INCREMENT OF THE INDEPENDENT VARIABLE
C     X  -- DEPENDENT VARIABLES ARRAY, X(120,M)
C        NXDIM -- FIRST DIMENSION OF X
C     M  -- NUMBER OF FUNCTIONS TO BE PLOTTED
C     N  -- NUMBER OF POINTS PER FUNCTION
C     IF XXMIN=XXMAX AUTOSCALE
C     OTHERWISE PLOT BETWEEN     XXMIN AND XXMAX
C
C  NOTE.. WHERE TWO OR MORE FUNCTIONS INTERSECT ON THE GRAPH ONLY THE
C  LAST ONE WILL APPEAR
C
      DIMENSION X(NXDIM,M),ILINE(20),IDIGIT(9)
      LOGICAL ERR
      COMMON /FLAGS/ ERR
      COMMON // LINE(102),XREF(11)
C
C     LOAD INVARIANT SYMBOLS
C
      DATA IZERO,IDIGIT/1H0,1H1,1H2,1H3,1H4,1H5,1H6,1H7,1H8,1H9/
      DATA ILINE(1),ILINE(2),ILINE(3),ILINE(4),ILINE(5),
     2  ILINE(6),ILINE(7),ILINE(8),ILINE(9),ILINE(10)
     3  /1H+,1H-,1H-,1H-,1H-,1H-,1H-,1H-,1H-,1H-/
      DATA ILINE(11),ILINE(12),ILINE(13),ILINE(14),ILINE(15),
     2  ILINE(16),ILINE(17),ILINE(18),ILINE(19),ILINE(20)
     3  /1HI,1H ,1H ,1H ,1H ,1H ,1H ,1H ,1H ,1H /
      DATA III/1/
C
      XMIN=XXMIN
      XMAX=XXMAX
      ERR=.FALSE.
      CALL FIXUP(X,NXDIM,N,M,XMAX,XMIN,XSCALE)
      IF(ERR) RETURN
C
C     DETERMINE IF AND WHERE ALONG THE X AXIS X=0, AND SET A REGISTER
C
      JZERO=102
      IF(XMIN*XMAX.LT.0.) JZERO=1.5-XMIN/XSCALE
C
C     GENERATE X-REFERENCE VALUES AND PRINT A BORDER
C
      DO 14 I=1,11
      XREF(I)=XMIN+10.0*FLOAT(I-1)*XSCALE
      IF(ABS(XREF(I)).LE.XSCALE*0.1) XREF(I)=0.0
14    CONTINUE
      PRINT 15,        III,XSCALE,DT,(XREF(I),I=1,11)
```

Fig. B-3. Line-printer plotting routines. (a) subroutine PLOTXT plots arrays vs. an incremented independent variable.

```
15        FORMAT (5X,30HPLOTX-T ROUTINE -- PLOT NUMBER,I2,21X,21HSCALE FACTO
         1RS ... X =,  E9.2,5X,5H T = ,  E9.2///22X,11( E9.2,1X)/25X,1H+,10
         2(9X,1H+))
C
C        INCREMENT GRAPH NUMBER COUNTER.
C
         III=III+1
C
C        START GRAPH
C
         DO 22 LINES=1,N
C
C        DETERMINE THE VALUE OF THE INDEPENDENT VARIABLE FOR THIS LINE
C        OF THE GRAPH
C
         T=TO+FLOAT(LINES-1)*DT
C
C        TEST IF GRID IS TO BE PRINTED, IF SO, LOAD GRID INTO GRAPH LINE
C        BUFFER, IF NOT LOAD BLANKS.
C
         IS=10
         IF(MOD(LINES,10).EQ.1) IS=0
         DO 16 K=1,10
         I=K+IS
         DO 16 J=K,101,10
16       LINE(J)=ILINE(I)
C
C        SET ZERO IN POSITION FOR THE X AXIS
C
         LINE(JZERO)=IZERO
C
C        START SEARCH THRU X ARRAY FUNCTIONS AND DETERMINE FOR EACH WHERE
C        THE GRAPH MARKER SHOULD BE, AND LOAD IT INTO THE GRAPH LINE BUFFER
C
         DO 20 I=1,M
         IJ=(X(LINES,I)-XMIN)/XSCALE+1.5
         IF(IJ.LE.0)IJ=1
         IF(IJ.GT.101)IJ=101
20       LINE(IJ)=IDIGIT(I)
C
C        PRINT ONE LINE OF THE GRAPH
C
         PRINT 21,      T,(LINE(I),I=1,101),LINES
21       FORMAT(2X,  E20.8,3X,101A1,3X,I3)
C
C        IF GRAPH NOT COMPLETE, RETURN AND START A NEW LINE
C
22       CONTINUE
C
C        PRINT LOWER BORDER FOR GRAPH
C
         PRINT 23,         (XREF(I),I=1,11)
23       FORMAT(25X,101(1H=),/25X,1H+,10(9X,1H+)/22X,11( E9.2,1X)//)
         RETURN
         END
```

Fig. B-3. (a) (continued)

```
      SUBROUTINE PLOTXY(X,Y,NYDIM,M,N,XMI,XMA,YMI,YMA)
C
C X-Y PLOTTER ROUTINE WHICH CAN SIMULTANEOUSLY PLOT 6 FUNCTIONS OF AN
C    INDEPENDENT VARIABLE ON A COMPLETELY SCALED SINGLE PAGE GRAPH
C       WRITTEN BY D. CLARKE (PLOTER PACKAGE), MOD. BY J.V. WAIT
C       APRIL, 1976
C
C DESCRIPTION OF ARGUMENT LIST
C
C    X--THE INDEPENDENT VARIABLE
C    Y--THE DEPENDENT VARIABLE
C       Y IS AN ARRAY OF THE FORM Y(I,J), WHERE I IS THE DATA POINT
C       AND J IS THE FUNCTION NUMBER.  IF TWO FUNCTIONS CROSS THE
C       ONE WITH THE HIGHER FUNCTION NUMBER WILL TAKE PRECEDENCE OVER
C       ALL OTHERS.
C    NYDIM - - FIRST DIMENSION ON Y
C    M--THE NUMBER OF DEPENDENT FUNCTIONS TO BE PLOTTED
C    XMI,XMA,YMI, AND YMA ARE TO CONTROL AUTOSCALING
C    IF XMI=XMA  AUTOSCALE X
C    IF YMI=YMA, AUTOSCALE Y
C    OTHERWISE PLOT BETWEEN XMI AND XMA, YMI AND YMA
C    N--THE NUMBER OF POINTS CALCULATED PER FUNCTION
C
C PLOTER IS WRITTEN IN STANDARD FORTRAN (ANSI X3.9-1966)
C
      DIMENSION X(N),Y(NYDIM,M),IDIGIT(9)
      LOGICAL EPR
      COMMON /FLAGS/ ERR
      COMMON // LINE(102),XREF(11)
      DATA IBLANK,IZERO,IDIGIT/1H ,1H0,1H1,1H2,1H3,1H4,1H5,1H6,1H7,1H8,
     1 1H9/
C
      XMIN=XMI
      XMAX=XMA
      YMIN=YMI
      YMAX=YMA
      ERR=.FALSE.
      CALL FIXUP(X,N,N,1,XMAX,XMIN,XSCALE)
      IF(ERR) RETURN
C
C     CALCULATE A NUMBER TO BE USED FOR TESTING
C
      XTEST=XSCALE/50.
C
C     IF X=0. CAN OCCUR WITHIN LIMITS XMIN TO XMAX, SET A POINTER
C
      IX0=102
      IF ((XMIN*XMAX).LE.0.) IX0=ABS(XMIN)/XSCALE+1.5
      CALL FIXUP(Y,NYDIM,N,M,YMAX,YMIN,YSCALE)
      IF(ERR) RETURN
      YSCALE=YSCALE*2.
      YTEST=YSCALE/50.
      IY0=0
      IF ((YMIN*YMAX).LE.0.) IY0=ABS(YMAX)/YSCALE+1.5
C
```

Fig. B-3. (b) subroutine PLOTXY displays arrays vs. an array of independent-variable values.

```
C WRITE HEADING AND TOP BORDER
C
      PRINT 6,        XSCALE,YSCALE
6     FORMAT (50X,20HSCALE FACTORS .. X =,  E9.2,5H, Y =,  E9.2//21X,10(
     110H*--------),1H*)
C
C START OUTPUT OF THE GRAPH -- 51 HORIZONTAL LINES AND 101 VERTICAL LINE
C
      DO 12 I=1,51
C
C     DEFINE BOUNDARIES FOR THE CURRENT LINE OF THE GRAPH
C
      YMID=YMAX-FLOAT(I-1)*YSCALE
      YHI=YMID+0.5*YSCALE
      YLO=YMID-0.5*YSCALE
C
C     IF YMID IS ALMOST ZERO, SET IT TO ZERO
C
      IF(ABS(YMID).LE.YTEST) YMID=0.0
C
C     IF CURRENT LINE IS Y=0., INITIALIZE THE OUTPUT LINE TO ZEROES
C         OTHERWISE, INITIALIZE THE OUTPUT LINE TO BLANKS
C
      IA=IBLANK
      IF(I.EQ.IYO) IA=IZERO
      DO 7 J=1,101
7     LINE(J)=IA
C
C     SET X=0. INTO OUTPUT LINE
C
      LINE(IXO)=IZERO
C
C     SEARCH THRU THE Y ARRAY, ONE FUNCTION AT A TIME, TO FIND ANY Y VAL
C     THAT FALLS WITHIN THE BOUNDARIES FOR THE CURRENT LINE OF THE GRAPH
C
      DO 8 K=1,M
      DO 8 J=1,N
      IF(Y(J,K).LT.YLO) GO TO 8
      IF(Y(J,K).GE.YHI) GO TO 8
C
C     WHEN A Y VALUE IS FOUND WITHIN THE CURRENT BOUNDARIES, DETERMINE
C     WHERE THE X VALUE SHOULD BE AND PUT THE SYMBOL CORRESPONDING TO TH
C     CURRENT FUNCTION NUMBER INTO THE OUTPUT LINE
C
      IX=(X(J)-XMIN)/XSCALE+1.5
      IF(IX.LE.0)IX=1
      IF(IX.GT.101) IX=101
      LINE(IX)=IDIGIT(K)
8     CONTINUE
C
C WRITE ONE LINE OF THE GRAPH
C
C     WRITE LOWER AND Y REFERENCE MARKS ONLY IF I=1(MOD 5)
C
      IF(MOD(I,5).NE.1) GO TO 10
      PRINT 9,        YMID,(LINE(J),J=1,101)
```

Fig. B-3. (b) (continued)

```
9       FORMAT (8X,   E9.2,2X,2H**,101A1,1H*)
        GO TO 12
10      PRINT 11,        (LINE(J),J=1,101)
11      FORMAT (20X,1HI,101A1,1HI)
12      CONTINUE
C
C GRAPH COMPLETE --- WRITE LOWER BORDER
C
        PRINT 13
13      FORMAT(21X,10(10H*---------),1H*,/21X,1H*,10(10H        *),/)
C
C CALCULATE THE X REFERENCES
C
        XREF(1)=XMIN
        SCAL=10.0*XSCALE
        DO 14 I=2,11
14      XREF(I)=XREF(I-1)+SCAL
C
C       IF XREF(I) IS ALMOST 0., SET XREF(I)=0.
C
        DO 15 I=1,11
        IF (ABS(XREF(I)).LE.XTEST) XREF(I)=0.
15      CONTINUE
C
C WRITE THE X REFERENCES
C
        PRINT 16,        (XREF(I),I=1,11)
16      FORMAT (18X,11(  E9.2,1X))
C
        RETURN
        END
```

Fig. B-3. (b) (continued)

```
      SUBROUTINE SCALE(X,NXDIM,N,M,XMAX,XMIN)
C
C  SCALE FINDS THE MAXIMUM AND MINIMUM VALUES OF THE ARRAY X(N,M)
C
      DIMENSION X(NXDIM,M)
      LOGICAL ERR
      COMMON /FLAGS/ ERR
C     TEST FOR AUTOSCALING
      IF(XMIN.NE.XMAX) GO TO 2
      XMAX=X(1,1)
      XMIN=XMAX
      DO 1 I=1,N
      DO 1 J=1,M
      XMAX=AMAX1(XMAX,X(I,J))
1     XMIN=AMIN1(XMIN,X(I,J))
2     IF(XMAX-XMIN.GT.AMAX1(ABS(XMAX),ABS(XMIN))/10000.) RETURN
      PRINT 3
3     FORMAT(45H *** BAD PLOT/GRAPH DATA ... MAX .LE. MIN ***)
      ERR=.TRUE.
      RETURN
      END
```

Fig. B-3. (c) subroutine SCALE.

```
      SUBROUTINE FIXUP(X,NXDIM,LEN,NFUNC,XMAX,XMIN,FSCALE)
C
C FIXUP USES SCALE TO DETERMINE EXTREMES OF THE ARRAY X(LEN,NFUNC).
C THEN, FIXUP CALCULATES AN OPTIMAL SCALE FACTOR AND ADJUSTS XMAX AND
C XMIN.  THE SCALE RETURNED IS .01*(XMAX-XMIN) ROUNDED UP
C UNTIL IT CAN BE EXPRESSED BY ONE SIGNIFICANT DIGIT.
C
      DIMENSION X(NXDIM,NFUNC)
      LOGICAL ERR
      COMMON /FLAGS/ ERR
C
C 1.  FIND LARGEST AND SMALLEST X
C
      CALL SCALE(X,NXDIM,LEN,NFUNC,XMAX,XMIN)
      IF(ERR) RETURN
      SPAN=XMAX-XMIN
C
C 2.  ROUND SPAN UP TO ONE SIGNIFICANT DIGIT
C   2A.  FIND LARGEST POWER OF 10. LESS THAN OR EQUAL TO SPAN
C
C  CODE TO CALCULATE THE HIGHEST POWER OF TEN WHICH IS LESS THAN
C     SPAN. THE EXPONENT IS LEFT IN I, AND TEN TO THE
C     ITH IS THE VALUE OF POWER
      POWER=1.0
      I=0
      IF(POWER.GT.SPAN) GO TO 2
1     IF(POWER*10..GT.SPAN) GO TO 3
      POWER=POWER*10.
      I=I+1
      GO TO 1
2     POWER=POWER/10.
      I=I-1
      IF(POWER.GT.SPAN) GO TO 2
C   2B.   OBTAIN DIFFER USING AINT (TRUNCATION FUNCTION)
C
3     DIFFER=AINT(SPAN/POWER+.995)*POWER
4     IF(DIFFER/POWER.GT.9.5) POWER=POWER*10.
C
C  USE TENTH=POWER/10.     FOR MAXIMUM RESOLUTION
C  USE TENTH=DIFFER/10.    FOR ZERO AXES ALIGNED ON TIC MARK
C
      TENTH=POWER/10.
C
C 3.  FMAX IS THE NEAREST MULTIPLE OF TENTH
C     HALF THE DIFFERENCE GREATER THAN XMAX
C
      FMAX=AINT((XMAX+(DIFFER-SPAN)/2.)/TENTH+.5)*TENTH
      IF(FMAX.LT.XMAX) FMAX=FMAX+TENTH
C
C 4.  SET FMIN AND SCALE, CHECK FOR PROBLEMS, AND RETURN
C
      FMIN=FMAX-DIFFER
      FSCALE=DIFFER/100.
      IF(FMIN.LE.XMIN) RETURN
C
C 5.  DIFFER TOO SMALL, ENLARGE AND REPEAT
C
      DIFFER=DIFFER+POWER
      GO TO 4
      END
```

Fig. B-3. (d) subroutine FIXUP.

```
      SUBROUTINE INTEG
C     VERSION 2, DEC. 1970
C     MODIFIED JUNE,1971
C     MODIFIED AUG. 21, 1972
C     ASSUMES THAT DIFFEQ HAS BEEN CALLED PRIOR TO FIRST CALL
C     TO INTEG
C     RUNGE-KUTTA-MERSON VARIABLE STEP INTEGRATION RULE.
C     CALLS DIFFEQ BEFORE RETURNING
C     IF K3 .GT. 0, USES ABSOLUTE TEST ON Y(K3)
C     IF L3 = .TRUE. SUBROUTINE WILL PRINT DT CHANGES
      LOGICAL A,B,C,D,E,FO,SWX
      COMMON/STADER/G
      COMMON/STATEV/Y
      COMMON/UNDVAR/P
      COMMON/OUTVAR/NLIST,NPLOT,NOUT,TITLE,V,IV,ISEL,W
      COMMON/SYSVAR/T,DT,TMAX,TNEXT,DTMAX,DTMIN,EMAX,EMIN,S1,S2,S3,
     1NORDER,NPARAM,NPOINT,K1,K2,K3,INIT,OUTPUT,L1,L2,L3
      DIMENSION TITLE(32),V(10),IV(10),ISEL(25),W(101,4)
      DIMENSION G(20),Y(30),P(20)
      LOGICAL INIT,OUTPUT,L1,L2,L3
      DIMENSION RK1(20),RK2(20),RK3(20),RK4(20),RK5(20)
      DIMENSION TE(20),YOLD(20)
      COMMON/ERR/A,B,C,SWX,RK1,RK2,RK3,RK4,RK5,TE ,YOLD,D,E
C     STORE INITIAL CONDITIONS
      DO 1 I=1,NORDER
      YOLD(I)=Y(I)
    1 CONTINUE
C     INITIALIZE
      IF(.NOT.INIT)GO TO 2
      INIT=.FALSE.
      IF(DTMAX.GT.TNEXT)DTMAX=TNEXT
      IF(DTMAX.EQ.0.0)DTMAX=TNEXT
      IF(DTMIN.GE.DTMAX) DTMIN=0.0625*DTMAX
      IF(DTMIN.EQ.0.0)DTMIN=0.0625*DTMAX
      IF(EMAX.EQ.0.0)EMAX=1.0E-03
      IF(EMIN.GE.EMAX)EMIN=0.015625*EMAX
      IF(EMIN.EQ.0.0)EMIN= 0.015625*EMAX
      SWX=.FALSE.
      D=.FALSE.
      E=.FALSE.
      FO=.FALSE.
      IF(K3.GT.0) SWX=.TRUE.
    2 DIFF=TNEXT-T
      IF(DIFF.LT.DT.AND.DIFF.GT.0.0) FO = .TRUE.
      IF(FO)GO TO 3
      GO TO 4
    3 DTEM=DT
      DT=DIFF
    4 S2=0.5*DT
      S3=0.33333333333333*DT
      TIME=T
C     FIND K1
      DO 5 I=1,NORDER
      RK1(I)= G(I)*S3
      Y(I)=RK1(I)+YOLD(I)
```

Fig. B-4. Runge-Kutta-Merson integration method. (a) subroutine INTEG.

```
      5 CONTINUE
        T=TIME+S3
C   FIND K2
        CALL DIFFEQ
        DO 6 I=1,NORDER
        RK2(I)= G(I)*S3
        Y(I)=0.5*(RK1(I)+RK2(I))+YOLD(I)
      6 CONTINUE
C   FIND K3
        CALL DIFFEQ
        DO 7 I=1,NORDER
        RK3(I)=4.5* G(I)*S3
        Y(I)=0.375*RK1(I)+0.25*RK3(I)+YOLD(I)
      7 CONTINUE
        T=TIME+S2
C   FIND K4
        CALL DIFFEQ
        DO 8 I=1,NORDER
        RK4(I)=4.0* G(I)*S3
        Y(I)=1.5*(RK1(I)+R<4(I))-RK3(I)+YOLD(I)
      8 CONTINUE
        T=TIME+DT
C   FIND K5
        CALL DIFFEQ
        DO 9 I=1,NORDER
        RK5(I)= G(I)*S3
      9 CONTINUE
C   FIND NEXT POINT
        DO 10 I=1,NORDER
        Y(I)=0.5*(RK1(I)+RK4(I)+RK5(I))+YOLD(I)
     10 CONTINUE
        IF(FO)GO TO 11
        GO TO 12
     11 DT=DTEM
        FO=.FALSE.
C       IGNORE CALL TO STEP IF DIFF USED
        CALL DIFFEQ
        RETURN
C   FIND ERROR
     12 CALL STEP
C   CHECK RESULTS OF ERROR TESTS
C   IF C IS .TRUE. DO NOTHING
C   IF A IS .TRUE. HALVE DT
C   IF B IS .TRUE. DOUBLE DT
        IF(C)GO TO 19
        IF(A)GO TO 13
        IF(B)GO TO 17
        CALL DIFFEQ
        RETURN
     13 T=TIME
        DT = S2
        IF(L3)PRINT 14,DT
     14 FORMAT(20H DT HALVED,NEW DT = ,E20.7)
     15 DO 16 I=1,NORDER
        Y(I)=YOLD(I)
     16 CONTINUE
        GO TO 2
     17 DT=DT*2.0
        IF(L3)PRINT 18,DT
     18 FORMAT(22H DT DOUBLED, NEW DT = ,E20.7)
        CALL DIFFEQ
     19 RETURN
        END
```

Fig. B-4. (a) (continued)

```
      SUBROUTINE STEP
C     VERSION 2, DEC. 1970
C     FOR RUNGE-KUTTA-MERSON ONLY
C STEP CALCULATES ERROR OF FUNCTION AND DETERMINES WHETHER OR NOT
C   STEP SIZE NEEDS TO BE CHANGED.
      LOGICAL A,B,C,D,E,F,R,H,O,Q,X,SWX
      COMMON/STADER/G
      COMMON/STATEV/Y
      COMMON/UNDVAR/P
      COMMON/OUTVAR/NLIST,NPLOT,NOUT,TITLE,V,IV,ISEL,W
      COMMON/SYSVAR/T,DT,TMAX,TNEXT,DTMAX,DTMIN,EMAX,EMIN,S1,S2,S3,
     1NORDER,NPARAM,NPOINT,K1,K2,K3,INIT,OUTPUT,L1,L2,L3
      LOGICAL INIT,OUTPUT,L1,L2,L3
      COMMON/ERR/A,B,C,SWX,RK1,RK2,RK3,RK4,RK5, TE,YOLD,D,F
      DIMENSION TITLE(32),V(10),IV(10),ISEL(25),W(101,4)
      DIMENSION G(20),Y(30),P(20)
      DIMENSION YOLD(20)
      DIMENSION RK1(20),RK2(20),RK3(20),RK4(20),RK5(20), TE(20)
C CALCULATE ERRORS.
      IF(SWX)GO TO 10
      DO 1 J=1,NORDER
      TE(J)=0.2*(RK1(J)-RK3(J)+RK4(J)-0.5*RK5(J))
    1 CONTINUE
C DO TYPE OF ERROR CHECK
      IF(SWX)GO TO 10
C DO RELATIVE ERROR CHECK
    2 YMAX=ABS( TE(1))/(ABS(Y(1))+ABS(YOLD(1)-Y(1))+1.0)
      YMIN=YMAX
      JMAX=1
      DO 4 I=2,NORDER
      RELERR=ABS( TE(I))/(ABS(Y(I))+ABS(YOLD(I)-Y(I))+1.0)
      IF(YMAX.GT.RELERR)GO TO 3
      YMAX=RELERR
      JMAX=I
      GO TO 4
    3 IF(RELERR.LT.YMIN) RELERR=YMIN
    4 CONTINUE
    5 R=YMAX.LT.EMIN
      H=YMAX.LE.EMAX
      O=DT.GE.DTMAX
      A=.FALSE.
      B=.FALSE.
      C=.FALSE.
      X=.FALSE.
      C=(H.AND.(.NOT.R)).OR.(O.AND.R)
    6 IF(C)GO TO 7
      Q=DT.GT.DTMIN
      A=Q.AND.(.NOT.H)
      IF(A)GO TO 7
      X=.NOT.(H.OR.Q)
      IF(X)GO TO 7
      B=R.AND.(.NOT.O)
      IF(DT.GT.0.51*DTMAX) B=.FALSE.
    7 IF(X)GO TO 9
      F=(A.AND.E).OR.(B.AND.D)
```

Fig. B-4. (b) subroutine STEP.

```
      IF(F)GO TO 8
      D=A
      E=B
      RETURN
    8 C=.TRUE.
      D=.FALSE.
      E=.FALSE.
      RETURN
    9 C=.TRUE.
      RETURN
C     ABSOLUTE ERROR CHECK
   10 TE(K3)=0.2*(RK1(K3)-RK3(K3)+RK4(K3)-0.5*RK5(K3))
      YMAX=ABS(TE(K3))
      GO TO 5
      END
```

Fig. B-4. (b) (continued)

REFERENCES

1. American National Standards Institute, "U.S.A. Standard Fortran," *USAS Report X3.9*, U.S.A. Standards Institute, New York, 1966.

2. FREUND, D. A., "An Interactive FORTRAN Package for Continuous System Simulation," Department of Electrical Engineering, University of Arizona, Tucson, 1974 (available from the authors; see the address following the preface).

C

Tricks and Treats:
Some Numerical Techniques

C-1. Avoiding Division.[1] Since division operations often cost extra execution time (at least in minicomputers) and may cause stability and scaling problems, it is sometimes useful to replace a differential equation of the form

$$\frac{dY}{dX} = \frac{F(X, Y)}{G(X, Y)} \tag{C-1}$$

by the system

$$\frac{dX}{dT} = aG(X, Y), \qquad \frac{dY}{dT} = aF(X, Y) \tag{C-2}$$

with $X = 0$ for $T = 0$. Also, differential equations

$$\frac{dYI}{dT} = FI(X, Y_1, Y_2, \ldots) \tag{C-3}$$

where FI is an unbounded function, can often be rewritten in the form of Eq. (C-1).

C-2. Function Generation, Constraints, and Steepest Descent.[1] FORTRAN-based languages approximate common functions such as sin X by Chebyshev polynomials or, on larger computers, by rational-function expansions.[2] Some block-diagram languages employ table lookup/interpolation algorithms (Sec. 6-6). Sometimes it is preferable to generate functions as *solutions of differential equations.* Thus, in flight simulation, integration of a roll rate $\dot{\psi}$ may produce an uncomfortably large range of angles ψ, while

$$X = \cos \psi, \qquad Y = \sin \psi \qquad \text{(C-4)}$$

stay within -1 to $+1$. We can obtain X and Y by solving

$$\frac{dX}{dT} = -\dot{\psi}Y \qquad \frac{dY}{dT} = \dot{\psi}X, \qquad \text{(C-5)}$$

with $X(0) = 1$, $Y(0) = 0$ ("rate-resolver" program).[1]

When a defined variable Y is implicitly defined by an equation

$$\varphi(X1, X2, \ldots, T; Y) = 0 \qquad \text{(C-6)}$$

which might represent a physical *constraint* in a simulation, one can often avoid the awkward iteration technique of Sec. 3-18a through *steepest-descent minimization* of the function

$$F(X1, X2, \ldots, T; Y) \equiv |\varphi(X1, X2, \ldots, T; Y)| \qquad \text{(C-7)}$$

If Y is suitably differentiable, we introduce the desired variable Y as a state variable in the differential equation

$$\frac{dY}{dT} = -K\frac{\partial F}{\partial Y} = -K\frac{\partial \varphi}{\partial Y} \text{ sign } \varphi \qquad (K > 0) \qquad \text{(C-8)}$$

which will continuously minimize Eq. (C-7) and thus enforce Eq. (C-6) (assuming that a reasonable solution exists). The correct initial value $Y(0)$ must be *precomputed* either by iteration or by a preliminary run with Eq. (C-8). $K > 0$ is chosen by trial and error for best accuracy.[1]

It is sometimes possible to reduce integration and roundoff errors substantially by using similar steepest-descent techniques to enforce constraints which express mathematical identities or energy conservation. Thus X and Y in Eq. (C-4) must satisfy

$$X^2 + Y^2 = 1 \quad \text{or} \quad X^2 + Y^2 - 1 = \min. \qquad \text{(C-9)}$$

We modify the state equations (C-5) by adding steepest-descent terms to enforce Eq. (C-9):

$$\frac{dX}{dT} = -\dot{\psi}Y - KX \text{ sign } (X^2 + Y^2 - 1) \qquad (K > 0)$$

$$\frac{dY}{dT} = \dot{\psi}X - KY \text{ sign } (X^2 + Y^2 - 1) \qquad (K > 0) \qquad \text{(C-10)}$$

The correction terms will be small as long as the condition (C-9) holds; we chose $K > 0$ by trial and error for best accuracy (*digital Gilbert-Howe rate-resolver technique*[1]).

C-3. Perturbation Techniques for Improved Accuracy.[1,2] Given a state equation (or system of equations)

$$\frac{dX}{dT} = F(X, T, \alpha) \tag{C-11}$$

where α can be a function $\alpha(T)$ of T, it is often possible to rewrite

$$\alpha = \alpha_0(T) + \delta\alpha(T), \qquad X = X_0(T) + \delta X(T) \tag{C-12}$$

where $X_0(T)$ is the *accurately known* solution of

$$\frac{dX_0}{dT} = F(X_0, T, \alpha_0) \tag{C-13}$$

We can then find the *perturbed solution* $\delta X(Y)$ resulting from the *perturbution* $\delta\alpha$ by solving

$$\frac{d}{dT}\delta X = F[X_0(T) + \delta X, T, \alpha_0 + \delta\alpha] - F(X_0, T, \alpha_0) \tag{C-14}$$

If $|\delta X|$ is small compared to $|X|$, then errors in solving Eq. (C-14) will have a relatively small effect on the total solution $X = X_0(T) + \delta X$; *the accuracy improvement can be dramatic.*

In particular, it may be possible to replace the *exact* perturbation equation (C-14) by a Taylor-series approximation

$$\frac{d}{dT}\delta X = \frac{\delta F}{\delta X}\bigg]_{X_0, \alpha_0} \delta X + \frac{\delta F}{\delta\alpha}\bigg]_{X_0, \alpha_0} \delta\alpha \tag{C-15}$$

(*linearized* perturbation equation), as was done to derive the simple flight equations of Sec. 5-6. Such techniques are especially useful in space-vehicle-trajectory computations.[1,3]

C-4. Difference Equations and Sampled-Data Systems.[2] Continuous-system simulation languages are directly applicable to the solution of *difference equations* (*or systems of difference equations*)

$$^{k+1}X = {}^{k}X + Q(^{k}X, k) \tag{C-16}$$

with given initial values ^{0}X. It is only necessary to solve the differential equation (or system of differential equations)

$$\frac{dX}{dT} = \frac{1}{DT}Q\left(X, \frac{T}{DT}\right) \tag{C-17}$$

using the *Euler integration routine* (Appendix A), so that

$$X[(k + 1) DT] = X(kDT) + Q\left(X, \frac{kDT}{DT}\right) \qquad \text{(C-18)}$$

Solution of difference equations is the main reason for including the Euler integration routine in a simulation-language library file. An important application is to the design of recursive digital filters.

The situation becomes more complicated when we want to simulate systems *with some state variables defined by differential equations and others by difference equations*, e.g., sampled-data control systems with "continuous" plants and digital controllers or filters. We program the differential equations as usually done. Assuming uniformly spaced *sampling times* $T = 0, I*DT, 2I*DT, \ldots$, difference equations will be of the form

$$X[(I + 1)DT] = P[X(IDT), Y(T), I, T] \qquad \text{(C-19)}$$

with given initial values $X(0)$. It is only necessary to write a FORTRAN function (Sec. 3-10.a) or block-operator macro (Sec. 6-6) which reads an input P at $T = 0$, $I*DT, 2I*DT, \ldots$ and produces the sampled-data output (C-19) for

$$(I + 1)DT \leq T < (I + 2)DT \qquad (I = 0, 1, 2, \ldots) \qquad \text{(C-20)}$$

(*unit-delay operator*), with the suitably entered initial value $X(0)$. One can also use separate derivative-file programs to represent the continuous and discrete portions of a simulation problem.[4]

REFERENCES

1. KORN, G. A., and T. M. KORN, *Electronic Analog and Hybrid Computers*, 2nd ed., McGraw-Hill, New York, 1972 (note bibliography for Chap. 8).

2. KORN, G. A., and T. M. KORN, *Mathematical Handbook for Scientists and Engineers*, 2nd ed., McGraw-Hill, New York, 1968.

3. FOGARTY, L. E., and R. M. HOWE, "Analog-Computer Solution of the Orbital Flight Equations," *IRETEC*, Aug. 1962.

4. MOORE, W. R., "An Expanded Simulation Language for Partitioned Systems," M.S. thesis, Electrical Engineering Department, University of Arizona, Tucson, 1972.

Index

References in the index are to section numbers, not page numbers. Note that section numbers are displayed at the top of text pages for convenient reference. Note also that there are several useful reference tables in Chapter 3–6, which summarize DARE language features.